ORGANIZING FOR PEACE

WITHDRAWN

Syracuse Studies on Peace and Conflict Resolution
Harriet Hyman Alonso, Charles Chatfield, and Louis Kriesberg
Series Editors

ORGANIZING FOR PEACE

Neutrality, the Test Ban, and the Freeze

Robert Kleidman

WITHDRAWN

ṢỵU

Syracuse University Press

Copyright © 1993 by Syracuse University Press
Syracuse, New York 13244-5160

ALL RIGHTS RESERVED

First Edition 1993
93 94 95 96 97 98 99   6 5 4 3 2 1

The paper used in this publication meets the minimum requirements of American National Standard for Information Sciences — Permanence of Paper for Printed Library Materials, ANSI Z39.48-1984. ∞™

Library of Congress Cataloging-in-Publication Data

Kleidman, Robert.
    Organizing for peace: neutrality, the test ban, and the freeze /
Robert Kleidman.
       p.   cm. — (Syracuse studies on peace and conflict resolution)
    Based on the author's doctoral dissertation, University of
Wisconsin-Madison.
    Includes bibliographical references and index.
    ISBN 0-8156-2573-1
    1. Peace movements — United States — History — 20th century.
I. Title.   II. Series.
JX1961.U6K55   1993
327.1'72 — dc20   92-40181

Manufactured in the United States of America

To My Parents

Robert Kleidman is Assistant Professor of Sociology at Cleveland State University. He received his Ph.D. from the University of Wisconsin-Madison. He participated in the nuclear freeze campaign at the local and national levels and remains active in the movement for peace and justice.

Contents

Preface

In 1983 I heard two talks that strongly affected me. Helen Caldicott, president of Physicians for Social Responsibility, presented a riveting and frightening description of the consequences of nuclear war, and argued that the deployment of a new generation of nuclear weapons by the United States was greatly increasing the chances of nuclear war. The second talk was by a youth leader of the British Campaign for Nuclear Disarmament. He urged those like me who were joining the growing antinuclear movement to find a way to maintain our activism for many years and to be prepared to face many setbacks.

These speeches illustrate a basic dilemma of organizing for peace — the tension between quickly mobilizing to respond to threats and building a movement for long-term fundamental change. The modern American peace movement has been most successful in generating activism when, like Dr. Caldicott, it has made eloquent appeals that raise fears, and then presented simple solutions. In 1936, with World War II approaching, peace groups united and launched the Emergency Peace Campaign, calling for American neutrality and greater international economic cooperation. In 1957, after fallout from atomic tests had created public health scares, peace organizations again came together, and started a campaign for a ban on atomic testing. The Nuclear Freeze Campaign was begun in 1979 by peace groups seeking to reduce the threat of nuclear war by halting and reversing the escalating superpower buildups and rhetoric.[1]

The effects of the campaigns are debatable. They did not achieve their main goals, but did have some impact on policy. They swelled the ranks of the peace movement by making simple appeals and establishing short-term structures. Some, however, believe that these brief and shallow mobilizations have hindered efforts to convey comprehensive alternatives and to strengthen long-term organizations.

While participating in the freeze campaign I began researching the histories of the earlier campaigns. I found that this basic dilemma could be seen as a series of strategic and organizational tensions. Both my concerns as an activist and my scholarly interests led me to focus on the organizational tensions: I had developed notions about how the groups in which I participated might better organize themselves, and I had been trying to integrate ideas from the sociological literature on formal organizations with social movement scholarship. This book is about how the peace campaigns managed organizational tensions, and how this affected their courses and outcomes.

Writing about a movement in which one has participated has its advantages and disadvantages. My participation in the freeze gave me a feel for the campaign I could not have otherwise obtained, and helped me develop insights into campaigns and campaign organizations.[2] On the other hand, it was difficult to gain critical distance from a movement in which I strongly believed. Conversations with friends and colleagues sympathetic with the goals of the campaign but outside the Nuclear Weapons Freeze Campaign (NWFC) organization helped me achieve this distance, as has the passage of time. Nevertheless, I do not pretend to be objective, nor do I believe that it is possible to be so, if objectivity means having no opinion on the value of a nuclear freeze.

I hope that this book will shed new light on the dynamics of these campaigns and on the constraints and options faced by peace organizers and other social movement activists. Like many scholars I also hope that a greater understanding of the past will guide future activists toward more informed choices and better results.

I wish to acknowledge with gratitude the assistance and support I have received while working on this book, which began as my doctoral dissertation at the University of Wisconsin-Madison (Kleidman 1990). Three faculty members at Madison were especially generous with their time, good ideas, and support. Gerald Marwell was my major professor. I benefited greatly from his support and encouragement, his great ability to identify key issues and themes, and his willingness to read chapters quickly and thoroughly. Ronald Aminzade had been my major professor before he chose to leave Madison. He was a critical influence early in my graduate career, encouraging me to believe that I had something to contribute. He worked with me when this project first took shape and continued to read and comment on my work, and he taught me about historical sociology. I also owe a large intellectual and personal debt to Professor Pamela Oliver, who has been a source of many insights and much help.

My thanks for important comments and ideas on earlier drafts go also to Ann Orloff, David S. Meyer, Mark Furman, and John D. McCarthy. Others at Madison who helped with ideas and encouragement include Lawrence Wu, Paul Boyer, and Harvey Jacobs. I am grateful for the support I have received from William Morgan and my colleagues in the sociology department at Cleveland State University. I have benefited from formal and informal discussions with numerous fellow students and activists.

Cynthia Maude-Gembler, Charles Chatfield, Louis Kriesberg, and the staff at Syracuse University Press have been very generous with their encouragement and advice. I respect and appreciate their commitment to publishing books on peace and conflict resolution.

My research was greatly helped by the generous cooperation of the staffs of the Swarthmore College Peace Collection and the Nuclear Weapons Freeze Campaign, and by those activists kind enough to grant me interviews. The research was supported by a National Science Foundation Grant for Doctoral Dissertation Research in Sociology (SES-8516934) and small grants from the Sociology Department of the University of Wisconsin-Madison.

Above all I would like to thank my friends and family, especially my parents, Howard and Goldie Kleidman; my brother, Richard Kleidman; and my wife, Kathy Rosner, for their unconditional love and support.

Robert Kleidman

Cleveland, Ohio
December 1992

Abbreviations

ABM	Anti-Ballistic Missile
ACDA	Arms Control and Disarmament Agency
AEC	Atomic Energy Commission
AFSC	American Friends Service Committee
APS	American Peace Society
APT	American Peace Test
CND	Campaign for Nuclear Disarmament
CALC	Clergy and Laity Concerned
CEIP	Carnegie Endowment for International Peace
CFR	Council on Foreign Relations
CLW	Council for a Livable World
CPD	Committee on the Present Danger
CNVA	Committee for Nonviolent Action (first called Nonviolent Action Against Nuclear Weapons
CORE	Congress of Racial Equality
EPC	Emergency Peace Campaign
FAS	Federation of American Scientists
FCNL	Friends Committee on National Legislation
FOR	Fellowship of Reconciliation
FPA	Foreign Policy Association
IDDS	Institute for Defense and Disarmament Studies
INF	Intermediate Nuclear Forces Treaty
LNA	League of Nations Association

MFS	Mobilization for Survival
MIRV	Multiple Independently Targetted Re-entry Vehicle
NAACP	National Association for the Advancement of Colored People
NATO	North Atlantic Treaty Organization
NCCW	National Committee on the Cause and Cure of War
NCPW	National Council for Prevention of War
NPC	National Peace Conference
NWFC	Nuclear Weapons Freeze Campaign
NWFTF	Nuclear Weapons Facilities Task Force
NSA	National Security Agency
PSMO	Professional Social Movement Organization
PSR	Physicians for Social Responsibility
SALT	Strategic Arms Reductions Talks
SANE	SANE, the Committee for a Sane Nuclear Policy
SANE/FREEZE	SANE/FREEZE, Campaign for Global Security
SCLC	Southern Christian Leadership Conference
SCPC	Swarthmore College Peace Collection
SDI	Strategic Defense Initiative
SMO	Social Movement Organization
SPU	Student Peace Union
SDS	Students for a Democratic Society
START	Strategic Arms Limitations Talks
TTP	Turn Toward Peace
UCAM	United Campuses Against Nuclear War
UCS	Union of Concerned Scientists
UNA	United Nations Association
UWF	United World Federalists
WAND	Women's Action for Nuclear Disarmament
WILPF	Women's International League for Peace and Freedom
WRL	War Resisters League
WSP	Women Strike for Peace

ORGANIZING FOR PEACE

Modern American Peace Campaigns

Throughout the twentieth century, the American peace movement has sustained major cycles of public attention and support, with the peaks taking the form of campaigns initiated by established peace leaders and organizations and focusing on limited but critical goals. In 1936 the leaders of the two major wings of the movement, pacifist and liberal-internationalist, joined amid growing international tensions to launch the Emergency Peace Campaign (EPC) in support of United States neutrality. The EPC, working with labor and other organized constituencies, held hundreds of meetings in cities and on college campuses around the nation, sponsored national radio addresses by prominent figures, and lobbied Congress with some effect. The EPC ended after two years when the sponsoring coalition split. With war approaching, most liberal-internationalists abandoned neutrality and embraced collective security with the Allies. Pacifists who continued to promote neutrality found themselves, to their distress, on the same side of a still strong but declining cause as right-wing isolationists.

In 1957 the atomic test ban campaign pulled the peace movement out of its Cold War, McCarthy-era doldrums. Reports of the spread of radioactivity from atmospheric tests had raised public fears; the decline of McCarthyism and the end of the Korean War had created some political space. The leaders of the established peace groups, in coalition, created two new organizations to spearhead an anti-testing campaign. One was SANE, the Committee for a Sane Nuclear Policy. For six years SANE led public protest against testing and the nuclear arms race. This campaign helped produce the 1963 limited test ban treaty, which banned atmospheric testing but permitted underground testing. Although this treaty did not end the arms race, it calmed public fears by reducing the threat of fallout and by providing symbolic reassurance that cold war tensions were easing. After mobilizing public support for the treaty, which the Senate ratified in September 1963, the campaign ended. SANE and other organizations rapidly decreased in size and visibility.

In the late 1970s the peace movement was struggling with problems of strategy and structure in the aftermath of the movement against the Vietnam War. The Carter administration was under pressure from a resurgent right wing to reverse the post-Vietnam decline in military spending and to regain nuclear superiority over the Soviet Union. The right prevailed, aided by international events including the Iran hostage crisis, the Soviet invasion of Afghanistan, and the overthrow of Nicaragua dictator Somoza by a left-center revolt. The election of Ronald Reagan in 1980 led to an increase in both the United States nuclear buildup and in anti-Soviet, war-fighting rhetoric.

The peace movement's Nuclear Weapons Freeze Campaign, begun in 1979, mobilized tens of thousands of activists in opposition to Reagan and in support of a superpower halt to testing, production, and deployment of new nuclear weapons. The campaign peaked in 1983 when it moved the freeze to the top of the national agenda and Congress passed a nonbinding freeze resolution. The Reagan administration began to moderate its rhetoric, promoted the Strategic Defense Initiative (SDI) as a means of eliminating the threat of nuclear war, and reopened arms control talks. These measures and political setbacks including Reagan's 1984 reelection and a failure to push Congress into stronger measures robbed the campaign of its momentum and hastened its decline. No freeze was achieved, but the superpowers again negotiated arms control treaties that reduced public fear of nuclear war without ending the development of new weapons.

These three campaigns were the peacetime peaks of the modern American peace movement — the post–World War I, secular and political era of a movement that started in colonial times as a religious pacifism based on individual witness. They were both a consequence and a cause of increased mobilization, as they turned threatening events and public fears into opportunities for gaining greater visibility, support, and impact. Each campaign affected American policy and politics in important ways. World events, domestic politics, and factors internal to the campaigns, however, combined to demobilize them and frustrate the peace movement.

All social movements are shaped and constrained by their political and social environments. Within these limits, the ability of movements to mobilize and sustain activism depends in part upon the structure of each one. Without strong indigenous organizations such as the southern black church, for example, the civil rights movement might never have been able to benefit from the political opportunities opening up in the 1950s and 1960s (McAdam 1982, Morris 1984). The building of effective, formal social movement organizations (SMOs), such as the Southern Christian Leadership Conference (SCLC), allowed the movement to continue mobilizing activism and support, and the structure of these organizations allowed the movement to retain its mass base despite political setbacks.

The peace campaigns were likewise profoundly shaped by the nature of the preexisting and emergent peace movement organizations. Small but enduring groups like the American Friends Service Committee (AFSC) provided an important base of resources and expertise for the emergent campaigns. As they developed, each formed one central organization to coordinate work: the Emergency Peace Campaign (EPC), SANE, and the Nuclear Weapons Freeze Campaign (NWFC).

Organizational tensions within the campaigns resulted from the interaction of three pairs of potentially incompatible tasks. First, holding together and broadening the sponsoring coalition threatened to conflict with developing an independent campaign organization. Second, operating nationally to focus political pressure on national policy makers complicated maintaining a strong base of local support. Third, each campaign sought to mobilize professional expertise and raise money to pay for it, as it also encouraged grassroots participation. These tensions operated as intervening variables, mediating between political opportunities outside the groups and the course, impact, and legacies of the campaigns.

How the tensions were managed depended in part on choices made by leaders and activists, particularly on those made at key moments such as the start of a campaign. When handled similarly, they led to similar outcomes. For example, both SANE and the NWFC developed federated structures, but local chapters did not provide much financial support for the national office. This organizational weakness accelerated the decline of each campaign when political setbacks led to the loss of outside support.

Different circumstances and choices also led to different outcomes. Unlike the test ban, the freeze campaign began with a strong network of local peace and antinuclear groups. Choosing to build local support before turning to national politics, the freeze leadership established a more extensive chapter structure, which left a much larger organizational legacy.

This book makes a detailed assessment of the organizational dynamics of these campaigns. By studying three cases of the same class of events, modern American peace campaigns, I have been able to develop appropriate analytic categories and trace complex patterns of causation in order to shed new light on their histories and to develop insights generalizable to other social movement campaigns and social movements.[1]

Time enters the analysis of the campaigns in two ways.[2] First, organizational structures and choices have different impacts at different stages in the campaigns. Second, because fifty years passed from the outset of the EPC to the end of the nuclear freeze campaign, these cases offer the opportunity to identify and analyze important trends within the peace movement.

The data that I use come from four kinds of sources: primary documents from archives and personal collections, interviews with key actors, secondary accounts of the campaigns, and my own observations of the Nuclear Weapons Freeze Campaign. I was fortunate to have the opportunity to examine the papers of the EPC and the key test ban campaign organizations at the Swarthmore College Peace Collection, and to examine the papers of the NWFC at its national clearinghouse office at its first location in St. Louis, and later in Washington, D.C.

2

The American Peace Movement

> Volunteer citizen peace activism figures as one of the
> more enduring features of American national life.
> First fashioned in the aftermath of the War of 1812
> and persisting well into our own times, the tradition
> of organized citizen peaceseeking has operated as
> one of the most irrepressible and effervescent — if un-
> derexplored and underrated — forces in the country's
> history.
>
> —Charles DeBenedetti (1984, 75)

The American peace movement ordinarily has been a movement
of a tiny minority, but at times peace and antiwar activism have
dominated the political agenda.[1] It is part of an international movement, although it often has been insular and ethnocentric. An over-
whelmingly white and middle class effort, it nonetheless profoundly
influenced the labor and civil rights movements by shaping and passing on the strategy and tactics of nonviolent protest.[2] The core of the
movement consists of groups interested in building peace through developing and promoting comprehensive alternatives to international
violence, yet the most widespread mobilizations have been reactive
and single-issue focused, resisting specific wars or threats to peace.
Opposed to war, the peace movement nevertheless has seen some of
its core groups and constituents supporting specific wars to defeat evils
such as slavery and totalitarianism.

The three peace campaigns that are the focus of this book crystal-
lized the contradictory characteristics of the American peace movement, especially the tensions between short-term crisis response and

long-term reform. Founded by a core of enduring peace organizations, the campaigns built upon public fears — of world war, atomic fallout, and nuclear war — and mobilized masses of people to pressure the government to avoid or end these perils. Yet the campaigns' founders also saw these crises as providing the chance to plant seeds for fundamental changes in foreign and military policy, changes some saw as inextricably linked to reforms toward greater social justice.

Understanding the campaigns requires some comprehension of the larger movement and its contradictory characteristics. Conversely, analyzing them will help illuminate the history of the movement, both because of their important role in the history of the movement and because of the ways in which they incorporate its potentials and problems.

The Modern American Peace Movement

The campaigns were the peacetime peaks of the modern — post-World War I — American peace movement. Although peace seeking can trace its roots back to early Christian pacifism, what we would recognize as a peace movement — organized secular activism — arose in the Western world in the early nineteenth century, in response to the Napoleonic wars and the introduction of mass conscription. The first wave of widespread support for the peace movement came after the turn of the century, as international rivalries moved ominously toward World War I. The unprecedented devastation caused by the war led to a reshaping of the peace movement into its modern form: a political, generally liberal to leftist endeavor, actively seeking to build coalitions with domestic reform constituencies. Four major aspects of the modern movement shaped its leading campaigns: its intellectual traditions, the organizational vehicles carrying the movement, its social base, and the relationship between peace and antiwar activism.

The three intellectual traditions at the core of the American peace movement are pacifism, antimilitarism, and internationalism.[3] Other ideas and movements such as feminism, liberalism, socialism, and environmentalism also have fed into the peace movement; isolationism and ethnic ties to various European nations at times have strengthened antiwar sentiment.[4]

Pacifism has been a key part of peace and antiwar activism in America since colonial times. Originating in early European Christian sects, pacifism has transformed itself from a religious tradition of individual witness into a secular, activist (and at times revolutionary) orientation that has shaped social movements around the globe.

Members of religious pacifist sects including Anabaptists, Mennonites, and Brethren emigrated to America beginning in the early seventeenth century. The most important of these groups was the Society of Friends, or Quakers. Quaker pacifism wove together key strands from religious pacifism: a universalism stressing the unity of human beings, consequent opposition to war as a crime against all, a commitment to oppose war both individually and collectively, belief in humanity's ability to end war, and a strong sense of social reform linked to the establishment of peaceful relations between individuals, groups, and nations (Young 1987). While retaining their religious roots, Quakers have helped shape secular, reform-oriented pacifism. Both religious and secular pacifism have sustained the American peace movement during times of war.

Antimilitarism is the second major strand. Opposition to the presence of imperial troops helped fuel colonial resistance to British rule, and the early republic witnessed major struggles over whether a standing army would be established. Although antimilitarism declined as a major force in American political life after 1800, it has periodically resurfaced in popular sentiment.

The third core tradition is internationalism. In sharp contrast to a strong isolationist sentiment in America, internationalism, like pacifism, has changed over time while retaining its main thrust, the belief that violence between nations can be reduced or eliminated through greater international cooperation and interdependence and peaceful resolution of disputes. Most pacifists have also been internationalists, although during the interwar period "internationalist" referred specifically to the nonpacifist wing of the movement.

More than pacifism and antimilitarism, internationalism frequently has been embraced by elements of the economic and political elite. Conservative internationalists have favored the imposition of order by major powers; liberal internationalists have worked toward establishing more equitable economic relations between states, disarmament, and development of multilateral institutions such as the United Nations. Conservative internationalism dominated the nonpacifist peace movement in the late nineteenth and early twentieth centuries, envisioning a world order based on Anglo-American economic hegemony and, if necessary, military force. From World War I through the onset of the cold war, liberal internationalism moved to the fore.

Pacifist, antimilitarist, and internationalist traditions have expressed themselves through enduring organizations and transient coalitions including the peace campaigns. Organizations founded during and just after World War I have sustained the movement during low moments and formed the nucleus of widespread mobilizations during upswings.

Throughout this era, the pacifist segment of the movement has centered on the American Friends Service Committee (AFSC), the Fellowship of Reconciliation (FOR), and the War Resisters League (WRL). After World War I, a second distinct segment was formed by internationalist groups including the League of Nations Association (LNA) and later the United World Federalists (UWF). The rise of the cold war disrupted the internationalist movement, and in its place arose a looser collection of antiwar and antinuclear organizations. Like some older groups including the Women's International League for Peace and Freedom (WILPF), these organizations did not fit neatly into any one wing or tradition.

With memberships ranging from several thousand to tens of thousands, and in some cases with a few paid staff, peace groups have carried the movement forward, expanding in membership and influence during upswings in movement activity and declining during downturns. Although the evangelical nature of the early peace movement made coalition-building difficult, the modern movement has been more pragmatic. Peace groups have entered coalitions with each other and with other social change organizations, in pursuit of specific goals and broad reforms. The peace campaigns began as coalitions.

The peace movement has no "natural" social base: no group clearly stands to benefit disproportionately from the achievement of the movement's goals in the same way that specific constituencies' interests have been represented by the labor, civil rights, and women's movements. The American peace movement's activists and leaders have come primarily from the educated white middle class, although peace groups have formed important coalitions with sectors of the working class and racial minorities as represented by organized labor and civil rights groups.

Since Quakers and members of other pacifist religious sects came to colonial America, there has been a complex relationship between ongoing peace activism and sporadic antiwar movements. Peace organizations have been important in movements of opposition to war and the preparation for war, but two kinds of tensions have persisted between peace groups and antiwar movements.

First, antiwar movements often appeal to beliefs and feelings distasteful to most peace activists. Coalitions with isolationists, communists, and others have been short-lived, as peace groups grappled with the moral and practical issues involved in working with these groups. On the one hand, the short-term crisis-management goals of the movement may be served by broad-based coalitions appealing to popular sentiments such as isolationism or fear of nuclear weapons. On the other hand, peace groups fear they may lose legitimacy through close association with fringe groups, and submerge the basic philosophies and programs of the movement by focusing too narrowly on one issue, however critical.

Second, most peace activists have been sympathetic to some war aims, such as abolitionism during the Civil War and antifascism during World War II. As peaceful means of achieving their goals disappear, many throw in their lot with military approaches. Even pacifists have been torn by this dilemma.

In the late 1930s, the neutrality movement gained great popularity and influence, uniting the peace movement and rallying a large sector of society. As war broke out in Europe and Asia, however, the peace movement split, and the neutrality movement faded. After American entry, as during World War I, the peace movement was sustained by a tiny pacifist community. The Vietnam War produced a different pattern. At the start of the war, the peace movement was a marginal voice of dissent, but opposition grew enormously after major escalation of American involvement.

Early American Pacifism and Antimilitarism

The roots of the American peace movement are in Christian pacifism, which emphasized individual witness and absolute resistance to war. The social upheavals associated with the collapse of traditional authority and the Protestant Reformation in sixteenth- and seventeenth-century Europe led to a proliferation of Christian pacifist sects, including both inward-looking, retreatist Anabaptists, and more worldly Quakers. Subject to severe repressions by political and military authorities, more than 60,000 members of these groups had emigrated to British North America before the American revolution.

Quakers have been critical to the development of western pacifism and the American peace movement. In the middle of the eighteenth century they abandoned their attempt to make Pennsylvania a "holy experiment" in harmonious relations between all peoples, and many scattered to other parts of North America. Quakerism then established itself as a vigorous tradition in North America, providing practical methods for resolving interpersonal and intergroup differences and an ethical basis for war resistance and peace-seeking. Few in number, Quakers have worked for social reforms from abolitionism to desegregation, as well as for peace. Furthermore, the commercial success of many early Quakers established a few wealthy families whose financial contributions to the peace movement were critical as formal movement organizations came to play a greater role in the twentieth century.

Pacifism remained a sectarian creed until the beginning of the modern peace movement. Despite the efforts of early religious pacifists, the right of conscientious objection was only gradually accepted by the government of the United States. Quakers and other pacifists who refused military service were subject to the confiscation of their property and harsher measures during the War of 1812, although the Union made the first provisions for alternative service during the Civil War.

Although the United States was established in a violent revolution, antimilitarism was widespread and powerful through the early nineteenth century. Popular opposition to a standing military limited the size and the pace of formation of the Continental Army, and Washington's postwar efforts to institute a national military were rebuffed. Instead, Federalists established a system of "federal volunteers," more than a militia but less than the kinds of armies European nation-states were developing. Antimilitarism declined, however, with the election of 1800, as the peaceful transition from a Federalist regime to Thomas Jefferson and the Republican faction eased fears of the antidemocratic possibilities of military establishments (DeBenedetti 1980, 27).

The War of 1812 provoked opposition "as vehement and widespread as any in American history" (DeBenedetti 1980, 28). Concentrated in New England, this opposition crossed class lines, and was fed by conservative antipathy toward the French revolution, religious denunciations of the immorality of war, and widespread skepticism toward possible gains from the war. Many northeastern financiers who would not loan money to the federal government made large loans to Britain, while popular resistance was expressed in mob actions, widespread refusal to enlist in military service, and local declarations of neutrality. Nevertheless, western farmers interested in expansion, suffering economically from the American boycott of both sides in the European wars, were able to rouse sufficient anti-British feelings among the public and in Congress to gain a declaration of war.

At the end of the war, jingoistic nationalism proclaimed the United

States divinely chosen to bring enlightened republicanism to the world as a basis for a new, more peaceful, international order. This attitude, which DeBenedetti (1980) traces to the dual American heritage of evangelical Protestantism and Enlightenment rationalism, and to the popularity of the war once won, has since furthered and rationalized continental expansion and overseas interventions as a strong counterpoint to the various peace and antimilitarist traditions.

The Rise of Secular Peace Activism

Although the War of 1812 set these militaristic forces in motion, it also led to the establishment of the first secular volunteer peace societies, as did the Napoleonic wars in Europe. In the nineteenth century there was a major shift in forms of political contention in the western world, including the rise of what Tilly (1984) calls "national social movements"—movements spanning entire nation-states—and a proliferation of local social movements. Responding to new forms of political and economic rule, including the consolidation of power in central governments, and paralleling new forms of political organizing, notably a focus on national electoral politics, deprived groups and others excluded from policy making began to create enduring national movement organizations to press their demands. Previous movement activity had been more exclusively local, scattered, and defensive. The peace movement was no exception to this transition.

In 1828, the American Peace Society (APS) was formed as a national organization, after several dozen city- and statewide nondenominational peace societies were established. The APS, strongly influenced by Christianity, approached peace in a heavily moralistic rather than a pragmatic and political manner. Before the Civil War, the organized nondenominational peace movement was part of a cluster of movements such as the temperance movement, centering around voluntary societies founded by Protestant, northeastern urban middle-class leaders "committed to moral improvement through gradual enlightenment" (DeBenedetti 1980, 34).

To these leaders, peace was a means toward social salvation; war was a "barbarous anachronism that destroyed good order, subverted human liberty, and inhibited Christ's global victory" (DeBenedetti 1980, 35). Believing in their evangelical mission, peace leaders spurned coalitions with other reform forces whose agenda might be less inspired. Its evangelical and humanitarian character made this movement more outward-looking than its sectarian predecessors, but the pre–Civil

War nineteenth-century American peace movement was still "a community without a polity" (Chatfield 1978, 115).

In the 1830s, the peace movement allied itself with abolitionism, which had similar intellectual roots, evangelical spirit, and middle-class social base. Leaders of both movements tended to come from the ranks of northern Protestant clergy, and most activists were women. This alliance strengthened the appeal of the peace movement in the Northeast and the West, and limited it elsewhere.

As abolitionism became a more heated issue, it also attracted violent reaction, and the APS endured its first split. The dividing issue proved enormously consequential for the peace movement thereafter: whether there was such a thing as a "just war." A small number of absolute pacifists whose answer to this question was negative formed a separate organization, the New England Non-Resistance Society. Thus the peace movement of the early and middle nineteenth century experienced the beginnings of trends that would shape its twentieth-century counterpart: secularization, increased reliance on formal, voluntary organizations, including national organizations (or organizations with pretensions to national scope), and factionalism. Also at that time, the movement, in general profoundly nationalistic, began to form international ties, especially with British peace societies.

Abolitionism helped spark opposition to the Mexican-American War of 1846–1848, as a small but vocal minority denounced the war for having opened more land for slavery. Focused in New England, opposition included tax resistance, later publicized by Henry David Thoreau's "Resistance to Civil Government." The antiwar movement had no coherent political expression, however, and the pull of territorial conquest and popular support for the war prevailed. Nevertheless, some credit the movement with forcing Polk to accept less than total conquest of Mexico (DeBenedetti 1980, 52–53).

The Civil War and Postwar Internationalism

The Civil War again divided the young peace movement. As sectional tensions increased throughout the 1850s, many pacifists decided that war would be justified if it led to the end of slavery. Membership in peace groups plummeted. Most of those remaining in the APS reluctantly voted to support the Union as southern states seceded.

There was little organized opposition to the Civil War. Fifteen hundred Quakers and other sectarian pacifists claimed conscientious objector status (DeBenedetti 1980, 58). Many were harassed; some were killed. Treatment was better in the North, which passed the first legislation providing for alternative service as well as the first national conscription program.

The bloody Civil War marked the end of the moralistic, "humanitarian" peace movement (DeBenedetti 1980). Although the pacifist tradition continued among Quaker and other religious sects, the American peace movement of the late nineteenth century came to be dominated by conservative internationalists.[5] Elite Anglophiles, they responded to America's rise to world power and the growing industrial interdependence between nations by promoting international order presided over by Britain and the United States. Economically liberal in the classic sense of belief in free-market capitalism and individualism, these business and political leaders were socially and politically conservative. Until World War I ended, the American peace movement remained conservative under the influence of these leaders. It stood apart from domestic reform currents such as the labor movement and agrarian populism.

New internationalist organizations grew under the sponsorship of leaders like Andrew Carnegie. In the 1860s and 1870s, they worked for the negotiation of treaties and the establishment of institutions such as international arbitration and a world court, achieving limited success. Meanwhile, the APS did not adjust well to the industrializing world and the growing trend toward empire. It failed to formulate any coherent policy toward post–Civil War violence between labor and capital and the wars against the Indians. Both the APS and pacifist organizations declined in strength.

The Spanish-American War and American Imperial Power

A turning point for American foreign policy and the American peace movement occurred in 1898 when the United States declared war on Spain. The Spanish-American war marked the emergence of the United States as an imperial power, and the defeat of a strong anti-imperialist coalition that only partially overlapped with the peace movement.

Some peace leaders actually supported President McKinley in his military conquest of Cuba and the Philippines, and many who did join the opposition were less than militant. Although some historians see the Spanish-American War as a critical event in American history, marking the triumph of a militaristic, interventionist foreign policy, prominent peace leaders of the time hoped it was a temporary aberration that could not stop the movement toward international order.

The anti-imperialist movement expanded dramatically with the bloody suppression of the Philippines. Even without the full support of the established peace movement, the Anti-Imperialist League grew to a membership of 30,000 members, the first peace or antiwar group in American history with a true mass base.[6] The movement split during the presidential election of 1900, as conservative elements of the coalition would not back populist Democrat William Jennings Bryan despite his anti-imperialist platform.

As this historic antiwar effort rose and fell, conservative internationalist groups looked toward Europe and the establishment of international peacekeeping mechanisms. In the prewar Progressive Era, however, a new, left-oriented peace movement gained strength, promoting social reform and a different vision of international order. This movement only slowly developed a mass base, as it shared with the conservative internationalists and with many progressives a deep-seated elitism.[7] Nevertheless, as nations continued arming and forming the alliances that set the stage for World War I, new peace groups in Europe and the United States grew in size and diversity. Socialists, feminists, and others on the left began to play a greater role in organized peace-seeking.

World War I

As the First World War began in 1914, the peace movement divided over the question of America's role. When President Wilson in late 1915 announced a program of military preparedness, most of the liberal factions of the peace movement joined a range of progressive constituencies in a broad antimilitarist, anti-interventionist coalition, while the conservative internationalists supported Wilson.

The antipreparedness coalition itself soon split over the presidential election of 1916. Liberal antiwar activists opposed Wilson's foreign policy, but many saw him as a domestic reformer and supported his reelection over Republican Charles Evans Hughes.

A second and decisive split occurred in April 1917 when the United States entered World War I. Internationalists, both conservative and liberal, endorsed Wilson's declaration of war, and hoped to play a role in shaping a new postwar international order. The Socialist party and pacifist groups formed the core of a much-diminished peace movement, which focused on support for conscientious objectors and civil liberties and plans for postwar reform.

The wartime peace movement, with other progressive forces, was subjected to severe government repression and right-wing vigilantism. Gaining momentum after the Russian revolution, the "Red Scare" included a potent combination of mob violence and new legal measures allowing the censorship, jailing, and deportation of thousands of Socialist, labor, and peace activists. This continued past the end of the war in 1918. Singled out for especially harsh treatment were foreign-born Americans who made up the core leadership of the Socialist party and African-Americans who were moving in unprecedented numbers from the South to northern cities.

The Red Scare created a very unhealthy climate for renewed peace activism. So did public opinion. Although ten million people, including 100,000 American soldiers, died during World War I, initial American reaction was not strongly antiwar. American intervention, in fact, was hailed (by Americans) as decisive in bringing the war to a close. The war's unprecedented carnage and civilian casualties did lead to the formation of the modern American peace movement, however, which in the 1920s helped turn public opinion against war.

Many leaders of the prewar peace movement had become demoralized. Others were in jail or deported. Some felt that the scope of the war had dwarfed their previous efforts. A new generation of leaders, radicalized by World War I, rose to shape the new movement. Their task, as described by DeBenedetti (1980, xiv), was to resolve "the most disturbing paradox of this century: The very processes of modernization — including industrial interdependence, advancing science and technology, and the bureaucratic organization of mass violence — which made peace a simple necessity of survival had intensified the kind of tribal nationalism and military influence that placed highest value upon state security and protracted struggle."

The Rise of the Modern American Peace Movement

Like its prewar predecessor, the modern American peace movement was split into two factions. Both internationalism and pacifism were profoundly influenced by progressivism and the experience of war and repression, and the peace movement reflected these influences.[8] The philosophies and organizations formed in wartime proved enduring and important.

Liberal internationalism overshadowed the conservative version. Instead of relying on Anglo-American force, it assumed that nations would cooperate voluntarily through enlightened self-interest to achieve economic and political harmony. Liberal internationalism included an elitism reflecting the faith of many progressive leaders in the ability of experts to fashion a rational, enlightened capitalism.[9] Its advocates claimed to offer a more democratic alternative to both revolutionary socialism and the prewar autocracies on which they blamed the war. To promote the formation of international bodies to facilitate international cooperation, they established organizations such as the League of Free Nations Association (1918, renamed the Foreign Policy Association in 1921), and supported Wilson during and after the war.

A new generation of leaders also transformed pacifism between the wars by fashioning a left-leaning activist pacifism. Influenced by their wartime coalition with socialists, they saw strong connections between international inequalities and violence and domestic injustice. During the 1920s and 1930s, key pacifists remained close to the Socialist party, often moving back and forth among the peace, labor, women's, and civil rights movements. Within pacifist groups and the Socialist party, debates raged over the morality and strategic role of violence in the class struggle.

Tensions over these issues intensified the search for a philosophy and practice of nonviolent social change. As early as 1917, notes Chatfield (1971, 203), American pacifists learned about the work of Mohandas K. Gandhi, and "endowed [him] with a mystique born of their need for a political model and enhanced by distance." Gandhi's influence over pacifists grew as his campaign for Indian independence progressed, and his philosophy offered pacifists a much-needed alternative to violent social change.

These new philosophies were embodied in peace organizations formed just before, during, and after World War I. In 1915, religious absolute pacifists founded the Fellowship of Reconciliation (FOR), which served as the common meeting ground of action-oriented pacifists. The American Friends Service Committee (AFSC) was founded in 1917 to provide alternatives to military service for conscientious objectors. It became the primary action arm of Quakers. The War Resisters League (WRL) emerged in 1924 from FOR as a coordinating committee for pacifists then turned to a program of recruiting pledges to refuse military service. These groups and their overseas affiliates have remained active throughout the modern peace movement.

The wealthy Carnegie Endowment for International Peace supported internationalist organizations including the Foreign Policy Association and the League of Nations Non-Partisan Association (1923, renamed the League of Nations Association in 1929). Three key groups represented liberal reformers outside the two main camps. The American chapter of WILPF (founded 1919) combined feminism with peace seeking. The National Council for Prevention of War (NCPW), organized in 1921, became the common lobbying arm of peace groups and civic organizations supporting peace initiatives. The National Committee on the Cause and Cure of War (NCCW) was established in 1924.

The Modern American Peace Movement Between World Wars

After World War I, peace groups focused on reconstruction and a search for ways to prevent another devastating war. Most pacifists opposed the Versailles Treaty ending World War I and Wilson's campaign for American membership in the League of Nations, believing that the punitive measures in the treaty negated any benefits of the league, and that the league placed too much power in the hands of major states. Liberal internationalists split over league membership. Even the League of Free Nations Association failed to help Wilson try to overcome nationalist and isolationist sentiment in the Senate, working instead for changes in the structure of the league and the treaty. The victory of antileague Republican Harding over pro-league Democrat Cox in 1920 ended the campaign for American membership. The peace movement instead promoted more modest measures: American membership in the league's World Court, and democratic reforms to limit the coercive role in the league of the great powers.

During the 1920s, pacifists divided their energies between reconstruction efforts abroad, domestic economic reform including labor struggles, and campaigns for disarmament and against universal military training. Under pressure from both wings of the peace movement, President Hoover in 1921 convened the Washington Disarmament Conference, which led to reductions in the navies of the United States, Great Britain, and Japan. Disarmament work continued until the mid-1930s, with limited success.

More effective were attempts to develop and popularize revisionist histories of World War I. Working mostly through churches, pacifists helped to revive antimilitarism by promoting the view that an unchecked arms race had been a prime cause of World War I. Internationalists in the 1920s cooperated with some pacifist initiatives, but focused their energies on two legal projects: American accession to the World Court and a treaty outlawing war. Despite efforts by pacifists and some internationalist leaders to reconcile their supporters, "the better part of a decade was wasted in internecine controversy" (Chatfield 1978, 120). Neither approach led to important policy changes, although the World Court issue remained alive through the mid-1930s.

American intervention in Nicaragua in December 1926 temporarily reinvigorated anti-imperialism. A broad coalition including both pacifists and internationalists successfully lobbied a receptive Congress for the removal of American troops and the peaceful settlement of differences with Mexico.

During the 1920s, the peace movement built coalitions, extended its public outreach, sharpened its political skills, and made inroads on policy. During the 1930s, however, under the press of international events, the peace movement turned to a defensive effort to prevent war, then an even more limited attempt to keep the United States out of the war.

Economic depression and the approach of World War II shaped the peace movement of the 1930s. The Depression cut into the resources and the organizational strength of the peace movement, the labor movement, and others. The Japanese invasion of Manchuria in 1931 dimmed activists' hopes of peacefully reforming the international order. Soon the economic discontent that spurred a resurgent labor movement contributed to the popularity of revisionist histories of World War I, in which big munitions makers played a sinister role. Increasing international tensions fed growing antiwar sentiment. The peace movement enjoyed at best a shallow popularity, though, one more receptive to isolationist than internationalist tendencies. President Roosevelt's preoccupation with domestic matters gave the peace movement greater room to maneuver and pressure Congress throughout the 1930s, but the start of World War II reduced this room dramatically.

One major peace effort of the 1930s was an attempt, headed by WILPF and pacifist groups, to regulate the arms industry. Under pressure from the peace movement, in 1934 Republican Senator Gerald P. Nye of North Dakota convened hearings on the role of arms manufacturers and merchants in World War I. Evidence presented at the "Nye hearings" of the arms merchants' use of bribes and political influence in lobbying for larger military budgets and their collusion with British arms dealers in sharing patents and dividing profits and sales territories received tremendous publicity and raised antimilitarist sentiment.

Despite the Depression, liberal internationalists avoided domestic reform issues and pressed for reform of the Versailles system and for

American accession to the World Court. Although their leaders gained influence in policy-making bodies, internationalists in the 1920s and 1930s found many of their plans blocked by growing isolationist sentiment. After the Senate rejected American participation in the World Court in 1935, they briefly formed a coalition with pacifists to mobilize public support for international reform and American neutrality, the Emergency Peace Campaign.

The Emergency Peace Campaign

The final rejection of the World Court by the Senate shocked the peace movement. At the same time, the Senate passed the 1935 Neutrality Act, which abandoned claims to neutral shipping rights, mandated an arms embargo on all belligerent states, and constrained presidential discretion in these matters. Most peace groups favored neutrality, but they thought the act did not go far enough. They launched an all-out effort to avert war or, at least, to keep the United States out of war.

Fearing both the rise of isolationism and the approach of war, in 1936 and 1937 both wings of the peace movement joined in the EPC, which had two key goals. The first, international reform to remove great economic disparities as a motive for war, was easily agreed upon if not easily achieved. The second, American neutrality, was more controversial, with weaker support among internationalists than among pacifists. Pacifists led the EPC, however. They had taken the initiative in forming it, and the pacifist groups were well-financed and better-equipped than the internationalists for mounting a public outreach and congressional lobbying campaign. As a result, internationalists temporarily put aside their misgivings over neutrality and joined the campaign.

The EPC was the largest peace coalition in the United States to that date. EPC leaders used church and other networks and mass communications to reach most corners of America with their internationalist-neutralist message. By the end of 1937, however, tensions within the coalition — primarily but not exclusively over the neutrality issue — ended the Campaign.

Internationalists embraced the doctrine of collective security with the Allies. Although they still hoped that war could be averted, they chose to support the Allies and looked toward shaping a reformed postwar order. Pacifists worked to maintain a left-wing, internationalist neutralism, but by 1940 right-wingers had captured the neutrality movement. Pacifism, which reached unprecedented popularity in the 1930s, dwindled again to a marginal creed embraced by a relative handful, and divisions within the Socialist party weakened the anti-war Left. In 1941, membership in the United States section of WILPF dropped by half, and Socialist party membership fell to six thousand (DeBenedetti 1980, 140).

World War II and the Postwar Peace Movement

After Pearl Harbor, the remaining pacifists again focused their efforts on establishing and protecting the rights of conscientious objectors and on providing aid to refugees. They also publicly criticized saturation bombing and what they saw as the refusal of the Allies to pursue a negotiated peace.

Wartime developments in the pacifist community helped shape postwar pacifism and American politics. As happened during World War I, a younger generation of pacifists became radicalized through their experience as conscientious objectors. Pacifists and civil libertarians successfully pressed the government to allow for alternative service, but were unable to persuade Congress to adopt British-style codes allowing for nonreligious objectors and complete exemption from service. Between 1941 and 1945, more than 25,000 conscientious objectors served in the armed forces as noncombatants, another 12,000 worked in the Civilian Public Service (CPS) at forestry and similar jobs; 6,000 (mostly Jehovah's Witnesses) who refused any cooperation were jailed. Authoritarian work camps increasingly controlled by the military, lack of compensation, racial segregation, and work that ranged from monotonous to dangerous sparked strikes, walkouts, and other protests including fasts in a variety of CPS camps and jails.

Although these uprisings had little if any public visibility and impact, they gave younger pacifists the opportunity to develop tactics of nonviolent civil disobedience. These tactics, instrumental in a variety of postwar movements, were spread through close links that formed between pacifist leaders and leaders of the civil rights movement. In 1942, members of the Chicago chapter of the Fellowship of Reconciliation established the Congress of Racial Equality (CORE) in an attempt to bring Gandhian nonviolent resistance to the civil rights movement. FOR activists helped to set up CORE chapters and sponsored successful campaigns for the desegregation of public facilities in Northern cities. Through CORE and FOR, key civil rights leaders, including James Farmer, Bayard Rustin, and Martin Luther King,

Jr., deepened their commitment to nonviolent civil disobedience.

At the end of the war, pacifist organizations declined in membership. Older, more traditional pacifists retained control of FOR; the War Resisters League became a haven for radical pacifists, who started new, socialist- and anarchist-pacifist journals and organizations, and added to their repertoire tactics such as tax resistance.

As pacifism developed a revolutionary current, liberal internationalists planned for the easing of economic rivalries and the establishment of a strong international association. They formed the United Nations Association (1943), which in 1944 absorbed most of the members of the League of Nations Association (renamed the American Association for the United Nations in 1945).

Some internationalists, along with pacifists who had supported the idea of an international association, were disappointed by the final United Nations (U.N.) Charter, signed by delegates from fifty-five nations in June 1945 in San Francisco and ratified by the U.S. Senate in July. They believed the U.N.'s structure would ensure domination by the five major powers (China, Great Britain, France, the Soviet Union, and the United States) granted permanent seats on the Security Council.

Despite their close ties with national policy makers and their extensive local contacts, internationalists had lost out to Roosevelt and others who favored plans for a postwar pax Americana based on unilateral military power and a monopoly on atomic weapons. However, by the late 1940s world federalism would capture the imagination of leading internationalists and a large segment of the American public.

The widespread support for world federalism was surprising because, as after the First World War, the political climate did not appear promising for a revived peace movement that incorporated internationalism. Once more, a common belief that American intervention had ended the European war encouraged pro-military nationalism.[10] There was little disillusionment with the war and its aftermath to mitigate these feelings. World War II was not viewed as a "war to end all wars." For all but a handful of absolute pacifists, the nature of the adversary and the attack on Pearl Harbor amply justified fighting. There also was a material basis for calling this "the good war," as Studs Terkel (1985) titled his oral history of the times. Although 80 million were killed and wounded in the war, U.S. casualties were relatively light at 1 million.[11] Domestic life was also relatively free of hardship, especially compared with the years of the Great Depression. High levels of unemployment did not end until wartime production revitalized American capitalism and the war effort absorbed large numbers of unemployed men. Unprecedented opportunities opened up in the labor force for women and minorities, and increased demand for food production meant that farmers finally recovered from the dust bowl and Depression.

Against these strong currents, which gained hegemony with the rise of cold war politics in the late 1940s, fears of the atomic bomb created a brief political opening for revived peace efforts by world federalists and in a movement among atomic scientists for international control over atomic energy.

Both world federalism and the scientists' movement were prompted by the first wave of "nuclear pacifism," the belief that nuclear weapons should never be used again and the hope that the existence of the bomb made war itself unthinkable. Although nuclear pacifism took hold mainly among intellectuals, including atomic scientists, much of the public also began to see war through new eyes. A September 1945 poll not only found that 83 percent of Americans believed that atomic warfare could kill most urban dwellers but also found that 64 percent saw such wars as less likely to occur precisely because of the devastating potential of these weapons. [12]

Closer to the established political discourse, nuclear pacifists reached a broader public than did the traditional or the radical pacifists. In particular, world government ideas, first broadly promoted by internationalist organizations in the aftermath of World War I, enjoyed brief but unparalleled success.

Toward the end of World War II, world government advocates lobbied unsuccessfully for American support of a strong international organization. After the atomic bombing of Japan, the campaign was reinvigorated; and by 1949, seventeen state legislatures had adopted a resolution urging Congress to establish a world government. Such a plan enjoyed significant support in Congress and by the public: an August 1946 survey found that 54 percent of Americans favored plans to make the United Nations a world government with control over all national armed forces. [13]

If the substantive achievements of this movement were minor, the UWF developed the closest thing to a mass movement seen in the immediate postwar era. In 1947, sixteen world government organizations merged to form the UWF, with about 17,000 members and 200 chapters in thirty-nine states. By late 1948, membership had expanded to 40,000 in 659 chapters.

The atomic scientists' activism also began as the war drew to a close. After the defeat of Germany, some atomic scientists opposed the use of atomic weapons on a Japan already close to defeat. Several top scientists lobbied and circulated petitions among the community of atomic scientists against using the atomic bomb against Japan. These leaders formed the core of the Atomic Scientists of Chicago, which in 1945 merged with two other groups to form the Federation of Atomic Scientists. Besides publishing the *Bulletin of the Atomic Scientists,* they fought for international control of atomic energy. An early victory for this high-level movement came when Congress rejected the Truman administration's plans to keep control of atomic energy within the military and instead created civilian agencies for this purpose.

By mid-1946, the Federation of American Scientists, the successor to the Federation of Atomic Scientists, had two thousand members committed to preventing a dangerous nuclear arms race. The Emergency Committee of Atomic Scientists, chaired by Albert Einstein and including many other prominent scientists, was the most militant of the scientists' groups, issuing strong statements on the need for international cooperation and control over atomic energy and strenuously denouncing American foreign policy, which seemed to be heading toward a militarism based on atomic monopoly.

Despite initial public fear of atomic weapons, the scientists' movement quickly lost momentum. Wittner (1984) cites two key reasons for this. First, fear diminished. That atmospheric tests in the South Pacific seemed to produce few negative effects made the bomb less ominous. The government, meanwhile, had embarked on an ambitious "atoms for peace" program to give atomic energy a positive image. Second, the fear that remained could prompt calls for more weapons to ensure military superiority.[14] This occurred during the test ban and freeze campaigns.

The last major battle of the scientists' movement in this era was over formulating American proposals for internationalizing atomic energy. There was no clear policy immediately after the war, although many influential policy makers were intent upon preserving and increasing the American nuclear monopoly. They believed that such a monopoly would last — longer than the four years it took the Soviet Union to develop its own atomic weapon. An increasingly intransigent position emerged from these critical policy debates, and the proposal presented to the Soviets and the United Nations insisted on maintaining the United States' right to continue stockpiling atomic weapons while other nations submitted to international inspection and supervision. The Soviets rejected this proposal out of hand, and hopes of averting competition in nuclear weapons were dashed.[15]

The Cold War

By 1948, the escalating cold war began to divide and weaken the American peace movement. Analogies were made between the Soviet Union and Nazi Germany, and the Truman administration fashioned a plan for "containment militarism," calling for high levels of military preparedness and a vigorous nuclear weapons program.

Some were skeptical about claims of a Soviet military threat to Western Europe. Radical critics have argued that this threat was inflated to provide a pretext for continuing military Keynesianism at home, adopting an active role in rebuilding European capitalism, and intervening abroad in the interests of domestic capitalists.[16] These critiques were heard only on the margins of political discourse, however, and many liberals and even some pacifists embraced containment. Those who did not faced growing state repression and shrinking public support and sympathy. The failure to reach an atomic agreement with the Soviets, along with increasing government pressure including Truman's loyalty oath program, demoralized many active scientists. The majority became reluctant supporters of government policy, although a few continued to seek a means to internationalize control of atomic energy. Almost all continued to work on atomic weapons, prompting harsh criticism from pacifists.

The election of 1948 split the noncommunist Left and pacifist communities, and divided liberalism into a dominant cold war wing and a much-weakened group of "peace liberals." Cold war liberals, many of whom voted for Truman, favored a strong presidency, a large military, active American intervention abroad, continued buildup of a nuclear arsenal, and a domestic agenda including limited economic reform and public works projects based on large military budgets. Truman's election helped to consolidate power in a strong executive and a Republican–conservative Democrat coalition in Congress. It also helped put into place a cold war system that profoundly shaped the course of history and the nature and limits of peace activism.

Three aspects of cold war politics have been critical to the peace movement. First and most obviously, the East-West confrontation has dominated international relations, posed the clearest threat of precipitating major, even nuclear war, and provided the greatest obstacle to more cooperative international relations. Second, the rise of the "national security state" has subjected peace and other activists to government scrutiny and repression and has been accompanied by the intensified identification of patriotism with conservative, promilitary views. Thus opponents have tagged the postwar peace movement, with some success, as "subversive." Third, military spending provided a material base for elite and public support of cold war militarism.[17] Although critics have argued that high levels of military spending have harmed the American economy, diverting resources from civilian production and consumption and allowing competitors to capture international markets for consumer goods, a powerful sector of business and workers has profited from military-based profits and jobs.[18] The potent political component of this domestic constituency is what economist Gordon Adams (1982) calls the "iron triangle," top military and civilian Pentagon employees, major defense contractors, and leading members of Congress with large military outlays in their districts.

After 1948, the emergence of the military-industrial complex and the rise of nationalist feelings led to the incorporation into a cold war consensus of sectors of the public that had been supportive of the prewar peace movement (DeBenedetti 1980, 154). Most significantly, organized labor and the Protestant church became much more nationalist and conservative. Concern over holding onto wartime gains in employment shaped the interests of organized women. College campuses in the 1930s provided a strong base for pacifism; in the postwar years, they were filled with returned GIs whose primary interests were vocational.

Cold war politics intensified with the formation of the North Atlantic Treaty Organization (NATO) in 1949 and Truman's decision to proceed with development of the hydrogen bomb in spite of opposition from most atomic scientists. The outbreak of the Korean War in 1950 was a devastating blow to a weakened peace movement, widening its internal divisions and escalating the repression of dissenters.

The Emergency Committee of Atomic Scientists folded by the end of 1950, and the *Bulletin of the Atomic Scientists* ceased advocating end to the nuclear arms race. The world federalist movement became more conservative before virtually fading from the scene. For the next few years, the American peace movement was again reduced to a small core of activists, outside the mainstream of politics and culture but continuing to formulate alternatives to cold war militarism and the buildup of nuclear weapons. It kept alive traditions including nonviolent resistance, and in the late 1950s spurred a large-scale antinuclear campaign.

The Movement Revives

Although activism was limited in the early 1950s, pacifists formulated a coherent critique of the cold war, developing a "third camp" position, echoed later by much of the noncommunist Left in the United States. Pacifists also maintained their involvement in the civil rights movement, which gained momentum and visibility in the 1950s, escalating dramatically with the Montgomery bus boycott of 1955–1956.

A decline in cold war tensions produced a more favorable political environment for the peace movement in the mid-1950s. The Korean armistice and Stalin's death in 1953 were followed by Khrushchev's 1956 condemnation of Stalinism and declaration of a policy of peaceful coexistence. In the United States, the decline of McCarthy and McCarthyism opened some political space within which the peace movement could maneuver. On March 1, 1954, shifting winds during an American nuclear test conducted in the Bikini Atoll in the South Pacific caused radioactive fallout to contaminate several nearby Marshall Islands and the crew of a Japanese fishing trawler. When the U.S. government admitted that radiation levels had also risen over the American mainland, press and public turned their attention to atmospheric testing.

In 1955, public concern increased as Britain tested a hydrogen bomb. The Soviet Union proposed a test ban, which President Eisenhower rejected as not verifiable. Democrat Adlai Stevenson campaigned for a test ban in the 1956 election, giving the issue greater visibility. Although Eisenhower came to support a test ban during his second term, he never acted decisively. Opponents of the ban, primarily within the Atomic Energy Commission and the Pentagon, blocked significant progress during the second Eisenhower administration, despite increasing international and domestic pressure for a halt to atomic testing.

The Test Ban Campaign

It was during the second Eisenhower administration, in 1957, that the peace movement formed a coalition to end atomic testing and promote nuclear disarmament. Two organizations were established to lead the campaign. Pacifists who headed the Committee for Nonviolent

Action (CNVA) brought their direct-action tactics into the antinuclear movement, while the liberal Committee for a Sane Nuclear Policy (SANE) educated and lobbied for a test ban. For six years, the test ban campaign was the focus of a newly revived peace movement. SANE developed into a federated organization with more than 25,000 members, plus twenty-five chapters of Student SANE. The liberal-pacifist coalition fractured in 1960 when pacifists accused SANE's liberal leadership of caving in to congressional Red-baiting. Pacifists who had worked through SANE, including some of its leading figures, quit the organization, while Student SANE membership plummeted. Some pacifists and students changed the focus of their activism to other issues and movements, most notably the rising civil rights movement.

These splits critically weakened the test ban campaign, which sputtered to a halt after the 1963 Limited Test Ban Treaty robbed the issue of its immediacy. The treaty, signed by the United States, the Soviet Union, and Great Britain outlawed atmospheric and outer-space testing of atomic weapons. It fell far short of the goal of ending the nuclear arms race because it permitted the development of new weapons through underground testing. SANE's membership dropped, the Student Peace Union (SPU) disbanded altogether, and public attention shifted elsewhere. Not until the nuclear freeze campaign was launched in 1979 did the issue of atomic weapons again become a major national concern.

Although it failed to change the course of the arms race, the test ban campaign was the first major show of public opposition to cold war policies and atomic weapons. It provided an intellectual and organizational springboard for the social movement upheaval of the 1960s.

Vietnam

As the test ban campaign ended, the peace movement was caught up in the turmoil of the Vietnam War. In the summer of 1963, SANE called for American disengagement as the Ngo Dinh Diem government took repressive action against Buddhists. For the next year, SANE, with other established peace groups and radical students in the SPU and the newly formed Students for a Democratic Society (SDS), mounted a series of small protests against American sponsorship of the South Vietnamese government. In early 1965, President Johnson dramatically increased the American military role, introducing large numbers of ground troops and beginning the most intensive aerial bombings in history.

Between 1965 and 1975, the war moved millions of Americans to protest in a variety of ways ranging from letter-writing and electoral work, to massive national and smaller local demonstrations, to militant direct action. Although SANE and the established peace groups were important actors, "antiwar activism expanded in the United States during 1965–1970 with such rapidity, diversity, and spontaneity that it seemed to preclude the very existence of an organized movement" (DeBenedetti 1980, 175). Throughout the war years, activism was much more widespread and decentralized than during the test ban campaign—a pattern typical of historic differences between peace and antiwar movements.[19]

The radical (pacifist and student) vs. liberal divisions of the early 1960s persisted and intensified as the New Left emerged as an important social force, led in many instances by young veterans of the test ban campaign. The New Left included both mostly-black groups such as the Student Non-Violent Coordinating Committee (SNCC), which emerged in 1960 from the southern civil rights movement, and campus-based, mostly-white groups, including Students for a Democratic Society (SDS, 1962) that formed the core of the 1960s student movement. The Old Left was based in the labor movement and included Communists and a variety of socialist groups.

Reacting against the intellectualism and exclusionist policies of liberalism and the Old Left, student activists produced a politics of action and inclusiveness that alienated many in the liberal and Old Left wings of the movement, and much of middle America.[20] Although the war provided a common focus for the different elements of the movement, differences in goals, strategies, tactics, and styles, along with the rapid proliferation of activism, prevented the formation of more than short-lived, ad hoc coalitions. From the outset, radicals called for unilateral American withdrawal, and liberals pressed for a cease-fire and a negotiated withdrawal. And although some liberals eventually adopted the unilateral withdrawal position, differences between the factions persisted and in some ways intensified, as the left wing of the movement grew more radical.[21]

The movement began to decline in 1970–1971 with Nixon's "Vietnamization" policy, which promised and slowly delivered a withdrawal of American troops and an end to the draft. After a brief revival of intensive bombing of the North in December 1972, peace accords were signed in January 1973, and the following year the governement of the South collapsed. A diminished group of activists continued to focus on Southeast Asia, pressing for an end to American military action in Cambodia and Laos, reconstruction aid to Vietnam, and an amnesty for the record number of draft resisters and deserters.

Although the antiwar movement may not have ended the war, it did limit the ability of the Johnson and Nixon administrations to escalate the level of violence, and along with fear of Soviet and Chinese retaliation, it helped rule out the use of nuclear weapons. It had contradictory effects on public opinion: some support for the war was hardened by reaction against the protest, but the unruliness of protest also contributed to a growing mood of disdain for the war and its consequences.[22] As a result of the antiwar movement, the cold war consensus was weakened, if not shattered, and public support for military intervention in the Third World became harder to mobilize. The "Vietnam syndrome" made elements of the military and the public more reluctant to use overt military force over any prolonged period. Instead, planners developed the doctrine of "low-intensity warfare" in the Third World, using proxy forces.[23]

The antiwar opposition, as well as Watergate, strengthened Congress's role in making foreign and military policy, as exemplified by the passage of the War Powers Act in 1973 (Waller 1987). On the other hand, conservative reaction to the Vietnam syndrome and to a decade of détente and strategic arms accords between the superpowers led to a revived campaign for a more aggressive military posture, one that contributed to the 1980 election of Ronald Reagan and a Republican majority in the Senate.

During the Vietnam years, the peace movement again focused its efforts away from the long-term task of building peace and toward a short-term, crisis operation. Efforts to build a lasting coalition linking antiwar activism with domestic reform currents, including the civil rights movement, were only partly successful. The economic legacy of the war, including inflation brought on by the impossibility of raising taxes to pay for an unpopular war, weakened support for social spending. Along with the backlash against the antiwar movement, these conditions also helped to erode the liberal, Democratic electoral coalition of the 1960s.

Although the Nixon administration played a backlash against the excesses of the radical wing of the movement to gain public support for its policies, the antiwar, New Left, civil rights, feminist, and other movements of the 1960s and 1970s produced a lasting legacy in values of empowerment and participatory democracy and a large group of experienced activists who played key roles in the peace movement after Vietnam.

After Vietnam: The Turn to Local Organizing

Veterans of the antiwar movement shared with long-time peace activists a desire to return to the fundamental issues of internationalism and disarmament as they continued a newly revived antimilitarist, anti-imperialist tradition. They moved the peace groups toward organizing locally to build the broad and deep support that had been lacking not only during the Vietnam era but throughout the modern peace movement.

This local strategy reflected the New Left belief in participatory democracy and suspicion of centralization and hierarchy. It also reflected a general trend toward community-based organization around economic and environmental issues (Boyte 1980, 1982; Herbers 1983). For the peace movement, it offered strategic benefits that compensated for the fact that its issues were more exclusively the province of the federal government than were those of any other movement.

Local weapons facilities and proposed missile sites provided a focus for organizing. Campaigns against these facilities brought the issue of atomic weapons home more powerfully than at any time since the end of atmospheric testing. Furthermore, the peace movement was relatively strong at the community level. After Vietnam, it had many experienced activists and organizers and a strong network of contacts and supporters. Local elites (political, economic, media, etc.) were open to alternative ideas on foreign and military policy, as federal aid to cities declined while military expenditures soared in the late Carter administration. In contrast, at the national level the movement was greatly outmatched by the financial and propaganda resources of the military-industrial complex.[24]

During the 1970s, the peace movement organized outside the national limelight, laying the groundwork for the apparently spontaneous takeoff of the nuclear freeze campaign in 1980. Despite initial conflicts over issues and strategy, peace groups formed local coalitions with community-economic and environmental organizations. Military programs such as the proposed Anti-Ballistic Missile (ABM) system and the costly B-1 bomber provided targets for successful ad hoc national coalitions of progressive forces, including organized labor and mainstream religion.

One AFSC organizer saw the B-1 campaign as "a breakthrough in terms of grassroots work" because of its broad base and perceived success when President Carter canceled the program.[25] As this campaign was extending the new disarmament coalition, the AFSC launched local campaigns against nuclear weapons production facilities. With the aid of the Colorado AFSC and the national office of FOR, these campaigns linked up in a national network, the Nuclear Weapons Facilities Task Force (NWFTF). This network raised public consciousness of the dangers of the production, storage, and use of nuclear weapons, dangers officially acknowledged only after a series of incidents led to the closing of three plants in 1989.[26]

In 1977, the Mobilization for Survival (MFS) was established by the major pacifist organizations and more than one hundred local, regional, and national groups working on disarmament and economic issues and against nuclear power. Modeled on the Vietnam-era Mobilization Against the War, MFS was also intended to be a coalition. Its broad agenda reflected the dominance within the coalition of pacifists and radicals: "zero nuclear weapons, ban nuclear power, reverse the arms race, meet human needs."[27] MFS grew to encompass more than 40 national and 280 subnational-level organizations, and promoted a range of educational efforts. Nevertheless, without a focused program it could not find a way to reach a larger public.[28]

During the 1970s, then, a growing network of activists and organizations worked on peace, environmental, community-economic, and other issues through local, regional, and national organizations. Local organizing was emphasized and assisted by the parallel growth of a network of local social responsibility committees in religious congregations. In retrospect, it is clear that the groundwork for the nuclear freeze campaign's rapid proliferation was in place. At the time, especially at the national level, what was more apparent was the resurgence of the Right, marked most clearly by the elections of the 1980s. The peace movement was still marginalized.

Part of the perceived shift to the Right was the result of a conservative reaction to the movement against the war in Vietnam and the arms control accords of the 1970s.[29] A group of influential figures inside and outside government reconstructed the Committee on the Present Danger (CPD) to press for increased military spending and a major effort to regain American nuclear superiority over the Soviet Union, which by the mid-1970s had eroded to the point of essential parity (Sanders 1983). In public discussions, this was phrased in misleading terms about overcoming a Soviet advantage.[30]

By the middle of Carter's presidency, public support for increased military spending had risen to majorities not seen since before Vietnam, and Carter proposed the development and deployment of a new generation of nuclear weapons. Feeling pressure from the Right,

Carter was moved further this way by elite and public reaction to the dramatic events of 1979: the Nicaraguan revolution, the Iran hostage crisis, and the Soviet invasion of Afghanistan in December. He withdrew SALT II from Senate consideration; but despite taking a promilitary stance in the 1980 campaign Carter lost to the archconservative and unreconstructed cold warrior Ronald Reagan.

As president, Reagan halted the arms control process and began a program of massive increases in military spending, backed by a return to the language of the cold war. Several administration figures made offhand remarks concerning the alleged survivability of nuclear war. These policies and this rhetoric renewed public fears about atomic weapons and opened the door to the second major wave of antinuclear weapons activism.

The Nuclear Weapons Freeze Campaign

Starting in 1980, the leaders of established peace groups, along with the new generation of local peace, environmental, and community organizers, built a coalition around a simple demand for a mutual, verifiable halt by the superpowers to the testing, production, and deployment of new nuclear weapons. The freeze campaign built upon the networks established by these movements in the 1970s and adopted a deliberate strategy of organizing local grassroots support.

Growing rapidly, the movement far outstripped the test ban campaign in size and influence. Tens of thousands of volunteers worked through almost two thousand local groups, and a June 1982 rally drew 1 million to New York City for the United Nations Second Special Session on Disarmament. By 1983, the freeze proposal had moved to the very top of the national political agenda, with Congress hotly debating a freeze resolution.

Almost as quickly, however, the freeze disappeared from the political landscape. The Reagan administration allayed much of the public fears it had engendered, moderating its rhetoric, proposing "Star Wars"—the Strategic Defense Initiative—as a defense against nuclear weapons, and resuming the arms control process. Most Democrats in Congress and on the 1984 presidential campaign trail had been lukewarm to the freeze at its peak, and their enthusiasm waned rapidly. Nominee Walter Mondale's support for the freeze was halfhearted. By the end of 1984, Reagan's reelection seemed to show the impotence of the movement; and by 1985, the national media were asking what had become of the freeze.

It is hard to assess the effects of the nuclear freeze campaign. Conservatives credit the Reagan and Bush administrations' hard-line policies for hastening the breakup of the Soviet Union and the end of the cold war. However, Meyer (1990B) and others argue that the international peace movement, of which the freeze was a part, prevented a drastic escalation of the arms race and encouraged democratic forces in Eastern Europe. Either way, despite recent progress between the United States and Russia in reducing strategic arsenals, the world is still threatened by the remaining weapons, by political instability in the former Soviet Union, and by nuclear proliferation in such dangerous areas as the Middle East.

The challenge mounted by the antinuclear movement of the 1980s became institutionalized in areas ranging from Congress to elementary school curricula, and the campaign left behind a residue of local and state peace organizations with a greater membership and broader base than had ever existed before. Nationally, the Freeze Campaign organization merged with SANE to produce the largest membership organization in the history of the American peace movement, although one beset with organizational and strategic problems. On the other hand, the military-industrial complex appears to have emerged from the 1980s with its power and prestige largely intact.

The Peace Movement and Peace Campaigns

The modern American peace movement has oscillated between periods of relative quiescence and periods of high visibility and widespread mobilization. During the "doldrums," the movement has been carried forward by organizations working to develop deep analyses and long-term solutions to the problem of modern mass warfare.[31] In the face of emergencies including wars, perceived threat of wars, or the prospect of atomic fallout from war preparation, the peace movement has joined with other forces in mobilizing broad segments of public opinion against prevailing policies. In the major peacetime peace campaigns, along with the movement against the war in Vietnam, the currents of peace activism have become more dilute and shallow: dilute in that these efforts have served as vehicles for a range of protest issues[32]; shallow in that to reach a broader public the fundamental analyses and solutions of the peace movement have been muted.

Peace leaders have hoped that these campaigns would avert immediate crises and establish first steps toward larger changes. Their success was limited by political and cultural factors that tend to incorporate reform movements after yielding few changes. Within those constraints lay the realm of apparent freedom to choose goals, strategies, and tactics. Nevertheless, choices were strongly influenced by the structural features and internal dynamics of the campaigns. How these features and dynamics, in complex interplay with strategic choices, affected the course and outcomes of the campaigns requires further analysis.

3

Social Movements, Campaigns, and Organizations

Social movement scholarship provides both perspectives from which to explain the role of organization in the peace campaigns and a set of concepts and ideas with which to analyze the organizational dynamics of the campaigns. As Tarrow (1983A) observes, more than most fields of political analysis, social movement theory responds to the ebb and flow of political events. The upsurge of social movement activism in the 1960s catalyzed renewed interest and major changes in social movement theory. Several scholars, most of them sympathetic to these movements, formulated new perspectives that challenged more conservative views, typified by "collective behavior" theories developed in the 1920s by Robert Park and his students at the University of Chicago.[1]

Collective behavior theorists tend to view mass movements as threats to social order and integration, which, following Emile Durkheim, they see as critically important but fragile. This view is typified by LeBon's influential 1895 book *The Crowd,* a reaction against the excesses of the French Revolution. These theorists see religious cults, fads, riots, strikes, revolutions and other forms of collective action as mostly irrational, sporadic responses to the breakdown of existing norms and institutions during periods of fast social change. Because they see these forms of action as unstructured, they do not emphasize the role of social movement organizations.

The emergence of totalitarian movements in the first three decades of the twentieth century deepened the distrust many collective behaviorists felt toward social movements. Morris (1984, 276) claims that "the writings of Park and Burgess, Blumer, Lang and Lang, and Smelser have tended to discredit movement participants by characterizing their activities as crude and elementary and as tension-relieving devices for pent-up frustrations."

After the "stormy sixties,"[2] however, a new generation of scholars developed resource mobilization and political process perspectives that separated social movements from other forms of collective behavior. They treated social movement activism as a mostly rational extension of institutionalized politics. These perspectives assume that movements are made up of people acting to redress grievances caused by institutionalized inequalities in power relations, and that such grievances are ubiquitous. Therefore, the rise and fall of movements — the issues most commonly addressed — depend on changes in groups' resources, organization, and belief structures, and changes in political opportunities for action.[3] The social impact of movements, which depends on strategic and political factors, may be significant.

Resource mobilization and political process perspectives emphasize the role of formal organizations as carriers of social movements. This growing interest in the role of formal institutions parallels developments in several areas of social science. In reviewing work in political science, sociology, and anthropology, March and Olsen (1984) remarked on the emergence of a "new institutionalism," combining new insights about class structure, individual decision making, and other aspects of politics with an older emphasis on political institutions. For example, political sociologists in the Weberian and Marxist traditions have paid increasing attention to the state's potential autonomy (or "relative autonomy") from economic and social determinants. They have come to see the state as an institution that shapes social and political processes, and does not simply respond to larger forces (see Evans, Rueschmeyer, and Skocpol 1985).

Zald (1987) and Tilly (1978, 1984) analyze the rise of formal organizations as the main vehicles of movement activism in the United States and Europe.[4] By the mid-nineteenth century in the United States the institutionalization of the two-party system closed off third parties as a likely option for the expression of dissent. Meanwhile, developments such as industrialization and urbanization provided a denser associational field and more resources for leaders building movement organizations. Along with the proliferation of professional reformers during the Progressive Era, these developments helped produce the key features of contemporary social movements: an ongoing social movement sector (SMS) dominated by formal social movement organizations (SMOs) and the frequent presence of paid movement staff.

Many SMOs operate on a national scale. Tilly (1984) describes the rise of national social movements — movements actively challenging the national state for new rights and advantages, not just defending traditional rights and customs — as a nineteenth- and early twentieth-century innovation, the result of the development of the modern state and mass electoral politics and the accompanying erosion of local political autonomy. By the early twentieth century in both Europe and the United States, formal, national movement organizations took over the center of the political scene.

Some scholars now criticize resource mobilization and political process views for overemphasizing the role of formal organizations in social movements.[5] Organizations are important, but so are crowds, diffuse collectivities, and other less well-ordered phenomena (Oliver 1989). Marwell and Oliver (1984) urge that social movement scholars shift their emphasis to a unit of analysis between organization and social movement — the "collective campaign," defined as "an aggregate of collective events or activities that appear to be oriented toward some relatively specific goal or good, and that occur within some proximity in space and time" (Marwell and Oliver 1984, 12). By looking at campaigns, they contend, scholars can move toward developing theories of social movements while avoiding the trap of identifying movements with organizations.[6]

Enduring social movements typically launch campaigns to concentrate their forces on limited, realizable goals and to draw upon a broader base of support than that ordinarily available to a movement with many and possibly far-reaching goals. Although the civil rights movement in the United States, for example, has a long history of organized struggle, its most recent peak occurred in the 1950s and 1960s as a campaign for the desegregation of the South. McAdam (1982) analyzes the "civil rights phase of the black movement" as a specific campaign: by focusing on limited goals and a specific geographic area, it overcame significant political disadvantages and achieved substantial gains. Although parts of the feminist movement have worked for the passage of an Equal Rights Amendment since 1920, in the late 1960s a concerted campaign for an ERA developed once political prospects brightened.

The Study of Social Movement Organizations

Oddly enough, "despite the concentration on SMOs over the last decade, literature on them as organizations is still scarce. In particular, empirical studies of the organizational characteristics of SMOs are lacking" (Klandermans 1989, 2). An early model of SMOs that remains influential emerged from the "institutional school" of the 1950s and 1960s.[7] Scholars in this tradition produced single-case studies of organizations that appeared to fit what Zald and Ash (1966) called the Weber-Michels model. Based on Max Weber's discussions of the routinization of charisma and Robert Michels's "iron law of oligarchy," this model holds that social change organizations over time become dominated by an oligarchical leadership. Powerful leaders chart a cautious and conservative course for the party, labor union, or SMO to ensure organizational survival, minimize elite opposition, and maximize their career chances. Organization, in this view, leads to the political incorporation of strongly oppositional movements, including socialist and labor movements.

Zald and Ash argued that conservatism was not inevitable even in oligarchical organizations. Because of competition between SMOs, or changes in public opinion, or both, an organization might adopt more radical goals. Jenkins (1977) found that the staff of the National Council of Churches exercised oligarchical power in pursuit of an agenda more liberal than that favored by the congregations of the member churches. As Wilensky (1956), Wilson (1973), and others have observed, staff members of church, labor, community, and other organizations are often attracted by the opportunity to use their jobs to promote social change — and these jobs typically provide relatively low pay.[8]

Another widely cited generalization about SMOs is that of Piven and Cloward (1977), who argue that organization building demobilizes movements of the poor. It diverts energy from the sole useful strategy of disruption and produces leaders who can be coopted by the state. This argument has been effectively criticized for overgeneralizing, ignoring cases where organizing has helped the poor.[9] Although they generalize, both the Weber-Michels and the Piven and Cloward models offer important cautions to movement scholars and activists. McAdam (1982, 53–54) proposes a balanced view of the potentials and problems of movement organizations. On the one hand, formal movement organizations seem necessary to sustain a movement beyond the enthusiasm and energy that typically accompany its rise.[10] Political efficacy requires the direction and coordination provided by a certain formalization. On the other hand, the establishment of formal organizations does raise the possibility of oligarchy and cooptation by the state or by external sponsors or both.

More recent scholarship has abandoned notions of inevitable evolution and necessary outcomes and has recognized instead many possible patterns of organizational change and impact, demanding contingent generalizations based on closer studies of existing organizations. The dynamics of social movement organizations reflect tendencies and countertendencies internal to organizations, interactions with other organizations and external forces, and strategic choices.

Organizational Tensions

Three sets of organizational tensions affected the rise, course, fall, legacy, and impact of the peace campaigns. During my research I came to see interactions between professional and grassroots tendencies and elements in the campaigns as an organizational tension, an interplay between forces pulling campaign organizations in different directions. This tension can also be seen as a pair of potentially incompatible tasks, in this case the task of recruiting and paying for professional expertise as against the task of mobilizing grassroots participation.

As my research progressed, I discovered two other sets of organizational tensions critically important to the campaigns: first, tensions between the campaigns as coalitions of existing organizations and as independent organizations; second, tensions between a national focus and local mobilization. All these tensions interacted with each other and with strategic tensions such as those in choosing between short-term and long-term social change goals.[11]

Coalition-Organization

A coalition is "an enduring arrangement requiring that choices over some common set of interests, for example, resources, goals, strategies, or the like, be made by explicit mutual agreement among the members" (Wilson 1973, 267). Movement organizations form coalitions with each other and with other organizations with various motives, among them increasing their ability to cope with threats and take advantage of opportunities.

As each peace campaign began, the peace movement faced both a perceived threat to peace and a political climate potentially favorable for mobilization against the threat. Established peace groups overcame a reluctance to form coalitions that is typical of SMOs (Wilson 1973, Staggenborg 1986). Coalitions do allow member groups to expand their influence through joint action and to conserve resources by dividing labor and sharing overhead costs. On the other hand, coalitions tend to produce organizational and ideological conflict.

Organizational conflict grows from the new demands a coalition places on the resources of movement organizations. Any serious commitment to a coalition requires such things as staff time, volunteer time, money, and office space. In principle, the division of labor and sharing of overhead costs within a coalition may balance these costs by multiplying the impact of the contribution and reducing other costs for member organizations. Nevertheless, the member organization's ability to retain activists and contributors may be threatened by loss of visibility if the coalition takes credit for accomplishments, or by blame for the coalition's failures.

Contributions to a coalition are likely to be unequal and possibly out of proportion to member groups' size and capacity to contribute; member organizations have some incentives toward acting as free, or at least cheap, riders.[12] What constitutes ability to contribute may be a source of friction. Larger groups may be expected to contribute more, but these organizations may be large because they have emphasized organization-building. They may find a coalition a greater threat to their organizational base than would smaller groups with a smaller resource flow. They also may fear that their voice in decision making will not match their material contributions. Although smaller groups may expect larger ones to shoulder the major burdens, they may simultaneously fear that the bigger organizations will take over the coalition (Staggenborg 1986).[13]

Large or small, a group that does most of the work in return for a small portion of the credit will continue to do so only if the goal is very important to that group — perhaps more important than to other groups — or if other groups control strategic resources such as legitimacy or both. During the Mississippi Summer Project in 1964, four major civil rights groups formed the Conference of Federated Organizations (COFO) to coordinate voter registration and other work. Most of the work nominally done by COFO was in fact performed by the Student Nonviolent Coordinating Committee (SNCC) (McAdam 1988). To SNCC, however, the ability to use the names of more established, mainstream groups, such as the NAACP, may have made this a fair deal, at least over the short run. The NAACP also provided resources like legal aid that SNCC saw as strategically crucial, even if the cost to the NAACP did not match SNCC's contributions of the majority of staff time and personal risk-taking. Control of some key resources can give organizations leverage within a coalition, although other groups may resent it.

An umbrella organization like COFO typically deals with the maintenance needs of a coalition (Staggenborg 1986). Although umbrella groups may be expected only to maintain and coordinate the sponsoring coalitions, they establish themselves as independent organizations if their staff members, out of ideological or material motives or both, wish to prolong the umbrella group's life beyond the brief span of most coalitions. Turn Toward Peace, a coalition of peace movement groups in the early 1960s, attempted to set up its own local chapters, but the established peace groups rebuffed this effort. Mobilization for Survival, a coalition of Left-leaning peace groups in the 1970s, did become an independent organization despite the wishes of some members of the original coalition.

The potential rise of a new organization thus exacerbates the tensions inherent in coalitions. The umbrella group can become a rival for resources, leadership, and publicity. Although it did not progress very far toward independence, the EPC was perceived as such a threat by the peace groups of the 1930s. When an umbrella group does become independent, it becomes a locus for new tensions. Both SANE and the NWFC developed a dual structure, part umbrella group and part new organization with chapters and members. This created strong tensions for leadership and staff between accountability to the member groups of the coalition and accountability to the new chapters and individual members.

Ideological conflicts within coalitions also act as centrifugal forces. Coalitions typically include organizations with a range of ideologies, goals, strategies, and tactical repertoires and preferences, even if the coalitions are limited to organizations within a particular movement "industry," the set of groups with a common issue focus.[14] Each organization confronts the danger of appearing to be linked with organizations from which they ordinarily wish to distance themselves. A continuing problem for many groups on the Left, for example, is whether to include the Communist party in coalitions. The much-cherished autonomy of organizations in setting goals and strategies is threatened by a coalition; exit may be the only remedy. And even organizations that can accept the other member groups and endorse the coalition program may feel that their distinct message is lost (Wilson 1973). Whereas moderate groups may fear the taint of radical groups, Right or Left, radical groups may find that coalitions with the Center require them to abandon key parts of their analysis and prescriptions to find common ground. Decisions to join or not to join coalitions also can cause conflict within an organization.

All these ideological tensions carry material implications. To the extent that a movement industry operates on market principles, support may depend on maintaining a distinct message and avoiding the taint of association with certain other groups. Furthermore, ideological squabbling within a coalition may drain resources (Staggenborg 1986). Tension over resources within a coalition may be reduced by new funding, from foundations, for example, that want movement organizations to join forces. It may be eased by a coalition structure that allows member groups to participate according to ability and interest (Staggenborg 1986).

The peace coalitions chose to deal with ideological tensions by focusing on one or two key goals — neutrality and international economic cooperation, a test ban, a nuclear freeze — and by promoting those goals in a campaign: an effort designed to mobilize public pressure for a consensus goal that is significant but also considered achievable within several years. During this time, members of the coalition made the campaign their top priority, a commitment that is not a feature of every coalition. This strategy gives a campaign a few goals that are potentially popular and easily understood and that may be won quickly. It leaves unresolved underlying tensions over long-term goals and strategies.

Aldon Morris's (1984) study of the origins of the civil rights movement shows how an organizational base was crucial in establishing a movement that other analysts have seen as more spontaneous. Formal movement organizations such as the NAACP had been repressed in the South. The key organizational base for the movement proved to be the southern black church and "movement halfway houses," organizations that are socially marginal because of their radicalism and lack of a mass base but serve movements as repositories of ideas, visions, strategies, and skilled activists. Among the halfway houses important in the civil rights movement were three peace movement organizations: AFSC, FOR, and WRL. In the 1930s, 1950s, and 1980s, these and other peace groups entered formal coalitions to launch peace campaigns. The peace groups were not quite so marginalized as Morris suggests. Beyond the resources he discusses, they lent to the campaigns local networks, access to funding, and some measure of access to policy makers.[15] The peace campaigns therefore had a complex structure, combining elements of a coalition and an independent movement organization.

National-Local

Social movements and movement organizations have become national in scope to keep pace with the growing power of the nation-state. For the peace movement and its leading organizations, the nation-state's monopoly on foreign and military policy making and the rise of the national security state make a national focus imperative.[16]

Social movements are also local. Some are strictly local, with small organizations working on neighborhood issues. Others with a national scope organize locally around issues that may be local, regional, or national. Even movements that focus on national issues may organize locally for two reasons. First, grassroots organizing is generally local.[17] People live, work, and act in specific locales. Movements that mobilize popular participation therefore tend to be locally based. Second, it is often easier for social change movements to influence or even win over local elites than it is to sway the more powerful national elites. This has been a strategic advantage for peace activists in communities without major military contractors and bases.

In the United States, the decentralized system of government and the weakness of national political parties encourage local organizing. Local and state bodies retain considerable power relative to the federal government. Among national policy makers, members of the House of Representatives are susceptible to local pressure. In the words of Thomas P. ("Tip") O'Neill, former Speaker of the House, "all politics is local."[18]

For any movement or campaign of greater than local scope, a key concern is how to coordinate activity across locales. The social movement literature has debated the relative merits of centralized and decentralized coordination. Resource mobilization and political process theorists tend to argue that a movement must centralize to divide labor efficiently, minimize internal conflict, raise resources efficiently, and deploy them quickly and effectively in the political arena. The clearest statement of this position is Gamson's (1990), based on a study of a probability sample of fifty-three American "challenging groups" from 1800 to 1945.

Gerlach and Hine (1970) argue that movements that are decentralized, segmented, and reticulate (weblike), generate greater interpersonal bonds and therefore stronger commitment and are more flexible and less vulnerable to repression and incorporation than centralized organizations.[19] Gamson (1988) also contends that social movement scholars generally ignore the importance to many movements of loose structures of linked cells.

Jenkins (1983) argues that the merits of centralization depend on the goals of a movement and that organizations tend to adopt structures appropriate to their goals: personal change movements are usually decentralized; movements for institutional change are typically centralized. In addition, the diversity of SMOs within a social movement can produce a blend of centralized and decentralized structures. Many SMOs have an intermediate degree of centralization.

Although goals and targets may limit appropriate movement structures, these are broad limits. Loose networks have tied together not only movements of personal transformation but also more overtly political movements such as the struggle against nuclear power (Nelkin and Pollack 1981). Decentralized targets—a chain of atomic power plants—encouraged the formation of a decentralized movement. In campaigns with more centralized political targets such as the foreign policy establishment, most activists and scholars see a need for tighter coordination. Still, within any given movement organization there will be debate over the degree of centralization, and within movements there is much contention over the relative dominance of centralized and decentralized SMOs.

Planned as short-term mobilizations to influence national policy makers on one or two key issues, the peace campaigns were centralized; an umbrella organization coordinated local work and focused pressure on national policy makers. Even within such operations there is room for structural variation.

McCarthy and Zald (1977) describe national SMOs as "isolated" or "federated" structures. Isolated structures have no local chapters. The national office deals directly by mail or telephone with supporters, who do not normally meet. Federated organizations consist of local chapters and higher offices—regional, state, national. Federated organizations can be established when paid organizers bring together previously isolated adherents, or they can emerge more quickly when chapters form from preexisting groups (so-called group, or bloc, recruitment).

McCarthy and Zald (1977) hypothesize that federated organizations will be more stable than isolated ones because their constituents are more closely tied to the organization. These close ties consist in part of "solidary incentives," bonds with other activists in local chapters.[20] In the absence of such ties, the loyalty of isolated constituents to SMOs tends to be lower than political party identification, resembling preference for marginal consumer goods. Thus isolated organizations are more likely to follow the "issue attention cycles" typical of the political agenda (Downs 1972).

On the other hand, Barkan et al. (1988) argue that federation may reduce stability. From Gamson's (1990) claim that centralization improves organizational effectiveness because it reduces factionalism, they reason that it may reduce the power of a national office and therefore permit increased factionalism. They did not find such a pattern in Bread for the World, an organization combating world hunger. Their findings instead supported the McCarthy and Zald thesis: chapter members became more active and more committed to the organization than did members isolated from direct interaction with other members. Nevertheless, in some organizations, under some circumstances, federalism might reduce stability. Both SANE and the NWFC did develop federated structures; the EPC did not. My analysis explores the consequences of this difference.

Another important set of issues relevant to SANE and the NWFC involves the impact of federation on local organizing. Oliver and Furman (1990) argue that federation burdens local chapters because of key differences between organizing nationally and locally. Unlike freestanding local organizations, local chapters must report to higher offices. Access to national membership lists does not compensate for this maintenance effort. Local chapters generally depend upon volunteers, and national organizations are run by paid staff. Those who join national organizations are more likely to contribute money than time. They are unlikely to help local chapters that seek active members.

This analysis, based on the study of one federated organization, the John Birch Society, captures only part of a complex set of issues, however. Federation may impose even greater burdens on local chapters in the form of dues payments that require the locals to raise money and recruit volunteers. On the other hand, advantages other than membership lists may accrue to local chapters and not to unaffiliated local organizations. Oliver and Furman mention that supporting a national organization with long-range goals may rationalize the local chapter's long-term existence. And Morris (1984) quotes leaders of local civil rights organizations who found that by affiliating with the SCLC their local movement centers gained a sense of purpose, national visibility, leadership, and access to expert training in strategies, tactics, and organizational development. Furthermore, national offices typically research issues and prepare printed materials for local chapters to use in outreach, and package programs for politics, education, and fund raising.[21] They print and mail newsletters, and may help with expensive technical tasks, such as updating membership lists and targeting mailings. They also may provide access to the political and public opinion establishments.

Federation brings with it potential advantages as well as tensions over resources, governance, and local autonomy. Many federated organizations have had difficulty establishing and maintaining more than one level of organization because of the strain on financial resources and have experienced conflicts between local chapters and higher offices over organizational goals and local autonomy. Unfortunately, although many major SMOs are federated, few studies of the patterns and consequences of federation have examined the workings and outcomes of these tensions.

Freeman (1983) compared the National Women's Political Caucus (NWPC) and the National Organization for Women (NOW). The NWPC was founded in 1972 to elect more women to political office. It began with state-level groups and no national dues structure. When it moved to set up a larger and more effective national office, many state groups were reluctant to shift resources from state and local elections to supporting more work at the national level. Conversely, NOW had trouble setting up state affiliates during the campaign to ratify the Equal Rights Amendment. NOW was strong nationally and locally because from the start it required all members to pay national dues. Nevertheless, establishing state organizations was difficult and time-consuming, even though in states that had not ratified the ERA these state groups were crucial in coordinating the campaign. Thus initial patterns of organization are important. Resources that can support one or two levels of organization may not be able to support more, and the established levels may be unwilling to sacrifice on behalf of newcomers.

Some organizations have made a smoother transition. Common Cause, founded in 1970 as a national lobbying group, quickly developed a membership base of more than 200,000, largely through direct mail.[27] Many paper members were willing to do more than contribute dues and occasionally write Congress, however, and so coordinating committees were established in about three hundred congressional districts.[23] Starting in 1972, some local members decided to work on state-level "good government" issues. Although Common Cause had planned to be strictly a national lobby, the national office helped create about thirty state organizations.

Why Common Cause developed more smoothly than did NOW is not clear, but, first, there were "slack resources": Common Cause had a large and growing budget when it set up the state groups. McFarland speculates that, should the overall budget drop, tensions will increase between national office and state affiliates over the proportion of resources to be spent on state-level matters. Second, the organization is highly centralized: members pay dues to the national office, which distributes a share to state groups. Overall, Common Cause receives 90–95 percent of its funds in dues and small contributions from members, and the states' shares account for almost two-thirds of their budgets. Thus once the national office decided to set up state groups, it had the power and resources to do so.

In governance, because Common Cause depends on dues, it tends to be responsive to its members. The state and local affiliates were initially kept on a tight reign; they still are weak not only because the national office controls fund raising and distribution but also because the governance structure is not truly federated. Although the national board is member-elected, all are elected at large; each candidate competes against all the other candidates for the national board in a single national election. Without direct representation, the state groups lack the clout of their counterparts in organizations with state representatives on the national board.

Common Cause demonstrates one possible pattern of complex relationships among resource mobilization and distribution, national governance, and local autonomy. The NAACP shows another.[24] It too is centralized, although local branches, as they are called, collect member dues and pass on half to the national organization. In theory and probably in fact, this process gives the locals more leverage than state organizations enjoy in Common Cause. So does the more federated governance structure, which allows for roughly one-third of the board members to be elected by region. Nevertheless, the national office of the organization wields great power through its large bureaucracy, its control of strategic resources (including legal expertise), and its long tradition and high prestige. Wilson (1973) sees the NAACP branches as enjoying wide latitude in developing projects and incentive structures for members; Morris (1984) argues that the centralized, bureaucratized nature of the organization prevented local southern branches from moving quickly to organize or cooperate with direct-action projects initiated by local activists during the rise of the civil rights movement. After the arrest of Rosa Parks in Montgomery in 1955, for example, local leaders began organizaing a boycott of the segregated bus system, but they did so by forming a new local movement center. They were unwilling to wait for the Montgomery branch of the NAACP to go through channels — the New York office — to see if the boycott was an appropriate project.

During the peak years of the civil rights movement, moreover, the national offices of the NAACP and other civil rights groups received substantial "outside" funding from "conscience constituents" (white sympathizers) and institutions. This also gave the national offices greater leverage with local branches.[25] In the early years of the SCLC, according to Morris (1984), the central office relied on outside support in the form of contributions from northern black churches; local chapters relied on local activists and local funds, primarily from black congregations. There was no financial integration between levels, but branches continued to depend on the national office for many resources. Morris also describes the great power exercised within the organization by Martin Luther King, Jr. — in part a result of his ability to raise outside funds.[26] Morris does not speculate about the consequences of the nonintegrated financial structure, but the accountability of national leaders to local chapters probably decreases when the national supports itself by raising outside funds.

Within federated organizations, other factors including ideology further complicate the relations between tensions over resources, national governance, and local autonomy. Both CORE and NOW developed decentralized structures in part because the dominant ideology among members stressed participation and autonomy — for individuals and therefore also for local groups (Rudwick and Meier 1972, Carden 1978).

One final issue, not touched on by existing research, is the impact of federation on an organization's ability to achieve its strategic goals. In principle, federated organizations combine important advantages of national and local work. To the strategic location of a national office and the expertise that typically is the strength of a national staff can be added the legitimacy and potential power that come from a local base and the range of perspectives that local members can bring to a group.

Professional-Grassroots

One of the most important works in the revitalization of social movement scholarship was John McCarthy and Mayer Zald's 1973

"The Trend of Social Movements in America."[27] The trend detected was toward the "professionalization" of social movements. The movements of the 1960s, McCarthy and Zald argued, could not be accounted for by the traditional "hearts and minds of the people" view, which explained the rise and fall of movements by focusing on the sentiments and actions of volunteer activists, because there was no rise in volunteer activism in this era. Instead, during the 1960s there was a proliferation of professional movement activism, performed by paid staff in professional social movement organizations (PSMOs) that employed them.

The rise of PSMOs in the 1960s was caused mainly by an increase in "outside support"—money (from outside an active constituency) available to social movements as middle-class affluence and foundation, church, and government grants all grew. "Entrepreneurs" from the swelling ranks of the liberal clergy, community organizers, and reform-oriented professionals used these resources to establish PSMOs. They used new technologies, such as computer-based direct mail solicitation, to reach a wide audience and generate support without face-to-face organizing. Occasionally, they organized "transitory teams" of volunteer activists from the increasing numbers of college-age activists and independent professionals.

The claim that the growth of outside funding and PSMOs accounted for the rise of the 1960s movements touched off a major debate. Studies of the civil rights movement, for example, showed that it originated within the southern black community (Morris 1984), and that the major increases in outside support, important as they were in shaping the movement, followed rather than preceded the rise of black insurgency (McAdam 1982, Jenkins 1986, Jenkins and Eckert 1986). McAdam (1982) and others took issue with the suggestion that elite sponsorship is necessary for the emergence of social movements.

This debate has obscured the contributions of McCarthy and Zald. Empirically, movement professionalism predates the 1960s, something traditional hearts-and-minds perspectives tended to ignore. Furthermore, movement professionalism has been increasing; it may even have become the most important form of activism during the 1980s (Oliver 1988). A long view of historical trends requires us to ask whether what was (possibly) true of the 1960s (or the 1980s) is part of a longer secular trend and whether it is likely to continue. In comparing the three peace campaigns, much can be learned about trends toward (or away from) professionalism in one movement over a fifty-year span.

The concept of professionalism is useful in the analysis of movements and movement organizations. The meaning of professionalism and the relationship between professionalism and grassroots mobilization have, however, been neglected by students of social movements.

According to McCarthy and Zald (1973), professionalized SMOs are run by a full-time paid leadership and rely on resources from beyond the group the movement claims to represent. Frequently, the leader is an entrepreneur, someone who created not just the organization but also a job for himself or herself. PSMOs may have no actual members, or a "paper"membership consisting of people who contribute their names or their money or both, but not time. PSMOs work politically by hiring lawyers, lobbyists, publicists, and other experts to "impart the image of speaking for a potential constituency" and to affect public policy of interest to that constituency (McCarthy and Zald 1973, 20).

Grassroots organizations, unlike PSMOs, are vehicles through which indigenous volunteer leaders and activists arise from within an aggrieved group. They use mass-based tactics, such as rallies, demonstrations, and civil disobedience, to achieve gains for these groups.[28]

Professional and grassroots organizations are ideal types: models like Weber's bureaucracy that help to organize analysis but do not necessarily exist in pure form. Their constituent elements are separable; organizations may combine paid staff with an active grassroots base, for example. Furthermore, the ideal types are simplifications in that each element is posed as one side of a dichotomy. Resources are either indigenous or outside. In reality, there are more than two possibilities. For example, Oliver (1983) divides outside resources into two types, external sponsors (large donors, individual and institutional) and external markets (small individual contributions). Likewise, instead of a professional–volunteer dichotomy, real organizations know a range of activist types: leaders, paid or unpaid, have a base of support among constituents, set policy, and speak for the base; entrepreneurs start movements for varying mixes of purposive and material reasons; staff are hired to carry out policy but frequently influence and even make policy; organizers work to increase the base of support and active participants, and institutional activists work in nonmovement organizations, especially government agencies (Oliver 1983).[29]

In the analysis of movements and organizations, distinctions among types of resources and among varieties of activists are important. For example, organizations dependent on external sponsors are subject to constraints different from those that restrict organizations dependent on external markets (Oliver 1983). Staggenborg (1988) argues that one cannot understand the actions of many leaders of the pro-

choice movement without distinguishing between the roles and mo-
tivations of entrepreneurs and paid staff. Many leaders founded
organizations but did not take paid jobs in them. The interests of entrepreneurs who do not become staff members may differ from the
interests of those who do.

As ideal types professional and grassroots models establish two
ends of a continuum of organizational structures and convey meaningful differences between them. Real organizations, leaning toward
one end of the spectrum or the other, may therefore be described as
relatively professionalized or relatively grassroots-oriented.

Organizations tend toward one end or the other of the professional-
grassroots continuum, first, because the elements of one model hang
together to reinforce each other. An organization with paid staff will
invest time and energy into raising money to pay staff members. Given
this investment, the organization is likely to use these staff members
for professional-style political action rather than seek to mobilize volunteers. An organization with a strong grassroots base, conversely,
is likely to produce leaders from within its own ranks and to rely on
mass tactics to achieve its goals.

Competition between SMOs for resources and attention increases
the chances that organizations will specialize (McCarthy and Zald
1977). So far as professional elements reinforce each other and grassroots elements also fit together, organizations tending toward one pole
or the other are likely to be more efficient and therefore more able
to survive in a competitive environment. It is difficult for an organization to succeed at both raising money and recruiting volunteers because both require expertise and the expenditure of initial resources.
Organizations successful at researching issues and producing authori-
tative reports are rarely the same organizations that can readily turn
out huge crowds for a rally.

What determines which direction an organization will take? Mc-
Carthy and Zald (1973) claim that social trends create the conditions
for the establishment of new professionalized SMOs. These same trends
also may push existing SMOs toward greater professionalism. As more
families are headed by two wage earners, free time for volunteer activism declines while, for some families, disposable income increases.
Existing organizations may therefore try to substitute money for volunteers, particularly when external sponsors, public and private, and
external markets become more generous. The increase in numbers
of liberal professionals increases the numbers of potential entrepreneurs and of experts to be hired by existing organizations.[30]

These movement professionals become not just a resource but also a lobby for professionalism in both new and existing organizations. The Weber-Michels model reflects the tendency of paid staff to protect their jobs by sacrificing grassroots organizing and agitation to stay in favor with elite sponsors and the state.

SMOs also may become more professional to survive the cycles of grassroots enthusiasm typical of social movements.[31] Even organizations built upon activism may choose to develop professional fund-raising skills once a wave of volunteer activism has passed. Professionalism also may contribute to organizational survival because paid staff tend to create formal structures and procedures that make organizations more stable (Staggenborg 1988).

Elites inside and outside the state may try to domesticate movements by channeling money to moderate groups that use professional political strategies and away from more militant, grassroots-based organizations. McAdam (1982) and Jenkins and Eckert (1986) showed that during the civil rights movement elite support tended to go to moderate rather than radical organizations. Not only did this support increase the relative strength of moderate groups but it also increased tendencies toward professionalism. With large amounts of outside funds available, McAdam argues, groups like CORE and SNCC tended to neglect grassroots organizing. Finally, the centralization of power in nation-states has led to a corresponding nationalization of social movement organizations. Most major SMOs are national in scope, and many have a Washington office to lobby the federal government. Oliver and Furman (1990) argue that national-level organizing is professional — national offices hire professionals and raise money to pay for them — and local organizing involves recruiting and training volunteers. I would not make quite so strong a claim. National organizations that are federated may put significant emphasis on strengthening chapters and mobilizing grassroots activism; and local organizations, whether chapters of federations or independent, may emphasize paid staff and funding. Nevertheless, because national-level organizations do tend to be professionalized and local chapters or organizations to be volunteer-driven, the trend toward nationalization contributes toward professionalizing tendencies.

Just as resources, the goals and interests of activists, and political opportunities and strategies at times produce tendencies toward professionalism, at other times they drive organizations toward grassroots organizing. Although leaders may usually find it easier to mobilize money rather than time (Oliver and Marwell 1988, Wilson 1973), fund raising has its problems. Periodical financial crises at many SMOs lead to staff layoffs, program cuts, and sometimes the organization's demise.

For these and other reasons, even organizations with professional staff often seek to initiate grassroots activism. Staff members and volunteer leaders may see grassroots pressure as a necessary component of an effective political strategy. Oliver and Marwell (1988) note that some movement professionals, particularly New Left veterans, have an ideological predisposition toward grassroots mobilization. Paid organizers, of course, also have a career interest in creating a strong grassroots base for an organization.

This is not a universal tendency, of course. Instead of promoting grassroots activism, established leaders and professionals may ignore or even resist it if it seems to challenge their authority or strike out in unknown directions. According to Morris (1984), for example, the hierarchy of the NAACP did not at first welcome the rise of grassroots activism in the South in the 1950s and early 1960s. Professionals may try to develop the appearance of a grassroots base to legitimate their claims to speak for a constituency, but may resist the development of grassroots leaders or power within the organization.[32] Still, even organizations with paid staff may work to mobilize or capture grassroots activism, and grassroots upsurges may transform existing organizations despite the wishes of established staff and leaders. Finally, despite the trend toward nationalization and professionalization, some SMOs have emphasized local organizing for strategic purposes, encouraging grassroots mobilization.

A different pattern of organizational development is possible, however. Rather than being driven toward one extreme, an organization may be moved toward a middle or combined structure that includes significant elements of both models. Organizations that survive over time are likely to experience external pressures or incentives in both directions, simultaneously or in succession. For example, an organization that professionalizes when outside funding is plentiful may add a grassroots base during a subsequent popular upsurge.

Combined structures may be adaptive. Specialization is a common survival strategy; an alternative possibility for an organization is to become a good generalist. Organizations able to do two different kinds of things at once may be better able to adjust to external changes and thus be more politically effective than those that are specialized. If an organization includes advocates of both models or advocates of middle or combined structures or both, its internal politics may then lead to the development of a structure with significant professional and grassroots features.

One reason a middle structure may work — a reason some activists would work to promote one — is that in certain combinations professional and grassroots elements may reinforce each other. For example, paid staff may recruit and train volunteer activists who make the organization more effective by adding to its resource base and tactical repertoire.[33] Some SMOs hire paid organizers to increase the amount and quality of grassroots activism.[34] In principle, the increased visibility and effectiveness that result from effective grassroots organizing will enhance the organization's fund-raising ability, strengthening the professional end of the SMO. Going in the other direction, grassroots organizations may hire staff to give the organization more managerial and political expertise, to perform administrative duties volunteers are reluctant to take on, or to perform other tasks in the interests of organizational stability and political efficacy.

Even when these elements are brought together successfully, tensions are likely to arise between professionalism and grassroots elements because of resources and the needs and desires of activists. Activists may wish to establish organizations strong in professional and grassroots work, but limited resources often force choices between them. A given budget for example, may allow an organization to hire an organizer to strengthen its grassroots component or a lobbyist to do professional-style political activism, but not both. When outside resources do increase, grassroots groups may be tempted to take advantage of them even if they are not well equipped to do so. Conversely, PSMOs may try to capture volunteers during times of grassroots upsurges. In both cases, the organizations may experience problems in changing their methods.

Despite the strength in a diverse base of activists and resources, advocates of professional work and advocates of grassroots work will differ about values (e.g., participation and efficiency), political ideology, assessments of political possibilities and the effectiveness of different strategies, and material and power interests (paid staff want to keep their jobs, volunteer leaders feel threatened by hired experts, etc.). Organizations may manage these tensions most simply by moving toward one end of the professional-grassroots spectrum, by finding ways for elements of the two models to reinforce each other, or by letting different elements coexist without much interaction — although competition for resources is likely to cause friction.

In one analysis of the impact of professionalism on the internal dynamics and political direction of SMOs, McAdam (1982) argues that civil rights groups that received substantial outside funding tended to neglect grassroots organizing. The implication is that easy access to money presented a more attractive option than the difficult and often frustrating work of mobilizing volunteers.

Professionalism may contribute to organizational stability and survival.[35] It is unclear whether reliance on outside funding rather than a grassroots base makes an organization more stable: PSMOs can lose outside support because they fall out of favor with elites, because the media and public attention tend to follow issue-attention cycles, or for other reasons.[36]

McCarthy and Zald (1973) argue that a PSMO can survive declines in outside funding if it can establish a grassroots base by attaching itself to a major social cleavage.[37] Even this may not ensure survival: McAdam (1982) claims that civil rights groups that slighted grassroots organizing after receiving external sponsorship eventually weakened as sponsorship was withdrawn. A more likely reason professionalism adds stability is Staggenborg's (1988) argument that paid staff tend to formalize the operation of SMOs. Formalization, if it does not become stifling rigidity, makes organizations more efficient and therefore better able to survive over time.

A second organizational issue involves power and decision making within SMOs. Clearly, paid staff in professionalized organizations exercise great authority—checked somewhat, perhaps, by governance structures, such as volunteer boards of directors, and by the constraints imposed by external sponsors and markets. As the Weber-Michels model suggests and others have found (Wilson 1973, Oliver 1983), even in organizations with a grassroots base and a formal structure that limits paid staff to implementing decisions made by volunteer activists, paid staff tend to make policy and not just implement it. Staff power is limited, though, by the voluntary nature of SMOs with a grassroots base; members can always leave, taking with them time, legitimacy, and possibly money (Wilson 1973).

Staggenborg (1988) claims that organizations with paid staff are more likely to enter coalitions than are purely grassroots groups. She bases this claim on her observations of the pro-choice movement and hypothesizes that paid staff have the time to put in the additional work required by coalitions—attending meetings, for example. This is probably true as well for SMOs in other movements, but another factor suggested by Staggenborg may be as important. She believes paid staff are more likely to have a broad, ideological view of movement activism than are most volunteer activists drawn in by interest in a single issue. Jenkins (1983), Wilson (1973), and others have also argued that paid staff tend to have better-developed ideologies and broader politics than do volunteers.[38] Not just time, therefore, but also ideology would induce staff to bring their organizations into coalitions that would extend the range of issues on which they could act.

Thus the presence, attitudes, and actions of paid staff are likely to affect the politics of organizations. If the Weber-Michels model suggests that paid staff may exercise a conservatizing influence on an SMO to protect their jobs, critics including Zald and Ash (1966) and Jenkins (1977) argue that staff in many organizations are more radical than the rank and file, so that oligarchy may mean radicalizing of the SMO. These authors, however, observed organizations such as labor unions and the National Council of Churches, in which the central office was funded by contributions from individual or organizational members who, despite their contributions, exercised little control. In SMOs where paid staff are more dependent on outside sponsorship, elite control over funding may temper radical impulses in the staff (McCarthy and Zald 1973).

Paid staff may indeed move an organization in a direction more conservative or more radical than that preferred by members or volunteer boards. Across a social movement, therefore, the presence of paid staff in a variety of organizations may permit the survival of a range of ideologies and strategic preferences. Fainstein and Fainstein (1974) argue that paid staff are more likely than the rank and file to retain interest in a cause during periods of movement quiescence and activist discouragement.[39]

Professionalism may steer an organization away from radical and even some moderate tactics, if not radical goals. The tax status of many formal SMOs restrict lobbying and electoral work. Sponsorship of illegal activity such as nonviolent civil disobedience jeopardizes this status.[40] SMOs have become adept at pushing the limits of these restrictions, but organizations with paid staff are more likely to accept them because of their greater need to maintain a tax status that encourages member and outside contributions. The structure of an SMO influences political tactics more directly because professionalized groups are more likely to hire experts to lobby and litigate. Groups with a mass base are more likely to mobilize this base for both extrainstitutional and institutional tactics.

Organizational Tensions and the Peace Campaigns

The Emergency Peace Campaign and the test ban and nuclear freeze campaigns experienced tensions between their founding coalitions and the emergent umbrella organizations, between national and local organizing, and between professionalism and grassroots mobilization. They managed the tensions variously. For example, the EPC and the nuclear freeze campaign formed a single umbrella organization to hold together a coalition of peace groups, and the test ban founders set up both a radical and a moderate organization. The EPC developed an isolated structure to deal with national-local tensions, and SANE and the NWFC became federated. The NWFC mobilized extensive grassroots participation, and the EPC emphasized the use of experts and major-donor funding. For each peace campaign, how these tensions were managed influenced the campaign's rise, course, fall, and impact.

4

The Emergency Peace Campaign

The Emergency Peace Campaign (EPC) was the last major effort of the American peace movement between World War I and World War II. In the aftermath of World War I, the peace movement entered its modern phase as a new generation of leaders founded internationalist and pacifist organizations. In the 1920s, these organizations worked to build a lasting peace and a stable international system. The rise of international tensions in the 1930s forced the peace movement to a defensive strategy of working to prevent war.[1] In 1936, the leading peace groups launched an Emergency Peace Campaign around common goals of increasing international economic cooperation and maintaining American neutrality.

For two years, the EPC brought together the two main wings of the peace movement in a productive if uneasy coalition. Reflecting the political, activist tone of the modern American peace movement, the campaign organized mass meetings and other large-scale efforts to influence public opinion and generate public pressure on policy makers. By the end of 1937, however, the coalition broke apart, as leading internationalists rejected neutrality in favor of collective security with the Allies.

The end of the coalition would not by itself have halted the campaign. This demise was also brought on by the withdrawal of support by pacifist leaders concerned about the political and organizational impact of the campaign. Key pacifist groups continued to support neutrality, but they were afraid that the EPC went too far toward subordinating the pacifist analysis to a simplistic proneutrality message. As the major sponsors of the campaign, they came to see it as a drain on their limited resources and a potential rival for members and financial support. The organizational structure of the EPC had kept it dependent upon sponsorship by the major peace organizations; the loss of this sponsorship spelled the end of the campaign.

The larger political environment also affected the fate of the EPC. By the end of the 1930s, elite opinion had coalesced around collective security policies, and no peace effort could stand in the way of greater military preparedness and aid to the allies, although public opinion was still split. Nevertheless, in the years in which the EPC operated, elite opinion was sufficiently divided and tentative to leave political space in which to operate. As the EPC ended, this space started closing.

Historical Context

During the 1920s and 1930s, pacifists and internationalists often found common cause in promoting a variety of measures such as the World Court and international treaties outlawing war. The EPC represented both the strongest and the last coalition, a coalition formed in a time of domestic and international crisis.

By early 1936, the economy had begun to recover from the depths of the depression, but a new recession occurred that summer that resulted in a new collapse that fall. During the two years of the EPC, there were more than 10 million unemployed workers.

The international situation worsened throughout the 1930s. Japan invaded Manchuria in 1931. Three years later it established a "Co-Prosperity Sphere" and announced its decision not to renew international treaties limiting naval forces when those treaties expired in 1936. In 1935, Italy invaded Ethiopia, and Germany began rearming in contravention of the Versailles treaty. Then the Axis powers of Germany, Italy, and Japan were established formally in 1936 and 1937.

These events had created both problems and opportunities for the peace movement. The Depression made it difficult to focus the attention of the public and elites on international concerns until they became crises. It also limited the fund-raising ability of peace movement groups, forcing them to rely on a narrow base of major donors for most of their general revenues. On the other hand, economic troubles made it easier to revive antimilitarism by drawing attention to the excessive profits received by munitions makers during World War I. The growth of the labor movement after the National Recovery Act of 1933 gave the peace movement an important potential ally.[2] Although not all labor leaders were sympathetic to the aims of the peace movement, many were part of an anti-imperialist Left.[3] Furthermore, the generalized unrest of the middle 1930s helped legitimize the growing politicization of the peace movement and threatened to keep the Roosevelt administration off-balance and susceptible to political pressure.[4]

Proneutrality sentiment increased with international tensions. Public opinion reflected fear of entanglement in another overseas conflict and a rethinking of World War I. In the 1920s and 1930s, pacifist groups, who had opposed American entry, led a movement to popularize a revisionist history of the war.[5] In 1934, Dorothy Detzer, the Washington lobbyist for the American branch of the Women's International League for Peace and Freedom (WILPF), played an important role in establishing the Senate's Nye committee, which investigated the role of the munitions industry in World War I. The committee reported that private arms makers had defied neutrality policies, sold arms to both sides, received excess profits, and enjoyed governmental favoritism. It initiated legislation on the taxing of war profits and the regulation of the munitions industry.

The Nye committee findings, along with a burgeoning literature including *Merchants of Death,* a 1934 Book-of-the-Month Club nonfiction selection, and the popular novel *All Quiet on the Western Front,* fed a growing antiwar mood in the United States and abroad. Polls showed an increasing support for pacifism, particularly in the churches and among young people, and a widespread determination to stay out of foreign wars.

Nevertheless, as the leaders of the Emergency Peace Campaign themselves observed, the mood of the public was at most "a blind, unintelligent, and perhaps temporary determination to stay out of foreign wars."[6] There was significant pacifist and neutralist sentiment, but there was also a strong current of national chauvinism, which opened the door to militarist appeals.[7]

Although clergy and students were strongly antiwar, other sectors of the public were more ambivalent. Labor did include a Left, anti-imperialist current. Some leaders of organized labor, including John L. Lewis, were suspicious of what they saw as growing corporate control of foreign policy and opposed conscription as a means by which government and business might regulate the labor market against the interests of unions. Conservative labor leaders favored greater military production as a means to create jobs. The leaders of the Emergency Peace Campaign hoped that organized opposition from workers, religious congregations, and students, along with more diffuse antiwar public opinion, would exert sufficient pressure on Congress to prevent President Roosevelt from moving away from official policies of neutrality and toward an alliance with England, France, and other nations against the Axis powers. Their support of neutrality was not motivated by any sympathy with Germany, Italy, and Japan, of course. Rather they hoped that war could still be prevented or, at the very least, that the United States could be kept out.

Peace movements typically involve efforts to mobilize public opinion to shape foreign and military policy—but the policy-making process is well insulated from public scrutiny and participation, and the foreign policy establishment has generally molded public opinion.

American foreign policy making is more of a closed process than is the formation of the domestic agenda. Since World War I, a network of public and private institutions headed by the Foreign Policy Association (FPA, founded in 1918 as the League of Free Nations Association, and renamed FPA in 1921) and the Council on Foreign Relations (CFR, founded in 1921) has coordinated the formulation and debate of alternatives within elite circles and the dissemination of ideas to the public.[8] Over the course of this century, within government the executive branch has come to dominate the making of foreign policy, overshadowing the more-responsive Congress and lowering the visibility of policy deliberations and the chances for public participation. The greatest growth in executive power followed World War II and the establishment of the "national security state," but the shift away from a strong congressional role had been visible in the 1930s.[9]

Peace movements are more likely to try to use public opinion when they face a divided elite and a public united in opposition to official policy (Joseph 1981). Public opinion in the mid-1930s was diffuse and contradictory. Elites, however, split over neutrality, creating an opening that peace leaders seized. The rise of internationalism within the business and foreign policy establishments improved the political climate for the peace movement.

Throughout the 1930s, internationalism was a growing force in business and policy circles and a major current in the peace movement. It prevailed over isolationist, economic nationalist, and protectionist positions. Ferguson (1989) emphasizes the role of economic interest in the emergence of an internationalist-oriented New Deal coalition. According to this account, since 1896, American politics had been dominated by a coalition of protectionist commercial and investment banks and labor-intensive industries. Threatened by foreign competition, they united under the umbrella of the Republican party to defeat the Populist movement and to battle the growth of organized labor. By the 1930s, however, this coalition was threatened by the growth of capital-intensive industries and internationally oriented commercial banks. These dynamic economic forces did not risk losing business to foreign competitors; rather, they saw overseas expansion as the key to their continued growth. They fought for an economic internationalism based on free trade and low tariffs, and they were willing and able to reach accommodations with organized labor. The resulting New Deal coalition solidified with Roosevelt's reelection in 1936.

The formation of a stable New Deal coalition by the mid-1930s presented the peace movement with opportunities and problems. On the one hand, internationalism was strengthened. On the other hand, internationalists in government and in the peace movement were deeply ambivalent over neutrality. Although economic internationalists saw peace as essential to the open-door policies that would permit overseas economic expansion, most of them eventually concluded that only support for the Allies would ensure a more open postwar system (Williams 1962). Furthermore, proneutrality peace leaders hesitated to strengthen Roosevelt's hand politically because they suspected his professed commitments to peace and neutrality. By 1934, when a modest but real economic recovery seemed to be underway, Roosevelt turned more of his attention to foreign policy. He quietly began pushing for greater military preparedness, including the construction of a larger navy, while continuing to talk neutrality. The peace movement took the fight to Congress with some success; but although some Republican senators were vocal antimilitarists and anti-imperialists, the Republican party did not offer a consistent alternative to Roosevelt on foreign policy.

In this domestic political context, leaders of the peace movement looked for some way to address the growing international crisis and steer American foreign policy away from what they feared was becoming a path toward war. Both internationalists and pacifists developed strategies based on unifying the peace movement around common goals and using the combined strength of the two wings to reach a broader public and to pressure policy makers. The EPC was the result.

The Origins of the Emergency Peace Campaign

The peace movement of the mid–1930s seemed to be in a strong position to carry out a major campaign. A core group of ten or so organizations gave the movement leadership, visibility, and an established flow of resources. Internationalist groups had access to elite opinion shapers and policy makers and to significant funding from the Carnegie Endowment for International Peace (CEIP). Pacifist groups had some grassroots base; strong ties to other social movements, including labor, socialist, feminist, and student groups; and a stable funding source in wealthy Quaker donors. The value of these resources and assets was multiplied by the dedication, skill, and experience of the peace groups' leaders and staff. Stanley High's 1938 *Saturday Evening Post* article "Peace, Inc." estimated that without such leadership, the activity financed by the combined $2-million-per-year budget of the top sixty peace and affiliated groups would have cost five times as much (High 1938, 89).

The largest organization in the pacifist camp was the National Council for Prevention of War (NCPW), founded in 1921 by Quaker Frederick Libby to coordinate disarmament work. It had evolved from a coalition umbrella group to a more independent organization, although its membership continued to consist of other organizations, not individuals. In 1935, the NCPW had twenty-one participating and ten "cooperating" member organizations, including pacifist groups, professional associations, and farm and labor groups. The NCPW also had its own staff of 18, 5 branch offices, and 23,000 subscribers to its mailings.[10] In 1927, led by Frederick Libby, it had conducted a rapid, effective campaign to put pressure on the Coolidge administration to find peaceful means to resolve disputes stemming from Mexico's nationalization of American assets (Libby 1969).[11] The National Peace Conference (NPC), a clearinghouse for the movement, boasted a combined membership of its affiliated organizations of more than 40 million people.

Just as public opinion was deceptive, with wide but shallow support for neutrality and even pacifism, so was the apparent organizational strength of the peace movement misleading. Individuals belonging to more than one NPC member group were counted more than once in the NPC total, so the clearinghouse's claim of 40 million followers was inflated. More significantly, an organization's membership in the NPC typically reflected the views of leaders and not those of rank-and-file members.

Individual peace organizations had key weaknesses. Although they opposed the elitist composition and political strategy of the internationalists, the pacifist groups had only a small grassroots base. The largest pacifist membership group—WILPF—had only 15,000 members in 120 local branch organizations. The internationalists had an even smaller grassroots component. Of the internationalist organizations, the League of Nations Association (LNA) had the most members, 10,000 individuals in 23 branches covering 18 states (Kuusisto 1950, High 1938).

The peace groups had a steady flow of financial contributions, but they depended on a small set of individual and institutional funders. The internationalists counted on support from the CEIP for most of their funding.[12] Only the LNA had a significant alternative funding base through membership dues. Some key pacifist groups also depended on a small set of donors. The NCPW, for example, typically received only 15 percent of its budget from small contributions.[13] Like the AFSC, this group was funded mainly from large donations made by wealthy Quakers (Chatfield 1971). The WILPF was the only pacifist group with a substantial dues base.

Beyond the Nye hearings and the NCPW-led campaign against war with Mexico, the peace groups could count no major postwar political victories. Internationalists had been frustrated in their attempts, supported by the pacifists, to secure American affiliation with the League of Nations or acceptance of the World Court. Pacifists had been unable to block huge naval appropriations or enact strong neutrality legislation. Both pacifists and internationalists therefore felt the need to go beyond existing efforts to launch a major antiwar campaign. The EPC for two years united the internationalists and the pacifists in an attempt to mobilize public opinion and support for a program of comprehensive international economic reform and strict neutrality for America.

Planning the Campaign

The immediate catalyst for the campaign was the Senate's rejection of United States membership in the World Court, a body created by but independent of the League of Nations. Although the Senate had rejected membership in the League of Nations after World War I, internationalists hoped that senators could be persuaded to take the more modest step of court membership. In 1926, the Senate did vote for membership, but included an isolationist-sponsored reservation other nations found unacceptable, and the issue returned to the Senate. Opponents delayed consideration of compromise measures for almost a decade, despite strong pressure from both wings of the peace movement.[14]

In January 1935, the Roosevelt administration asked the Senate to reconsider court membership, and the Foreign Relations Committee reported a favorable bill. Under pressure generated by the Hearst press and the right-wing populist radio preacher Father Charles E. Coughlin, who claimed this would be a back door to league membership, the Senate failed by seven votes to give the two-thirds approval necessary for membership. This show of continued isolationist power alarmed the peace movement. So did the German military buildup and Italy's invasion of Ethiopia in 1935. By the end of that year both pacifists and internationalists were planning a united campaign, each side intending to bring the other in as a junior partner.

Most pacifists had abandoned the united front with Communists that they had worked to establish in the early 1930s. They decided that the American Communist party was cooperating mainly to recruit members, and that it was more interested in advancing the interests of the Soviet Union than in peace. Pacifist leaders decided instead to form a Left-Center coalition, with internationalists representing the Center. They valued the legitimacy and elite contacts the internationalists would bring to this kind of effort.

Under the leadership of Clark Eichelberger, director of the LNA, and historian James Shotwell, director of the Division of Economics and History of the CEIP, the internationalist wing of the peace movement had developed an interest in political pressure tactics. To Shotwell, this did not mean mobilizing a mass movement. Instead, he felt internationalists should go beyond their usual tactics of quietly circulating discussion papers and talking with national policy makers to directly lobbying local elites via chambers of commerce, professional associations, and similar organizations. Both Eichelberger and Shotwell recognized that by the mid-1930s the pacifist groups, pursuing less genteel tactics, had gained considerable experience and expertise in critical areas such as fundraising, media outreach, and government lobbying.

Shocked by the Senate's World Court decision, internationalist leaders realized that for all their elite contacts they were politically impotent. They appointed a committee to devise a program and organizational structure that would include the pacifist groups, although some internationalists considered these organizations too far to the Left. Their program centered on international economic cooperation and only incidentally mentioned opposition to collective sanctions. This resembled a proposal drafted by leaders of the NPC, the umbrella organization for both wings of the movement. Both, however, were to be put aside in favor of the campaign plan devised by pacifist leaders.

The pacifist program was devised by Ray Newton, a longtime AFSC staffer. During World War I, Newton had been fired from his instructor's position at Phillips Exeter Academy because of his pacifist beliefs. He had served with the Quaker relief project in Europe after the war, and later joined the Peace Section of the AFSC. At the October 1935 annual conference of the FOR, he spoke to a small meeting of members pondering how to participate in a national campaign without losing the pacifist message. Newton argued that on the eve of American entry into World War I, public opinion had shifted rapidly toward intervention, catching the peace movement off guard. He argued that to avoid a similar fate this time the peace movement would have to take the initiative. He proposed a united peace campaign that would cost between $500,000 and $1 million and would involve peace leaders, foreign policy experts, clergy, and students (Chatfield 1971, 266–267).[15]

The FOR endorsed Newton's idea of a coalitional peace campaign. On November 8, 1935, the AFSC added its approval and, equally important, its sponsorship. For two months, planning went forward while the AFSC paid Newton's salary and put its staff at his disposal. He brought in leaders, including Kirby Page, a "social evangelist" speaker and accomplished fund raiser; John Nevin Sayre, chair of the American section of the FOR; and Frederick Libby, founder and head of the NCPW. Detailed plans were drawn up at two conferences in November and December, attended by most of the key pacifist leaders.

By the time the NPC convened in mid-December, the pacifists had seized the initiative within the peace movement. Not only did they have a comprehensive plan, they had the organizational and financial resources and the extensive national network, mainly among the clergy, to carry it out. They also had enough representation at the conference to elect one of their own, Sayre, to chair the steering committee and to achieve numerical balance on the committee between pacifists and internationalists.

Funding gave pacifists the edge in setting the terms of the new campaign. The internationalist groups depended for funds on the CEIP. While the CEIP balked at providing the dollars needed for a large campaign, the pacifists gained the cooperation of the AFSC in soliciting some of its major donors. They raised more than $100,000 in pledges in time for the early December planning session convened by Newton.[16] These funds, mostly from a few families who had been sponsors of the pacifist organizations, were raised by Newton, Page, Libby, and Sayre, "the only four pacifists capable of raising the sums [the EPC] would require" (Chatfield 1971, 267).

At this December meeting, attended by more than one hundred pacifists at Buck Hills Falls, Pennsylvania, it was agreed that the EPC would be run by a council made up of leading pacifists. They would serve as individuals rather than as official delegates from their respective organizations, to speed and simplify decision making.[17] The council was to be self-perpetuating body, and several members were selected at the December conference. The council in turn selected an executive committee, including Newton, Sayre, Clarence Pickett of the AFSC, and Mildred Scott Olmsted of the WILPF. This committee directed the EPC in early 1936 by filling in the details of broad plans approved at the conference, and appointing staff. After the campaign's official start in April 1936, initiative passed to key staff members, especially Executive Director Newton and Kirby Page, who served as chair of the EPC speakers' bureau (Chatfield 1971, 268). The pacifist organizations cooperated closely with the campaign in terms of staff and programs. They continued to pay the salaries of Newton and a few other top EPC staff while releasing them to work full time for the campaign.

Certain tensions were evident from the outset of the EPC. Leaders of pacifist groups were concerned that the joint campaign might undercut their organizational and resource base, particularly in the WILPF, which had the most extensive local chapter structure of any of these groups and feared the establishment of rival EPC chapters. Both sides were concerned with the themes of the campaign. Internationalists were wary of a strong commitment to strict neutrality. Pacifists who considered war likely were already planning to aid conscientious objectors.[18] Determined to present a clear pacifist case for war resistance, they feared that their case would be muted by the campaign's emphasis on neutrality and international economic cooperation.

Because of these tensions, it was decided at the outset to limit the campaign to a two-year effort. Although the top leaders of the EPC came from pacifist groups, they agreed to subsume pacifism to the campaign's larger goals. The WILPF's concerns over local competition were reduced if not resolved when the EPC agreed to conduct its local work by forming committees of representatives of key groups already present in the community rather than by attempting to form new organizations. EPC leaders also thought that this approach would have the added virtue of facilitating a more rapid development of local committees.

Internationalist groups accepted the EPC program despite their growing doubts about neutrality, but only a few nonpacifists took important committee positions in the EPC. Nevertheless, the campaign worked to present a unified face to the public. The name Emergency Peace Campaign was adopted in January 1936 to broaden the appeal of what had been called a No-War Movement (Chatfield 1971, 269). In March the coalition was formalized when the EPC officially affiliated with the NPC and claimed the sponsorship of a united peace movement.

The EPC formally adopted three goals: to keep the United States from going to war, to bring about economic and political changes essential to a just and peaceable world order, and to build a united movement of individuals opposed to war. The goal of promoting international economic reform was based on the premise shared by most peace leaders that the growing international crisis could in large part be attributed to the economic inequities inscribed in the Versailles treaty ending World War I. They believed that comprehensive reform rather than piecemeal appeasement or reliance only on negative sanctions might avert another world war, even at that late date.[19]

At the start of the EPC, pacifists strongly supported neutrality; the internationalists were ambivalent. Neutrality had been a highly controversial issue throughout the 1920s and 1930s. That violation of American neutrality by German submarine attacks on American shipping had been the rationale if not the cause of American entry into World War I prompted a rethinking of the meaning and practicality of neutrality after the war. Some policy makers concluded that insistence on free trade and navigation was likely to compromise any neutral position and recommended that the United States adopt a position of strict neutrality that would not include these terms.

The pacifist position on neutrality had changed over the course of the decade. In 1931, pacifists had been among those urging collaboration with the League of Nations to enforce diplomatic sanctions against Japan after it invaded Manchuria. Some even went along with proposals for economic sanctions after the Japanese attacked Shanghai in early 1932, although many pacifists felt this would simply strengthen the hand of militarists within Japan. The failure of the league to take effective action, however, led most pacifists to embrace strict neutrality, including the embargo of military material to all hostile powers. They reasoned that in the absence of a just and effective international system, the only alternative to strict neutrality was to form military alliances, something they were not willing to do (Chatfield 1971).[20]

In the 1930s, proponents of strict neutrality had fought to make neutrality binding on the president once a state of hostility was recognized. The Senate had considered neutrality legislation throughout the decade, but disagreements over impartial vs. discriminatory sanctions and mandatory vs. discretionary rules prevented passage of any significant laws until 1935, when the first Neutrality Act prohibited the sale of arms to either side during a war. Neutrality advocates considered the act weak, and during the EPC they fought to strengthen it.

The addition of the third goal of building a united movement of individuals opposed to war was a further concession to pacifists who feared the campaign would smother their efforts to promote pacifism. The strategy designed to meet this goal was simple: pacifist "enrollment cards" would be distributed at EPC events to widen the organized network of pacifists around the nation.

The general strategy for achieving the first two goals involved mobilizing public opinion and focusing pressure on the government, particularly Congress. This would be done by complementing the educational and lobbying work of the peace groups with an extensive outreach effort aimed at communities and constituency groups and with political lobbying.

The EPC was planned to take place over a series of intensive "cycles" from April 1936 to February 1938. In three cycles, including the first, the central outreach technique was to be a series of public meetings in cities and towns in every state. Some of these would be mass meetings, at which national figures and local activists, primarily clergy, would address the key themes of the campaign. Also planned were smaller meetings organized and run by local contacts. The meetings were all to be coordinated by the national EPC offices in Philadelphia (donated by the AFSC), regional EPC offices opened in the early spring of 1937, and local contacts.

Supplementing the face-to-face interaction of the meetings would be a large-scale media effort. The peace movement had become adept at using the rapidly emerging national mass media — magazines and radio networks — and often received favorable coverage. Between 1931 and 1937, World Peaceways, the media arm of the pacifist wing of the movement, had managed to obtain $800,000 in free advertising from sympathetic media.[21] To inaugurate the campaign and its key cycle, the No-Foreign-War Crusade planned for the spring of 1937, the EPC would use national radio addresses, including speeches by important figures such as Eleanor Roosevelt and Admiral Byrd.

Finally, specific constituencies were targeted to help build a coalition beyond the peace movement. Pacifists experienced in outreach to labor, youth, blacks, and other groups were hired by the EPC or borrowed from sponsoring pacifist organizations. Churches would play a central role in the campaign because of the large number of clergy sympathetic to the peace movement.

The pressure generated from meetings, mass media, and constituency work was to be focused on Congress by the EPC's Legislative Department, headed by Dorothy Detzer. She brought to the campaign experience and skill gained as the WILPF's lobbyist. Also serving in this department were Libby and other NCPW staff members and William Stone of the internationalist FPA.

In addition to Detzer and other top staff on loan or leave from the peace groups, the rest of the national staff was filled primarily with people who took leave from jobs and careers outside the movement and agreed to work for the EPC for up to two years for subsistence wages, generally with no guarantee of returning to their former jobs.[22] Early plans for opening and staffing area offices were to be put off until the start of 1937, probably for financial reasons, although regional conferences of activists were held as early as December 1935 on the West Coast and in New England.

Early Stages of the Campaign

On April 20, 1936, Adolf Hitler celebrated his birthday by parading through Berlin the newly built-up German military, and on April 21 he took the title of supreme war lord. That same day, the EPC was launched publicly when the mayor of Philadelphia tapped the Liberty Bell to begin a national radio broadcast featuring a short message from Eleanor Roosevelt. The main address was delivered by George Lansbury, a longtime British pacifist, member of Parliament, and former leader of the Labour party, who spoke to the need to prevent war by removing its causes, especially economic inequalities between nations.

This broadcast kicked off the first cycle of the campaign, a two-month effort to publicize broadly the EPC's main goals, stressing the need to keep the United States out of any European war. Lansbury and leaders of the American peace movement toured the major cities in the East and Midwest, addressing radio audiences and mass meetings in venues such as New York's Carnegie Hall. Another prominent English Quaker and member of Parliament, Alfred Salter, took part in a West Coast tour of meetings. One- and two-day study conferences were held in 278 cities, and teams of two and three ministers, educators, and peace leaders traveled through every state but Wyoming, speaking to groups large and small.

The church network proved invaluable, as 3,500 ministers promised to give five talks each on peace over two months and to help the campaign in other ways. The Legislative Department put together a comprehensive program centered on proposals to limit military policy to continental defense rather than overseas intervention, increase cooperation with international bodies such as the League of Nations, further international economic cooperation and trade, control the munitions industry, and strengthen neutrality legislation. Congress had passed an extension of the 1935 Neutrality Act in February 1936, prohibiting loans as well as arms sales to belligerents and limiting presidential discretion. This bill satisfied neither the administration nor advocates of strict neutrality, who felt that the president still had too much latitude in the declaration of embargoes and that key materials easily converted to weapons were still excluded from these embargoes. The campaign intended to close what it considered key loopholes in these measures.

Detzer and her colleagues in the Legislative Department hoped that the spring meetings would focus on the upcoming fall elections, and to this end they compiled and distributed congressional voting records and furnished to local committees copies of bills and a questionnaire for candidate interviews. Detzer complained later that the spring meetings lacked a political emphasis. She felt that this initial cycle of the campaign had failed to generate much pressure on Congress.[23] The fall 1936 meetings did, however, satisfy her.

A Farm Department, operated jointly by the EPC and the NPC, distributed literature through local farm organizations. The Labor Department developed a labor press service that reached 420 newspapers and sent troupes of players through twenty-four states presenting antiwar skits. In the summer months, both Farm and Labor departments conducted institutes on foreign relations for their constituencies. The EPC added staff members to work with Jewish and African-American groups. According to historian Charles Chatfield (1971, 271), "Never had the peace movement been so united or so closely in touch with the people as it was during the Emergency Peace Campaign."

The opening of the EPC had been timed to coincide with a student strike against war, in which about half a million high school and college students left their classrooms to demonstrate, in some cases with the cooperation of college administrators. Students had already organized a "Veterans of Future Wars" organization; by the start of the campaign, it claimed more than 30,000 members in 375 college chapters. Many of these students had taken the "Oxford Pledge," named for the occasion in 1933 when undergraduates in Oxford University's Union voted almost two to one that "this House will not fight for King and Country in any war." This pledge was taken by many of the 175,000 U.S. students who participated in student antiwar strikes in 1934 and 1935 (Chatfield 1971, 260). Student activism continued after the first intense cycle of the EPC in the spring of 1936, and youth work became the focus of the campaign over the summer. Two hundred twenty-three young volunteers were trained at three college campuses to do peace education. Most then formed teams and went into rural communities targeted as critical in the upcoming elections and legislative efforts.

Other summer efforts emphasized preparation for the fall political season. The Legislative Department extended its earlier work and put together a program designed to attract broad support. Departing from a narrow focus on the key goals of the campaign, the program included support for an antilynching law to attract backing from blacks and backed off slightly from support of strict mandatory neutrality, as a concession to political reality and to the internationalist members of the coalition. Nevertheless, plans were made to pressure Congress into passing "an adequate neutrality measure" as well as legislation aimed at increasing international economic cooperation.

The EPC lobbied the presidential nominating conventions of both major parties, with little impact. The Democrats did maintain their rhetorical allegiance to neutrality, promising, "We shall continue to observe a true neutrality in the disputes of others, . . . to work for peace and to take the profits out of war; to guard against being drawn, by political commitments, international banking, or private trading, into any war which may develop anywhere."[24] This language greatly upset proponents of collective security such as Secretary of State Cordell Hull, but the party platform did not satisfy advocates of strict neutrality because it did not promise any measures that might restrict Roosevelt's latitude in conducting foreign policy.

At the Republican convention, Dorothy Detzer used her extensive contacts to gain an interview with Senator William Borah, who was to author the party's foreign policy platform, only to find that he planned to include a repudiation of the League of Nations and the World Court. Although she persuaded Borah to support modest pro-neutrality language, the foreign policy drafting committee rejected this idea before it reached the convention floor.

The second cycle of the EPC also centered on public meetings. More than 1,110 meetings were held in 424 cities, in every state. These numbers included 168 of the 278 cities reached by the first cycle of meetings and 256 additional cities. Most of these meetings were small, held in clubs, schools, colleges, and similar sites. Attempts in a few cities to hold large meetings were not very successful. The campaign attributed this to competition from the electoral campaigns, lack of adequate preparation, and a failure to enlist more than one main speaker. Nevertheless, the EPC Speakers Bureau concluded that this round of meetings represented a step up from the initial round: the campaign had employed only five field workers (operating out of Phila-delphia and regional offices in Los Angeles and Nashville) to coordi-nate the meetings.[25]

During fall 1936 plans were formalized for the remaining cycles. Counting the completed first cycle, there were six.[26]

1. April–May 1936: General discussion of the three major goals.

2. October–November 1936: Discussion of political issues, pres-sure on political candidates, national enrollment of pacifists.

3. January–February 1937: "Neutrality Campaign": Political pres-sure on the new Congress, with primary emphasis on "adequate" neutrality measures, also aiming for international economic coopera-tion, and "changing basic policy of army and navy"; strengthening community organizations.

4. April–May 1937: "No-Foreign-War Crusade," planned to be-gin on the twentieth anniversary of American entry into World War I.

5. November 1937: emphasis on international economic coop-eration.

6. January–February 1938: Building an effective peace movement in every community.

The third and fourth cycles were special campaigns-within-the-campaign, designed to highlight key themes, build broader coalitions, and generate greater publicity and political pressure on Congress. Both were to be headed nominally by prominent figures — the Neutrality Campaign by Charles P. Taft II, the No-Foreign-War-Crusade by Ad-miral Richard E. Byrd. This crusade would be the culmination of the campaign's work for stricter neutrality measures and military policies limited to defense of the United States.

The Campaign Peaks

The size, intensity, and influence of the EPC grew during the winter of 1936–1937 and the spring of 1937, with the Neutrality Campaign and the No-Foreign-War Crusade. After this, tensions inside the sponsoring coalition and shifting public opinion led to a rapid decline.

The Neutrality Campaign began in January 1937. To manage it, the EPC expanded its national staff to include 150 members, and increased the number of area offices to twenty, with ninety-one staff members. Local committees had formed in 1,200 cities; 600 more had EPC "contacts."[27]

The strategic focus of the Neutrality Campaign was to persuade Congress to extend and strengthen the neutrality acts of 1935 and 1936, which had left unresolved the tensions between two popular goals, neutrality and foreign trade. Debate revolved around a "compromise" devised by Bernard Baruch in June 1936.[28] Baruch proposed a "cash-and-carry" policy that would permit the United States to continue trading with belligerent nations but would require them to pay cash rather than use credit, and to transport the material on their own ships. This, it was argued, would avoid the problems over interference with trade that had led to American entry into World War I. The plan met with some support but also with opposition from two sides: those who thought it conceded too many traditional neutral rights to navigation, and those, including the pacifist groups, who thought it put neutrality too much at risk by favoring naval powers such as Britain and France who could meet its terms.

Congressional committees began considering these issues in mid-January. They focused on an administration-backed bill that gave the president wide discretion over when to enact embargoes and what materials would be permitted under cash-and-carry provisions. The two wings of the peace movement now moved significantly apart. In public hearings in February, representatives of the pacifist groups, including Florence Boeckel of the NCPW, testified against the pending legislation, arguing that it gave the president too much discretion. She and other pacifists lobbied instead for strict neutrality, including the extension of mandatory embargoes to strategic materials such as oil and limiting cash-and-carry to nonstrategic trade items. Meanwhile, some internationalists were moving away from neutrality altogether toward a collective security position. The LNA sent every member of Congress a pamphlet urging the adoption of laws that would allow the administration to declare selective embargoes against aggressor nations.

The sharp divergence of views between pacifists and internationalists raised tensions within the EPC. Because pacifists predominated in leadership positions, however, the campaign continued its work for strong neutrality legislation. Although internationalist leaders feared that this continued proneutrality stance might strengthen isolationism, they did not formally withdraw from the campaign, perhaps feeling that the shared work for international economic cooperation was important enough to justify maintaining the coalition. Meanwhile, they remained to take positions (as individuals and organizations) different from those of the EPC — and plans called for an end to the campaign in February 1938.

Under these circumstances, the Neutrality Campaign went forward, with well-known speakers touring the country for a third series of meetings and with intensified work in outreach to farm and labor groups. This time, the meetings were more closely tied to the political goals of the EPC, and many passed resolutions in support of specific legislation. The Legislative Department kept a close eye on congressional debates on the neutrality bill and used its own newsletter and those of the NCPW and other member groups to generate letters and telegrams to legislators. EPC staff directly lobbied senators and representatives and provided information and "even whole speeches" to sympathetic legislators (Chatfield 1971, 276). These legislators were also given access to some of the free radio airtime enjoyed by the peace groups. The print media were addressed through press releases and the No-Frontier-News Service, an independent wire service operated since 1933 by pacifist Devere Allen with AFSC support.

Public opinion supported neutrality. A January 1937 Gallup poll found that 69 percent of U.S. citizens thought that Congress rather than the president should formulate neutrality policy; the same organization reported in March that 94 percent preferred a policy aimed at keeping the United States out of war to one with the more ambitious goal of preventing war abroad (Divine 1962, 180–181).

Nevertheless, in March both houses passed bills that included cash-and-carry policies. The final version of the House bill gave the administration much greater latitude in the application of these policies than did the Senate version. This bill passed after a last-ditch effort to send it back to a House committee for strengthening had failed by a vote of 275 to 118. The House and Senate then sent the bills to a conference committee to iron out the differences.

The conference committee was still deliberating when the EPC launched its final and most intensive effort, the No-Foreign-War Crusade, on April 6, 1937, the twentieth anniversay of American entry into World War I. Again there was a national radio broadcast, which included messages from Eleanor Roosevelt and Admiral Byrd. Around the nation, large meetings and small discussion groups drew upon the network established by earlier cycles. There were now committees or contacts in almost two thousand cities and towns, on five hundred college campuses, and in many farm and labor organizations (Chatfield 1971, 276).

The EPC Speakers Bureau told more than six hundred volunteer speakers to focus their message on the questions of whether the United States should go to war as a last resort and how the United States could, without resorting to war, help to decrease Axis belligerence. Meeting organizers were urged to include speakers with different perspectives on these issues, apparently on the premise that the campaign's message would prevail over opposing views.[29] A twenty-five-page outline prepared by Kirby Page and distributed to speakers and discussion group organizers emphasized neutrality legislation, revising military policy, lowering trade barriers, economic equality, and transforming international agencies from instruments for the preservation of the status quo into agencies of justice (Chatfield 1971, 277).

Despite the best efforts of the campaign and its allies, the conference committee reported out a weak neutrality bill containing a "curious mixture of mandatory and permissive features designed to insulate the United States from contact with future wars" (Divine 1962, 193). Once the president used the authority to certify that a state of hostility existed between nations, several prohibitions on trade with these nations automatically took effect. Rather than extending embargoes to strategic material, the bill also gave the president great latitude in extending cash-and-carry provisions to selected belligerents. President Roosevelt and his supporters were satisfied. The bill was passed by Congress in late April and signed into law by Roosevelt on May 1.

The Campaign Declines

After passage of the 1937 neutrality legislation, the No-Foreign-War-Crusade ended in May, having failed to accomplish its main goal of strengthening American neutrality. Mounting financial pressures on the EPC led to the closing of most of the area offices in June (the rest closed that summer) and the furloughing of most of the ninety-one field staff. Throughout the campaign, the goal of raising money in small amounts at the public meetings had proven elusive, as the Depression economy continued.[30] Meanwhile, families and individuals who had provided the campaign's initial funding balked at continued requests to give at levels that would be "sacrificial"—cutting into capital—to support both the campaign and the established pacifist groups. Behind the financial problems were exacerbated tensions over policy and organization within the campaign, tensions that drove both wings of the movement to hasten the end of the EPC.

First, the gap between internationalists and pacifists had widened. Although internationalists had put aside their misgivings over neutrality for a larger effort to prevent war, they had continued to move toward the collective security position; pacifists, on the other hand, had more strongly embraced strict neutrality. The differences could no longer be compromised or ignored by the end of this fourth cycle of the EPC.

Second, there were growing tensions between the pacifist organizations and the campaign. Although some 23,000 persons had signed pacifist enrollment cards at EPC-sponsored events, some leaders thought that their initial fears were justified: the campaign was hurting their cause by obscuring the pacifist message. Sayre and others had been particularly offended by the selection of a military man, Admiral Byrd, to serve as figurehead for the No-Foreign-War Crusade. The pacifist groups felt financially drained by sponsoring the campaign; they feared that continued EPC appeals to their key donors would damage their own fund raising.

Finally, disputes over organizational turf had continued. When the EPC area offices had been established, Mildred Scott Olmsted of the WILPF had charged that the campaign's staff had ignored the wishes of the EPC council in going ahead with an extensive regional outreach program.[31] Frederick Libby had expressed concern that the EPC had tapped into the NCPW donor network. He insisted that in some of its activities the campaign merely duplicated the NCPW program, with less expertise.[32] In February 1937, Olmsted had declared her intention to pull the WILPF out of the EPC at the end of the year, even if the campaign were to extend beyond its initial two-year limit.[33]

The fiscal responsibility for the campaign that had given the pacifists the upper hand in the organization became a wedge between the EPC and some pacifist groups. As the EPC dissolved, Newton and Page tried to guide the momentum it had generated into a new unified peace movement coordinated by the NPC, with political action to be coordinated by an expanded NCPW. They urged those local EPC groups that had survived to affiliate with the NPC. Neither pacifist nor internationalist groups were willing to join another coalition, however. In May, their leaders approved much more modest plans to designate the NPC as a clearinghouse for the movement and to have it take over the fifth and last EPC cycle, a campaign for an international economic conference. The Campaign for World Economic Cooperation did begin on October 1, 1937, and ran for fifteen months under the leadership of Clark Eichelberger. The proposed international conference never materialized, largely because of British opposition, although Roosevelt actively pursued the idea in early 1938.

The EPC itself formally continued for the remainder of the year but at a much smaller scale, conducting another round of youth work in the summer and then winding down in the fall. It officially disbanded at the end of 1937.

Aftermath

After the official end of the EPC, pacifist groups continued working together in support of neutrality legislation, and pressed for application of existing laws in the Far East. In October 1937, Roosevelt delivered an ambiguous speech that pacifists interpreted as moving toward collective security. The NCPW then decided to support the Ludlow amendment, a proposed constitutional reform that would require passage of a national referendum before Congress could declare war, except in the case of invasion. With a Gallup poll showing 73 percent of the public supporting the amendment, the administration launched an all-out lobbying effort against it. The House effectively killed the amendment by voting 209 to 188 against a measure to discharge it from committee. The close vote that showed continued support for neutrality and concern over the growth of presidential power in making foreign policy also may have represented the high-water mark for both sentiments.

Internationalists joined the administration in lobbying for collective security. The tide turned against strict neutrality, but it turned slowly. Despite the German occupation of Czechoslovakia in March 1939, the arms embargo remained in effect. Not until November 1939, two months after the German invasion of Poland and the outbreak of war, did Congress repeal the arms embargo. By the time the Japanese attacked Pearl Harbor, the president had gained the legal power and public support to give the Allies all aid short of direct military intervention.

Once the EPC ended, pacifists had felt so embattled on the neutrality issue that they put aside their misgivings and entered formal coalitions with the Right. In the Ludlow amendment struggle they were dismayed to find themselves on the same side as right-wing isolationists. As the war in Europe began, their ranks shrank. Those who remained turned to supporting conscientious objectors at home and preparing postwar reconstruction efforts abroad.

The Impact of the Emergency Peace Campaign

For two years, 1936 and 1937, the EPC focused the efforts of the U.S. peace movement on the twin goals of reforming the international economic order as the key to preventing another world war and maintaining neutrality to keep the United States out of any hostilities. The start of World War II and the subsequent entry of the United States meant, of course, that the EPC had failed to achieve these goals. The campaign had strengthened proneutrality forces; it did not manage to toughen neutrality legislation.

Despite these failures, the EPC represented an important step in the growing politicization of the peace movement. It unified peace groups, broadened their outreach into local communities, and strengthened their ties to other organized constituencies. World War II wiped out most of these gains and split the movement, but in Chatfield's view the EPC nevertheless remained "the most important and impressive effort in the history of the American peace movement" before the movement against the Vietnam War (Chatfield 1965, 321). The EPC had its main impact in three areas: public opinion, policy and policy making, and the peace movement itself.

Systematic public opinion polling was just emerging at the time of the EPC, but there are some studies of attitudes toward neutrality and related issues. Several polls cited by Divine (1962) and Wittner (1984) show that support for strict neutrality was high during and after the campaign, as the 73 percent support for the Ludlow amendment suggests. By early 1939, polls showed declining support for an arms embargo applied impartially to all belligerents. This support, however, remained substantial, ranging from 34 percent to 50 percent even after the outbreak of war. Divine interprets these results as reflecting a continued fear of direct involvement in war in conflict with an increasing identification with the Allied cause.

There is no direct evidence on the specific impact of the EPC on public opinion. I have seen no data suggesting a great increase in support for neutrality during the campaign, but it seems likely that an organization with the size and scope of the EPC affected attitudes toward neutrality. It may have increased the number of those who supported neutrality or simply delayed the reduction. It probably did increase the resolve of those who were proneutrality and gave them more channels to express their views.

More complicated is the question of the impact of the campaign on the isolationism-internationalism issue. Before the EPC, peace leaders recognized that much proneutrality sentiment was linked to a simplistic isolationism among those determined to avoid involvement in another European war. The difficult task of the movement and the campaign was to strengthen neutrality while linking it with an internationalist outlook, most directly through the goal of international economic reform.

The impact of the peace movement on increasing public understanding and support for internationalism is hard to assess, but it seems small. A common view is that internationalism became a consensus position only after the war. Chatfield even speculates that the efforts to promote an internationalist-oriented neutrality in the 1930s backfired: "[Perhaps the peace groups] helped to lay grounds for public acceptance of collective security in the face of a totalitarian threat to the international order to the degree that they successfully communicated their internationalism, just as they inadvertently contributed to isolationism to the extent that they established World War I as proof of war's essential futility" (Chatfield 1971, 141). This speculation illustrates the difficulty of the job facing the peace movement as well as a tension running through all three peace campaigns: how to achieve short-term goals by capitalizing on popular sentiment against war or the arms race while contributing to longer-term change by strengthening the deeper currents of internationalism, disarmament, and pacifism. Support for the short-term goals often stems in part from ideas and values that contradict these deep currents, such as isolationism.

The EPC certainly generated pressure on Congress to pass neutrality legislation. Although the 1936 and 1937 laws disappointed advocates of strict neutrality, they contained some mandatory measures. For example, the 1937 law required that once the president declared the existence of a state of war, the U.S. would embargo arms to all belligerents. Earlier measures had permitted selective embargoes. The campaign as a whole, however, may not have accomplished much more than the peace groups operating separately would have done. Early in the campaign, Dorothy Detzer had complained that at least one cycle of EPC meetings lacked political focus and that the campaign had "not been utilized for political action."[34] Halfway through the campaign, in October 1936, Frederick Libby complained that the EPC had drawn resources away from groups like his NCPW without matching their political savvy. He argued that "Many of the heads of departments of the Emergency Peace Campaign are amateurs in the peace movement, quite unfamiliar with local situations, so that in many places [the NCPW's] secretaries have had to go about and smooth things over where the EPC meetings had been held or where the young people had been."[35]

Libby's critique of the EPC was part of his effort to maintain the NCPW's role as the key political pressure group within the peace movement and to limit competition from the EPC. He did concede that the net contribution of the EPC to the peace movement had more than offset the loss of resources felt by some individual groups, including the NCPW. Nevertheless, the EPC may not have added that much to what the peace groups might have done alone, in translating opinion into effective political pressure and policy.

In policy making, the peace movement had hoped to check the trend toward greater presidential authority and to strengthen the role of the more-responsive Congress. The legislative branch, reluctant to challenge the administration over the growing military budget, did assert its role in making policy on neutrality. Any gains made here, however, were also wiped out by the dramatic increase in presidential power that accompanied entry into World War II.

The EPC brought pacifist groups closer together than ever before, although it also intensified interorganizational rivalries over funding and local chapters. And although 23,000 people had filled out pacifist "enrollment cards" during the campaign, there seems to have been little or no increase in actual membership of pacifist organizations. Not long after the campaign, in fact, pacifist groups began losing members and financial support as their positions became less popular. By 1939, the NCPW was almost a year's budget in debt ($70,000) and the WILPF, despite ambitious organizing plans to increase membership to 20,000, found itself with only about 14,000 members (Chatfield 1971, 298). With the outbreak of war, membership in and support of pacifist groups declined more precipitously.

On the surface, therefore, the EPC seems to have had little impact on the usual cycles of the pacifist groups: an increase in popularity and support as war approached, then a dramatic decline during wartime. Nevertheless, James Mullin, who served as assistant to the director of the EPC, thought the campaign did have a lasting positive effect on pacifism in the United States (Mullin interview). Although membership in peace groups did not increase greatly, the campaign did bring the pacifist message to a small but important group of people who became the next generation of pacifist leaders. Many of them refused induction into military service during the War (Mullin interview).[36] Some were jailed or sent to Civilian Public Service Camps, where they practiced nonviolent resistance to unjust or harsh conditions. In these settings, the philosophy and practice of nonviolent resistance were shaped, to be passed on later to leaders of the peace, civil rights, and other movements.

Beyond their shift to collective security, the internationalist groups did not change much during the campaign. After the war, however, a great upsurge in internationalism was led by established groups and new organizations such as the United World Federalists. Popular reaction to World War I may have had isolationist overtones; World War II was commonly seen as demonstrating the need for a stronger internationalism. Until the cold war, internationalist groups experienced a great increase in membership and support.

Because of both the tensions that disrupted the EPC and the effect of the war on the peace movement, the EPC did not create any new enduring organizations, philosophies, or strategies.[37]

Organizational Tensions in the Emergency Peace Campaign

Three sets of organizational tensions influenced the course and outcome of the Emergency Peace Campaign: coalition-organization, national-local, and professional-grassroots. The EPC was the strongest but also the last in a series of peace coalitions in the 1920s and 1930s. In launching a united campaign, the pacifist and internationalist wings of the movement set aside disagreements and misgivings about cooperating in a joint venture to confront the grave threat to peace. Because war seemed near but still avoidable, the peace groups made the EPC their top priority, giving it a fast start and sponsoring it for almost two years. The campaign was weakened, however, by tensions within the coalition, tensions present from the outset that intensified as time went on.

Coalitions, in principle, offer organizational and political advantages, allowing member groups to multiply the impact of available resources through a concerted division of labor and to expand their political influence through concentrated action. The peace groups brought a sophisticated division of labor into the campaign, with groups such as the NCPW emphasizing lobbying and political pressure and others such as World Peaceways specializing in mass media work. The major gain of the campaign was not so much in increasing specialization but in creating a common agenda between the two wings. This increased focus may have caused some loss of efficiency in the division of labor, as the remarks by Frederick Libby cited above show. Nevertheless, the campaign raised the political profile of the movement.

The advantages coalitions offer to their member groups are tempered by potential problems or tensions. Organizations may believe that their contributions to the coalition far exceed their returns in control over the coalition, credit received for the coalition's accomplishments, and risks taken for its failure; and they may lose freedom of action and visibility.

As a bloc, the pacifist groups made greater contributions of money, staff time, office space, and other resources than did the internationalists. In return, however, they gained effective control over the EPC, keeping neutrality at the center despite the ambivalence of the internationalists.[38] They achieved this control by taking almost all the leadership positions within the umbrella organization.

An umbrella organization is a typical device for managing a coalition. The increased coordination brings with it tensions between the member groups and their creation, which often establishes itself as a rival organization. Pacifist leaders, aware of this tendency from the start, took steps to counteract it, most importantly by agreeing with the internationalists to limit the campaign to two years.

In spite of this time limit, friction developed between the WILPF and the EPC over local organizing and between the NCPW and the EPC over fund raising and political work. Most pacifist groups came to see the EPC as a drain on their financial resources; many saw the EPC as a rival for funding, members, local presence, and national visibility. This assessment reinforced the initial decision to impose a time limit on the campaign.

Because pacifist groups continued to sponsor the EPC — their staff served as the top staff of the campaign and their donors provided most of the funds — they had the power and the will to keep the campaign from becoming a truly independent organization. The initial decision to avoid building an enduring organization reflected not just organizational rivalry but also the urgency felt by peace leaders — the belief that they had no time for major organization building. A member of the Executive Committee argued early in 1936: "If we were building an organization to go on functioning down through the years, that would be different. Our function is not comparable to the WIL[PF], the FOR, etc. If you start to build up state organizations, half the time would be taken setting them up."[39] Frederick Libby declared in early 1937: "I have been concerned about building a movement rather than an organization, and I felt that was the essential thing and the organization would take care of itself."[40]

The time limit did not eliminate tensions, but it helped the campaign manage them. Disgruntled member groups refrained from withdrawing sooner in the knowledge that the limit was there. Coalitions generally devise additional ways to manage tensions between groups and between groups and the umbrella organization. The EPC followed a common strategy for reducing conflict over goals and strategies by choosing a few key goals shared by member groups and focusing on them while ignoring differences over long-term goals and underlying ideology. This strategy helped to hold the coalition together, although the internationalists quickly lost enthusiasm for neutrality and later turned against it, and the pacifists remained concerned that these core goals would overshadow the pacifist message.

Another common strategy for reducing conflicts over resources is to seek outside funding, additional money that becomes available because sponsors hope that a concerted effort will be more effective than a divided movement. Complaints from pacifist groups make it clear that the EPC never solved this problem. Pacifists had already been pressing their sponsors for "sacrificial" giving because of the world crisis. These donors responded by providing start-up funds for the EPC, but there were limits to their generosity. If the CEIP, main sponsor of the internationalist groups, would not give them enough money for them to take leadership of the coalition, it was not likely to continue sponsoring a neutrality-oriented effort. Nor could the EPC use the expanded outreach of the movement to generate new funds because the Depression economy made it difficult to raise money, even in small amounts, from people of average means.

In one sense the EPC functioned exactly as a coalition should: as long as its member groups agreed on a common program, it focused the resources of the peace movement and widened its impact. The sponsorship of the established organizations gave the campaign a fast and effective start and maintained the EPC as its program developed. The inevitable tensions within the coalition were managed well enough to run a strong program for the first year and to keep the campaign together for two years. For the peace movement as a whole, the campaign coalition came up short: it failed to transcend differences between the two wings and to create new organizations or traditions.

The EPC was very much a top-down effort. Although its program revolved around public meetings in hundreds of cities and towns and it established 1,200 local committees, the planning, supervision, and fund raising for the campaign were done through the national office.[41] The regional offices were designed to help coordinate the program, not to start or service local chapters.[42]

Campaign strategy called for recruiting as local committee members people active in community organizations such as women's groups, labor unions, youth organizations, and service clubs. They would serve as individuals, not as official delegates of their organizations, in imitation of the national EPC leadership. On the national council, peace leaders served as individuals and not delegates, although they acted with the strong backing of the national peace groups. The local committees (or "councils") were created to help plan and run meetings and to distribute literature prepared and provided by the national office. They were not expected to plan and direct the campaign, to raise much money, or to hire their own staff. The EPC was not intended to be a federated organization with local chapters nor did it become one.

The 1,200 local committees that make an impressive number for a two-year campaign, on investigation consist of only one or two members.[43] Who these local leaders were is not entirely clear. Some reports suggest that religious congregations were the best source of volunteer organizers (frequently clergy) and of people who attend meetings.[44] The NPC reported in early 1937 that most of its local councils (some of them probably EPC locals also) consisted of formal representatives of community organizations, including the established peace groups.[45]

The local structure reflected campaign strategy, which was to avoid organization building in the interests of speed. Leaders who wanted to strengthen local activism met strong opposition from groups like the WILPF, which did not wish to see rivals to its own local chapters established.[46] Mildred Scott Olmsted of the WILPF had expressed concern that local EPC chapters might "squeeze out" her group because the more "conservative" program of the EPC would have broader appeal.[47] As a result, only a few local committees tried to build permanent local councils during the campaign.[48] And during the Campaign for a World Economic Conference, planned as the last EPC cycle but run by the NPC after the EPC's end, there was an effort to establish more of these councils, which made "painfully slow progress" because established peace groups resisted perceived competition (Masland 1940, 667).

The top-down structure of the EPC permitted a fast start to the public campaign. It made decision making more streamlined than in federated organizations. Without strong chapters, however, the EPC left no community-based legacy.[49]

On the surface, the EPC was highly professional. Full-time paid staff made all the key decisions. At its peak the campaign employed 150 national staff and 91 at area offices, many of whom served full time.

Almost all funding came from contributions from major donors. The EPC raised and spent a total of $543,600 at the national level.[50] About two-thirds of this money came from large gifts of $1,000 or more, and more than half of the first $400,000 received came from nine families.[51] This reliance on outside support rather than an active membership base is characteristic of professional movement organizations.

Nevertheless, the claim that the EPC was professional must be qualified in three respects. First, it was a sponsored professionalism. The top staff were only nominally EPC employees: they remained on the staff and payrolls of their home organizations. These groups provided critical sponsorship in the form of key donors, office space, and legitimacy. Second, it was a temporary, emergency-induced professionalism. Both key donors who gave at sacrificial levels and staff who worked for (barely) subsistence wages could not sustain their contributions to the campaign over a long period. Finally, this was not the "market" professionalism implied by McCarthy and Zald (1973, 1977).[52] The staff were longtime peace activists, not social movement professionals who moved in and out of careers in different social movements, government, academia, and other settings. The campaign (and some pacifist groups) relied on "outside sponsors" rather than an extensive base of volunteers and small donors, but these major donors were hardly "outside" the peace movement. Like the EPC staff, they were people with deep commitments to and long-lasting affiliations with the peace movement.

The political strategy of the EPC combined professional and grassroots aspects. The grassroots component was modest but important. Through meetings, radio addresses, and other forms of publicity, and through outreach to other organized constituencies, the EPC hoped to change public opinion and to attract supporters who would write to Congress. Mobilizing public opinion and pressure is not the same as recruiting people to sustained activism, but neither is it the same as the quiet, high-level lobbying characteristic of the more professional internationalist groups. The paid full-time lobbyists sent to Capitol Hill went as the representatives of a public campaign and not as policy-making insiders.

The structure and strategy of the EPC reflected the structure of existing peace groups. Few had an extensive membership base, but several had widespread local contacts through religious congregations, professional associations, and other organized groups. Top national staff tended to dominate the decision-making process of the peace groups, even those with local chapters.

In the balance of professional and grassroots elements as in the other structural features, the desire for a fast start led EPC leaders to build on existing strengths. Mobilizing grassroots activism is different from building local organizations, and the strategy of the EPC called for expanding the number of people taking at least sporadic action. Among college students, at least, numbers were expanded.

There were few if any important tensions between the professional and grassroots components of the EPC. The decision-making structure was fully professional. No grassroots leaders emerged to challenge the national leaders, and no vital local chapters arose to struggle over local autonomy. As there was little disagreement over general strategy, there were no tensions over allocating resources.

The history of the EPC supports Staggenborg's (1988) hypothesis that for pragmatic and ideological reasons, professionalism of social movement organizations facilitates the formation of coalitions: once the leaders of key peace groups decided to establish a concerted campaign, they quickly brought the groups into coalition. The EPC's balance of professionalism and grassroots activism also contributed to a rapid start and a steep decline. Professionalism facilitated the formation of the sponsoring coalition. Key leaders had the legitimacy and fund-raising ability to generate start-up money quickly, and the campaign chose its top staff from the rosters of peace groups instead of recruiting and training new staff.

The absence of a vital grassroots component (in local chapters or outside them) meant that the campaign ended when its top leaders decided it would. Professional organizations are commonly criticized for persisting beyond their usefulness, because of staff members' career interests and access to outside funds. The top staff of the EPC were ideologically and organizationally committed to their home groups, and so the EPC did not outlast its mission. To the contrary, the sponsored professionalism of the campaign helped put it out of business at the insistence of the sponsoring groups.

The organizational tensions in the EPC worked to generate a fast and effective start to the campaign, to enable the EPC to run a strong program for more than one year, and then to hasten its end. The existing groups could sponsor a major effort, the tensions within the founding coalition led these groups to keep the EPC under their control, and no upsurge of grassroots activism emerged to upset their plans. The campaign could therefore be organized and run as a short-term effort, replicating the structure of the existing peace movement.

5

The Atomic Test Ban Campaign

The atomic test ban campaign of the late 1950s and early 1960s was the first large-scale movement to confront cold war militarism. It emerged at the same time that the civil rights movement posed the first major challenge to the postwar domestic order. Fighting for a foothold just after the peak of McCarthyism, the test ban campaign encouraged significant local activism and substantial public opposition to nuclear testing, the buildup of nuclear weapons, and key aspects of American foreign policy. Although substantive achievements proved modest — it helped to produce a limited test ban, which eased immediate concerns over fallout but failed to prevent further nuclear buildups — the campaign did raise public consciousness of the nuclear peril and helped legitimize public participation in the formulation of nuclear weapons policy.

Historical Context

World War II affected the American peace movement in two key ways: directly, by dividing and weakening the movement, and indirectly, by promoting a militarized economy and political culture.[1] The collapse of the EPC in 1938 signaled the end of a vigorous antiwar coalition combining a growing pacifist movement with liberal internationalists. Although the liberals turned away from neutrality and toward collective security, the pacifists were losing numbers and visibility. By the time the United States entered the war, the pacifist and antiwar Left ranks had dwindled to a hard core. In 1941 alone, membership in the U.S. section of the WILPF dropped by half, and the Socialist party declined to a membership of six thousand (DeBenedetti 1980, 140).

The existing pacifist and affiliated organizations concentrated on aid to conscientious objectors and relief for war refugees and criticized war policies, such as saturation bombing and what they saw as the Allies' refusal to pursue a negotiated peace. The Friends Committee on National Legislation (FCNL) was founded in 1943 to lobby for relief, reconstruction, civil liberties, and racial equality. Pacifists forged a strong relationship with the civil rights movement when FOR activists helped establish CORE in 1942.

As during the First World War, a new generation of pacifists were radicalized by their wartime experiences. Between 1941 and 1945, more than 25,000 conscientious objectors served in the armed forces as noncombatants and 12,000 worked in the Civilian Public Service (CPS); 6,000 (mostly Jehovah's Witnesses) who refused any cooperation were jailed. Authoritarian work camps, lack of compensation, and work that ranged from monotonous to dangerous sparked protests in a variety of CPS camps and jails. These protests had little if any impact outside these institutions, but they profoundly affected the pacifist resisters, who became more firmly convinced that existing authority was unjust and that nonviolent resistance was the key to a more just social order. The newly radicalized pacifists played an important role in the postwar peace movement.

Liberal internationalists worked through organizations such as the LNA to develop plans for the postwar world and focused on easing international economic rivalries and developing an international military force to police world order. These elitist organizations had close ties with policy makers but failed to prevail over President Roosevelt and others who favored plans for a postwar pax Americana based on unilateral military power, including atomic weapons (LaFeber 1980, Kolko 1984).

After World War I there was widespread horror and disillusionment with war and growing suspicion of the motives of the American government in entering the war. The initial reaction to World War II was very different. It was "the good war" (Terkel 1985) in which we stood up to dictatorship and won, with (relatively) little cost. The United States emerged from the war with a dynamic economy, an inflated sense of its own role in defeating Germany, and a monopoly on atomic weapons.[2]

Even the use of atomic weapons on Hiroshima and Nagasaki prompted little protest from any but pacifists, a segment of the atomic scientists, and some religious leaders. A *Fortune* poll of December 1945 found only 4.5 percent of the American public opposed to the use of the bomb under any circumstances, 53.5 percent favored the use made of the weapons, 13.5 percent would have preferred a test demonstration before use on cities, and 22.7 percent wanted to "use many more of them before Japan had a chance to surrender" (Wittner 1984, 129). Nevertheless, the bomb left a legacy of fear.

Despite the danger posed by the new weapon, American leaders chose to maintain a high level of military preparedness as a cornerstone of the postwar pax Americana and to further the establishment and defense of a global "economic empire" in which American-based multinationals would have free reign in the Third World and, to a lesser extent, in the rebuilding European states. In the spring of 1947, President Harry S Truman overcame congressional resistance to continued high levels of military spending. He declared that the Greek civil war was a result of Soviet expansionism and asked for support of the "Truman doctrine," committing the United States to a global war against communism and constant military vigilance. The strategy of "scaring hell out of the American people" by inflating the Soviet threat to the West worked, and the broad outlines of postwar American foreign policy were set: a strategy of active intervention in the Third World and of "containment militarism"—confronting the Soviet Union by military rather than political and economic means— backed by the establishment of a massive military-industrial complex.[3] Despite this militarization of American society and the weakening of the peace movement, postwar activism for world government and the internationalization of atomic energy flourished briefly before the worst of the postwar political repression accompanying cold war militarism set in.

Two events profoundly affected the postwar American peace movement: the use of nonviolent resistance in India's struggle for independence from Britain, led by Mohandas Gandhi, and the atomic bombing of Japan. Gandhi's influence was felt most strongly by pacifists, particularly the younger more militant group returning from work camps and prisons. The older generation of pacifists retained control of the FOR, and the WRL became a haven for the younger generation, called "radical pacifists" because of their uncompromising commitment to the goal of social revolution and strategies of extrainstitutional nonviolent resistance. In addition to working within the WRL, radical pacifists started new, socialist or anarchist-oriented pacifist journals and organizations and promoted new tactics, such as tax resistance.

Despite the emergence of this group, membership in pacifist organizations declined even further at the end of the war. Postwar pacifists worked mainly in coalitions using institutional politics for limited goals. Along with some religious, labor, and veterans' groups, they fought unsuccessfully for a general amnesty for conscientious objectors like the one granted at the end of World War I. They made their biggest and most successful effort as part of a broad coalition against plans for universal military service promoted by the Truman administration.

The development and use of the atomic bomb produced widespread fear if not guilt. A September 1945 poll found that 83 percent of Americans believed that atomic warfare could kill most urban dwellers. This fear was tempered by a belief that atomic weapons might help keep the peace. In the same poll, 64 percent believed that worldwide wars were less likely to occur precisely because of the devastating potential of these weapons (Cantril 1951, 21–22, cited in Wittner 1984, 132). This ambivalence about nuclear weapons has persisted, providing both opportunities and problems for later arms control and disarmament movements, including the nuclear freeze campaign. The use of the atomic bomb did produce a wave of activism among two groups of intellectuals: world federalists and atomic scientists. Closer to the political mainstream than the pacifists, these groups reached a broader audience.

The idea of world government, first promoted by elite organizations in the aftermath of World War I, enjoyed brief but remarkable popularity. World federalists had been part of a centrist coalition that toward the end of the war lost the policy debate to unilateral militarists. They lobbied unsuccessfully for American support of a strong international organization. After the atomic bombing of Japan, the campaign was reinvigorated, and by 1949 seventeen state legislatures adopted a resolution urging Congress to establish a world government. An August 1946 survey found that 54 percent of the American public favored plans to make the United Nations a world government with control over all national armed forces. Nineteen United States senators and fifty to one hundred representatives also favored world government. Although the substantive achievements of this movement were minor, the world federalists developed the closest thing to a mass peace movement seen in the immediate postwar era. In 1947, sixteen world government organizations merged to form the United World Federalists (UWF), with about 17,000 members and 200 chapters in thirty-one states. By late 1948, membership had expanded to 40,000 in 659 chapters.

The leaders of the world federalist movement were generally from elite backgrounds. As part of the liberal internationalist bloc, they had embraced collective security in the late 1930s. A decade later, most became "cold war liberals," arguing that unilateral military deterrence would be necessary until an international government could be established. In addition to hardening the views of its leaders, the cold war eventually eroded the support of the world federalist movement.

The atomic scientists' activism also began as the war drew to a close. After the defeat of Germany, several top scientists lobbied and circulated petitions within the small community of atomic scientists, opposing use of the atomic bomb against a Japan close to defeat. These leaders formed the core of the Atomic Scientists of Chicago, which in 1945 merged with two other groups to form the Federation of Atomic Scientists. They published the *Bulletin of the Atomic Scientists* and fought for the international control of atomic energy. An early victory for this high-level movement came when Congress rejected the Truman administration's plans to keep control of atomic energy within the military, and instead created civilian agencies for this purpose.

By mid-1946, the Federation of American Scientists, the successor to the Federation of Atomic Scientists, had 2,000 members committed to preventing a nuclear arms race. Despite an initially positive response owing in part to public fear of atomic weapons, the scientists' movement quickly lost momentum. Wittner (1984) cites two reasons. First, public fear diminished as atmospheric tests in the South Pacific seemed to produce few negative effects and the government launched the "atoms for peace" program to give atomic energy a positive image. Second, as earlier disarmament movements had discovered, fear could lead to calls for more weapons in the hope of strengthening deterrence.[4]

The last major battle of the scientists' movement in this era was over United States policy on internationalizing atomic energy. They opposed top policy makers intent on preserving the American nuclear monopoly, which they believed would last for many years, and on building an arsenal of atomic weapons. An increasingly instransigent position emerged from these critical policy debates. Truman appointed Bernard Baruch to present the American proposal to the Soviets and the United Nations. Baruch further hardened the plan by insisting that the United States maintain the right to continue stockpiling atomic weapons while other nations submitted to international inspection and supervision to prevent their developing the bomb. The Soviets rejected this proposal out of hand, and hopes of averting a nuclear arms "race" were dashed.[5]

By 1948 the escalating cold war began to divide and weaken the

American peace movement again. Most liberals and even some pacifists moved toward support of government policies while the remaining activists faced growing state repression and shrinking public support and sympathy. The failure of the Baruch plan and increasing government pressure, including a loyalty-oath program instituted by Truman, demoralized many active scientists. The majority became reluctant supporters of government policy, although a few continued to seek a means to internationalize control of atomic energy. Almost all continued to work on developing atomic weapons, prompting harsh criticism from pacifists.

The 1948 election split the non-Communist Left and pacifist communities; some supported Henry Wallace and the Progressive party and others followed Socialist Norman Thomas. Truman's victory, coupled with the poor showing of Wallace and Thomas, further discouraged peace activists and solidified the power of cold war liberalism. Truman moved in 1949 to establish NATO as a primary instrument for containment militarism. Also in 1949, the administration proposed to develop a hydrogen weapon, or H-bomb. This thermonuclear device promised to exceed greatly the power of the atomic bomb, and many atomic scientists rallied to oppose this decision as an unnecessary and immoral step. Truman's decision in January 1950 to proceed with the bomb prompted small protests from pacifists and some scientists. The protests had little effect, and the government repressed dissent in the scientific community through political attacks on dissidents. The outbreak of the Korean War in 1950 was a devastating blow to a weakened peace movement, widening its internal divisions and escalating the repression of dissenters. Some Communists and die-hard isolationists joined the pacifists as the only vocal opposition to the war, but world federalists and even the Socialist party supported it.

Public support for dissident scientists and world federalists declined, as did their organizational bases. The UWF had grown to almost 50,000 members during 1948 and 1949, but it had also become much more conservative, supporting NATO and containment militarism. During the Korean War it began a dramatic decline, losing most of its recent converts. By 1952, sixteen states had repealed pro-world-government resolutions. The Emergency Committee of Atomic Scientists folded by the end of 1950, and *Bulletin of the Atomic Scientists* stopped calling for an end to the nuclear arms race. The ranks of both radical and more traditional pacifists thinned as well. For the next few years, the American peace movement was again reduced to a small core of activists. Although they were back on the margins, they worked to formulate and promote alternatives to cold war militarism and the buildup of nuclear weapons. They kept alive traditions including non-violent resistance and provided a group of experienced leaders to a resurgent movement in the late 1950s.

With prospects for peace activism limited in the early 1950s, pacifists turned their attention to the development of a "third camp" position critical of both sides in the cold war, a position later adopted by the non-Communist Left in the United States. Pacifists also maintained their involvement in the civil rights movement, which gained momentum and visibility in the 1950s. Groups like FOR and CORE were critical in teaching philosophies and tactics of nonviolence to civil rights leaders and those involved in the mass movement that began with the bus boycotts in Baton Rouge in 1955 and in Montgomery in 1955 and 1956.

Several events combined to produce a more favorable political environment for the peace movement in the mid-1950s. The Korean armistice and Stalin's death in 1953 were followed by Khrushchev's 1956 condemnation of Stalinism and declaration of a policy of peaceful coexistence with the West. In the United States, the decline of McCarthyism began with the Army-McCarthy hearings in the spring of 1964 and accelerated with the Senate's censure of McCarthy in December. On March 1, 1954, an American nuclear test in the South Pacific had produced fallout that contaminated residents of several of the Marshall Islands and sailors on a Japanese fishing trawler. After the American government admitted that winds had carried fallout over the American mainland, the press and public finally turned their attention to the dangers of atomic tests, all of them then conducted above ground.[6] In April 1954, Indian Prime Minister Jawaharlal Nehru called for a moratorium on testing. In 1955, Albert Einstein and Bertrand Russell issued a humanistic call for the prevention of atomic war, signed by prominent European, American, and Asian scientists and intellectuals. A conference of Nobel laureates called for the renunciation of force in international relations. Pacifists founded a new journal, *Liberation,* reflecting "the maturation of militant pacifism since its genesis in World War II" (Wittner 1984, 237).

Public concern over fallout heightened in 1955 when Britain tested a hydrogen bomb. The Soviet Union proposed an international ban on all testing of nuclear weapons. President Dwight D. Eisenhower rejected the proposal, insisting that a test ban would not be verifiable. Some Democrats, however, argued that a verifiable ban could be negotiated. Norman Cousins, editor of *Saturday Review* and an officer of the UWF, helped persuade Adlai Stevenson to make a test ban a major focus of his 1956 presidential campaign. Cousins had been working with Nehru since 1954 as part of a growing international movement for a test ban. Stevenson adopted the argument that a ban would end fallout and stop the development of new, more dangerous weapons.

Eisenhower's advisors were split, and despite a secret pro-test-ban report from the National Security Council (NSC), he rejected the idea during the campaign, at least in part to avoid giving the initiative to his opponent.[7] Toward the end of the campaign, two dramatic events eclipsed the test-ban issue: the October 30 attack on Egypt's Suez Canal by Israel, England, and France, and the November 4 Soviet invasion of Hungary. Eisenhower came to support a test ban during his second term, but he never acted decisively. Opponents of the ban, primarily within the Atomic Energy Commission (AEC) and the Pentagon, blocked significant progress during the second Eisenhower administration, despite increasing international and domestic pressure for a halt to atomic testing.

The Test Ban Campaign Begins, 1957–1958   *American Friend Service Committee.*

Although the test ban issue entered the policy debate via presidential politics, the peace movement raised it to high and sustained visibility. Members of the Chicago AFSC Peace Committee, including Homer Jack, a Unitarian minister who would later become a key leader of SANE, had been promoting disarmament since 1950. In the spring of 1957, they urged Lawrence Scott, the (paid) peace secretary of the Chicago AFSC, to lobby other pacifists for their help in organizing an antitesting campaign.[8] With the support of leaders of existing pacifist groups, he organized a meeting of pacifists in Philadelphia in April 1957, where they formed a Committee to Stop H-bomb Tests.[9]

As in the 1930s, pacifists recognized that a major campaign required a coalition with nonpacifists. They sought a way to attempt this without losing their distinct methods or message. This time they decided to pursue a two-organization strategy.[10] One campaign organization would be pacifist in membership and philosophy, relying on a core of committed activists who would express their opposition to testing and atomic weapons by pursuing Gandhian nonviolent resistance. The other campaign organization would be more mainstream, promoting a liberal analysis and pursuing an institutional strategy based on education and lobbying. Both organizations would work for a halt to testing as a first step toward nuclear disarmament. The established peace groups adopted this as their key goal and agreed to cooperate with the two new organizations, which took form as the Committee for Nonviolent Action (CNVA, first called Nonviolent Action Against Nuclear Weapons), and SANE, the Committee for a Sane Nuclear Policy. SANE became the major force behind the test ban campaign, developing an extensive network of local chapters as well as a national presence.

As SANE and CNVA were forming, some noted figures helped to raise the public salience of the test ban. In April 1957, Albert Schweitzer, after some urging by Norman Cousins, issued a "Declaration of Conscience" calling for the mobilization of world public opinion to help bring about arms control and other agreements. In June, Linus Pauling, a Nobel Prize-winning scientist, released a petition calling for a halt to nuclear testing, signed by more than 11,000 scientists, 3,000 of them Americans.

Members of the Committee to Stop H-Bomb Tests were meanwhile setting up the two new campaign organizations. The pacifist organization was in the hands of Lawrence Scott and A. J. Muste, a highly respected longtime pacifist and labor organizer. Although the second organization was not to be pacifist, the task of putting it together was assigned to another noted pacifist, Robert Gilmore, New York secretary of the AFSC. As in the 1920s and 1930s, pacifists were providing leadership to the peace movement by supporting a range of approaches. Scott and Muste also were part of this organization's initiating committee, which met in May 1957.

Initial modest plans envisioned a working committee made up mainly of those already active on the issue in the existing peace groups, supplemented by a list of prominent national sponsors. Noting that "a new dimension has been presented" by an upsurge in public interest in the testing issue, committee members recognized the possibility of expanding beyond these plans.[11] Before launching a more vigorous campaign, however, they agreed to sound out several national leaders. Scott was delegated to contact Norman Cousins and Clarence Pickett, secretary emeritus of the AFSC, and to ask them to recruit leading liberals and religious figures (respectively) for a larger organizing meeting.

Both Cousins and Pickett agreed to take on the job. Cousins talked of establishing a campaign that would be politically nonpartisan and primarily moral in tone. In June twenty-seven religious, scientific, business, labor, and other leaders met to decide how to proceed. This group made no binding decisions; instead, it appointed a steering committee to develop a plan. Led by Pickett and Cousins, the committee included Homer Jack, and Norman Thomas, longtime Socialist party leader. This committee had to obtain start-up funding and to determine the form and scope of the organization. At the start, the AFSC could offer office space and some cash, but the pacifists were not as strong as they had been in the 1930s, when they sponsored the EPC. The cold war had eroded their support among clergy and religious organizations. The wealthy Quakers who had funded the EPC and the pacifist organizations had died, their fortunes dispersed to family or given away in bequests.[12] Those liberals who had resisted the turn to cold war liberalism were also a small and poor minority. Norman Cousins borrowed against his *Saturday Review* stock, and Lenore Marshall, a wealthy New York activist, made a contribution. The kitty of several thousand dollars was nothing like the original funding enjoyed by the EPC, but it was sufficient to get SANE started. Decisions on organizational form and direction were mostly postponed until larger meetings could be arranged in the fall.

Meanwhile, the testing issue remained visible. In July 1957, Bertrand Russell organized the first in a series of conferences of scientists from both sides of the cold war at Pugwash, Nova Scotia. This Pugwash conference resulted in a consensus statement against atomic weapons. Nevil Shute's novel *On the Beach* was published, dramatically portraying the lethal consequences of nuclear war. Congressional hearings on fallout, conducted in the spring, had produced no consensus on fallout dangers, but had undermined public confidence in the AEC's claims of no danger. American public opinion was beginning to turn in favor of an international test ban, antitesting protests were beginning in England, and governments around the world were also making clear their concerns over fallout from American, Soviet, and British tests.

World opinion against testing had become a major source of pressure on the three nuclear powers to begin negotiations for a test ban. In March 1957, these nations plus France, which had been developing an atomic bomb but had not yet tested one, had begun meeting to work on issues of testing and international control of nuclear power. Although the talks broke down over the summer, pressure continued and the testing issue remained on the international agenda. SANE and CNVA became the heart of the organized part of the American test ban campaign. Along with international grassroots protest and diplomatic pressure, it helped produce a sequence of public postures, unilateral initiatives including testing moratoria, and multilateral negotiations, culminating in the 1963 limited test ban treaty.

The first public action of CNVA came on August 6, 1957, the twelfth anniversary of the Hiroshima bombings, when eleven pacifists were arrested for trespassing at the Nevada atomic test site. SANE, still limited to an organizing committee, restricted its summer activities to the publication and distribution of a newsletter and communication with potential activists and supporters. Homer Jack coordinated the work of this "Provisional Committee to Stop Nuclear Tests."

In the fall, encouraged by positive signs from the public and some national leaders, the committee decided to expand its effort beyond the initial plans for a small group of prominent volunteers who would stimulate public debate on a test ban. In a September meeting Cousins put forward his view that the campaign should be aimed at stopping testing by all nations, and should avoid "embarrassing" the United States (M. Katz 1973, 77). Although some participants, including the psychologist Erich Fromm, argued for a stronger posture against American policy, Cousins's more cautious approach prevailed. Fromm's suggestions for the name "The National Committee for a Sane Nuclear Policy" and the acronym SANE were accepted.

In a second organizing meeting in October, Homer Jack agreed to serve as SANE's part-time executive secretary, Cousins and Pickett were selected as cochairs, and an executive committee including these three was delegated to draw up a statement of purpose, select an organizing committee of fifteen to twenty, and hire a full-time director. In late October, Trevor Thomas, a staff member of the FCNL of northern California, was hired as temporary executive secretary. The organizing committee was formed, including some major business and educational figures as well as peace activists from both pacifist and liberal-internationalist organizations.

Although pacifists began and at first led SANE, its goals, strategy, rhetoric, and tactics were decidedly liberal-internationalist and conventional under the influence of liberals such as Norman Cousins and the agreed-upon strategy of making SANE a mainstream organization. At the October meeting, a statement of purpose was adopted that called for immediate cessation of all nuclear weapons tests by all nations, and the international control of missiles and satellites, both to be enforced by the United Nations.

Despite some debate about broadening their focus, the SANE leaders decided to restrict their major goal to an end to testing in the belief that this issue had the best chance of capturing public attention and support for a campaign that could build toward an end to the arms race. SANE added to its agenda each year of the campaign, to include, for example, a call for disarmament down to "police levels" and the pursuit of peaceful resolutions of international crises. Testing remained the major thrust of the campaign until 1963, though, and additional stands were carefully couched in terms of helping to avoid nuclear war.

The focus on testing proved to be both a strength and a liability. Mainly because people feared atmospheric fallout, the campaign mobilized extensive attention, support, and grassroots activism. On the other hand, when testing literally went underground after the 1963 treaty, the wind was taken from the sails of the campaign, and the arms race continued. Public fears of immediate danger were abated, but the threat of nuclear war was not significantly reduced.

The organizing committee also debated SANE's basic strategy. The more conservative members, including former AEC Commissioner Gordon Dean and the chairs of the boards of General Electric and General Mills, wanted to return to earlier notions of a quiet campaign of high-level lobbying. The majority, however, decided to continue with plans for a more widespread campaign. SANE would emphasize "top-level approaches to the administration" and it would also pay attention "as the way opens" to providing public information through newspaper ads and literature and coordinating and serving as a clearinghouse for local committees that might spring up.[13] The decision to conduct even a limited public outreach effort prompted Dean and the corporate leaders to leave SANE.

SANE went public on November 15, 1957, with a full-page ad in the *New York Times*. The ad, written mostly by Cousins, was headlined "We Are Facing A Danger Unlike Any Danger That Has Ever Existed." The lengthy text stressed the dangers of atomic testing and atomic weapons. It also argued that, as Americans, "we are not living up to our moral capacity in the world," because of our preoccupation with material pursuits and consequent failure to focus on "the big ideas on which our lives and freedoms depend." There was a strong internationalist message as well: "the sovereignty of the human community comes before all others — before the sovereignty of groups, tribes, or nations." Some test ban supporters, such as Hans Bethe, a leader of the postwar scientists' movement, objected to the emotional appeal and moralistic tone of the ad, and refused to sign it.

The ad included two coupons to be clipped. One was to be signed and mailed to President Eisenhower, urging him to go before the United

Nations to propose a halt to testing and the international control of missiles and satellites. The other was to be sent to SANE headquarters in New York and offered three boxes to be checked: one to show a contribution was enclosed to help SANE place the ad in other newspapers, one asking for information on any local organizing in the respondent's community, and one asking for further information on SANE. The coupons were the idea of Robert Gilmore. Gilmore's organizing background gave him a perspective significantly different from that of some other committee members, who, according to Sanford Gottlieb, "had the naïve view that all they had to do was publish a series of newspaper ads and government policy was going to change" (Gottlieb interview).[14]

Within six weeks of the ad's publication, the small SANE staff had received about 2,500 letters and $12,000 in donations. Supporters around the country ran the ad in their local papers and requested 25,000 reprints from SANE. Local committees were started in several communities. This large, unanticipated public response provided the leaders of SANE with an emerging grassroots base, and, as the more conservative elite sponsors unhappy with this development departed, it moved the campaign in a much more activist direction than its founders had envisioned.

Even before the ad was published, a few local test ban committees had formed in California and New York. In Larry Scott's view, they were "looking for national leadership."[15] These preexisting committees had been set up by members of the AFSC and other peace organizations. SANE's ad, however, reached beyond the modest local network of established peace groups. Most of those moved to act by the ad were new to peace activism, although many were members of civil liberties and other liberal/Left political groups (Gottlieb interview).[16] By January 1958, fifteen committees and forty-one "less formal groups" had formed "entirely through local initiative," and were looking specifically to SANE for this national leadership and direction.[17] By the summer of 1958, there were about 130 SANE chapters with combined membership of about 25,000.

The initial response and chapter formation were concentrated in Northeast metropolitan areas, with significant activity also in California. Geographical distribution broadened over time, but the demographic profile did not. Most SANE members were white and middle-class, and a disproportionate number were professionals.[18]

Although the November 1957 ad was timed well to capture existing local activism, the birth of SANE coincided with discouraging international events. In August, the Soviet Union had fired the world's first intercontinental ballistic missile. On October 4, the Soviets used a powerful booster rocket to launch the first orbital satellite, *Sputnik*, followed one month later by *Sputnik II*. Divine (1978) argues that, before *Sputnik*, Eisenhower was moving toward a pro-test-ban position, although his advisors remained divided. Opponents of the ban used *Sputnik* and alarmist predictions of a potential "missile gap" to arouse public and congressional support for an expanded military buildup and to check any movement that Eisenhower might have made toward a test ban.

The governments of Britain and France also opposed a test ban. Britain wanted to conduct tests of new weapons in 1958. France anticipated developing and testing its own atomic weapon by the end of that year. Leaders of nonnuclear nations, including Nehru of India, endorsed Soviet test ban proposals, but the governments of the United States, Britain, and France were not moved.

Despite these political setbacks, the public test ban campaign continued to grow. SANE urged local committees to solicit letters supporting a pro-test-ban speech by Senator Hubert Humphrey. The AFSC and the WILPF circulated petitions calling for an American halt to testing. A pacifist-led "walk for peace" to the United Nations building in New York attracted seven hundred participants.

SANE's leaders pursued their primary strategy of high-level lobbying of the administration and Congress, and they ran a second newspaper ad, this time in the *New York Herald Tribune* of March 24, 1958. Headlined "No Contamination Without Representation," the ad claimed that atomic tests were poisoning the atmosphere, and "we [Americans] do not have the right — nor does any nation — to take risks, large or small, for other peoples without their consent." Like the first ad, it was strongly worded and designed to appeal to public fears in order to rouse a response (Katz 1986, 27). Some supporters criticized this strategy, arguing that the time for basic education had passed; it was now time to direct concern into political channels. Among those who signed the ad was Martin Luther King, Jr., who had gained national stature as a civil rights leader after leading the Montgomery, Alabama, bus boycott of 1955–1956.[19]

One week later, the Soviet Union announced a unilateral halt to atmospheric testing. Although the United States had started testing atomic weapons underground in 1957, the Soviets had not developed the necessary technology. This halt therefore meant an end to all Soviet testing and development of new atomic weapons.

Test ban advocates, including SANE, pressured the United States government to reciprocate. Albert Schweitzer issued a second appeal for an end to testing. Linus Pauling, Norman Thomas, and others filed a lawsuit to stop the upcoming American nuclear tests. SANE staged a nine-day rally in New York, with public meetings and picketing at the United Nations, and on April 11 published a full-page ad in the *New York Times,* featuring a photograph of a huge mushroom cloud and urging postponement of the next series of American tests, an internationally monitored test ban, and an end to the spread of nuclear materials to other nations.

Despite this surge of activism, the Eisenhower administration refused to match the Soviet initiative. Public opinion supported continued testing: 60 percent of those sampled in a Gallup poll favored continued American tests in the absence of a negotiated ban, and only 29 percent opposed them and favored matching the moratorium. A pattern that continued throughout the campaign was established: public opinion supported the president (Rosi 1965, Divine 1978, Kriesberg 1985). Opinion shifted in favor of a test ban only when administration policy and rhetoric did, despite fear of the health effects of tests.

Even with public opinion on his side, however, Eisenhower felt pressure building from the growing American test ban campaign, from international opinion, and even from within his administration. In 1957, physicist Isidor Rabi had convinced Eisenhower to transfer his Science Advisory Committee from military to civilian control. This change gave a voice to a growing number of pro-test-ban scientists. Eisenhower therefore ordered a review of administration policy. Although opponents of a test ban continued to argue that verification would be impossible, a panel of experts reported to Eisenhower that the United States could verify a test ban with several seismographs on Soviet soil. Meanwhile, at the urging of Secretary of State John Foster Dulles, Eisenhower agreed (privately) to Soviet proposals to separate a test ban from other issues, such as the freeze on production of nuclear material.

As SANE pursued institutional channels, CNVA promoted direct actions, including two sailings of small boats into the Pacific test zones to protest announced H-bomb tests. These sailings received surprisingly favorable publicity from the press and prompted a series of small demonstrations in their support. Wittner (1984, 250) attributes the positive response to the appeal of simple idealism in an otherwise cynical time.

Meanwhile, SANE chapters continued to proliferate, although more slowly than at first. Because they were concerned about the participation of Communists (party members, nonmembers sympathetic to the party, and former members) in some chapters, the national leaders set up a closer working relationship with local activists to coordinate strategy and improve finances. SANE could not find money to hire more staff as organization grew, in spite of a policy calling for locals to return to the national office half the income produced by local reprints of national ads. Plans were made for a conference of local activists to work out these and other issues and to share information and organizing experiences.

In April, about forty-five representatives from locals in thirteen states, most from the East Coast and some from the West Coast and Midwest, met with national leaders and staff in a weekend conference in Pawling, New York. Other locals sent reports. Clearly, there was a groundswell of activity and interest in the test ban campaign, with delegates reporting up to forty activists and mailing lists of several hundred per chapter. These groups had been placing ads, distributing literature, and pursuing other forms of education and public protest. The metropolitan New York area was particularly strong, with many locals throughout the area and a coordinating Greater New York Committee. Several campus groups also reported increasing interest and activity, marked by the summer's founding of the National Student Council for a Sane Nuclear Policy, commonly known as Student SANE, as an organization with close ties to SANE. A New York-based group of physicians was publicizing radiation hazards, and SANE was getting cooperation from the Farmer's Union in distributing literature.

Some delegates expressed concern over SANE's stress on fallout. One scientist, although supporting SANE, contended that many claims about the health hazards of fallout had been exaggerated. A psychologist from Yale argued that fright could backfire, and that at his school the most frightened students were also the strongest advocates of aggressive foreign policies. Others argued that an emphasis on testing was too short-sighted and asked delegates to begin devising a post-test-ban strategy for nuclear disarmament. Despite these misgivings, SANE continued to emphasize a halt to testing as a key first step and to stress the danger of fallout in order to mobilize public attention and support.

Robert Gilmore observed that SANE was still a loose campaign rather than a formal organization and compared the conference to a "constitutional congress," urging delegates to help form a more demo-cratic structure. Local activists complained that a small group of na-tional leaders had been setting policy and pressed for a greater role.[20] Since the end of 1957, a ten- to fifteen-member executive council and a five-member executive committee had been making the key deci-sions. The top national leaders had appointed the members of both bodies. There was also a consultative national committee made up of thirty to forty representatives of local groups, most of them se-lected from East Coast locals because meetings were held in New York. It was agreed that the local representatives would form a federation to work with national leaders in devising a new structure. Locals would retain autonomy, and there would be periodic congresses of local representatives.[21]

National leaders pledged to add to the staff of two full-time pro-gram staff, in part to provide locals with more resources, such as lit-erature. Delegates agreed that the financial burden of supporting this increased effort would be taken up by strong locals, while the national would distribute some funds to locals in need. The Boston group offered to put out a national newsletter. The national statement of purpose and ad campaigns were endorsed, and locals were urged to begin to work on the 1958 congressional elections by identifying sympathetic candidates and publicizing candidates' positions.

In August, President Eisenhower offered to suspend testing for one year beginning October 31, provided the Soviets refrained from testing during that period. Buoyed by this shift in policy, more than one hundred persons from fifteen states met in September to establish SANE's new federation of local representatives. Because a permanent negotiated test ban seemed within reach, there was some debate over broadening the organization into a committee for a sane foreign pol-icy, a proposal Cousins had put forward in a smaller August executive committee meeting. This was rejected, however, as most felt it would detract from SANE's effectiveness on the testing issue. A compromise position was adopted, allowing the national committee to take posi-tions on aspects of U.S. foreign policy that affected the possibility of nuclear war but continuing the policy of encouraging other organiza-tions to take the lead on these matters.

A council of local SANE committees was formed as a coordinat-ing and fund-raising body. This council elected five representatives to the fifteen-member executive committee of national SANE. In re-turn for this representation on the official policy-making body and for the right to retain substantial autonomy, locals agreed to accept the lead of this committee in policy matters. The participation of Communists in SANE was discussed but not resolved.

Following through on pledges made at the Pawling conference, local representatives agreed to increase their financial support for the campaign; the stronger locals promised to contribute in proportion to their size. The failure of locals to meet these pledges would prove to be a continuing problem for national SANE well into the 1960s, contributing to periodic financial crises and staff cutbacks. Already in 1958, a lack of funds had cut the number of ads in a planned campaign from a national full-page newspaper ad per month to three for the year. Both national and Student SANE incurred operating deficits.

Despite fiscal problems, SANE moved toward a more independent, long-term structure, raising its own funds and hiring and paying its own staff instead of relying on the AFSC and other peace organizations. SANE had developed a modest fund-raising operation based on small contributions solicited through ads and other means.[22] Trevor Thomas, on loan from the FCNL, was replaced as executive director by Donald Keys, previously a staff member of the UWF. Over the next few years, SANE slowly increased its national staff.

With the new chapters and a more tightly knit structure, SANE confronted more political setbacks. Although the United States and the Soviet Union were, along with Britain, negotiating a permanent ban on testing, press reports on the negotiations were pessimistic. Both sides conducted a flurry of atmospheric tests before the planned start of the moratorium at the end of October. SANE leaders were concerned about keeping expectations and morale high. They began a petition drive and at the end of October published as another full-page *New York Times* ad a test ban appeal sponsored by prominent world leaders.

Organizational Growth and Crisis, 1959 and 1960

In the first two years of the test ban campaign, there had been a dramatic increase in public awareness of the dangers of atomic testing and arms buildups and an upsurge in activism far exceeding the expectations of national campaign leaders. Although these leaders and local activists may have been overly optimistic about the changes for a quick, permanent test ban, they managed to forge an effective organization out of the first wave of grassroots antinuclear activism. The year 1959 proved to be one of continued organizational growth and political frustration for SANE and the rest of the test ban movement.

In 1959, the test ban negotiations in Geneva bogged down over verification, with the United States insisting on on-site inspections and the Soviets rejecting them as a pretext for spying. Domestically, the AEC and the Pentagon continued their fierce resistance to a test ban. SANE's Donald Keys labeled as "barbaric" congressional proposals to limit the ban to atmospheric tests, arguing that underground tests would permit a continued arms race (Divine 1978, 245). SANE supported Senator Humphrey, who continued to press for a comprehensive ban. In February, SANE publicized a statement by twenty-two national leaders that "There are elements of risk in any agreement, but the risks of continuing the arms race are even greater."[23] In March, local SANE committees conducted a month-long campaign for a comprehensive ban, using the theme "Acts for Sanity."

In April, the Senate adopted a Humphrey-sponsored resolution implicitly endorsing a comprehensive ban. Nevertheless, Eisenhower offered the Soviets only a limited ban. When the Soviets refused the talks were deadlocked, prompting stronger calls from the American Right for a resumption of testing. Meanwhile a fallout scare grew in response to the October 1958 premoratorium testing flurry, as research showed that radioactive strontium-90 was moving from the food and milk supply into children's bones and teeth. SANE publicized this and other dangers through a storefront information center in Times Square in April and May, drawing much attention. Over the summer, the organization challenged government claims that fallout hazards were minimal. The goverment studies may have reassured some, but the fallout scare left as its legacy a public consensus that atmospheric testing was intolerable (Divine 1978).

The scare gave impetus to a campaign that, still growing, was beginning to broaden its base. The formation of the Student Peace Union (SPU) in the summer of 1959 provided an organizational niche for those students who saw SANE as too moderate. SANE had 150 local chapters plus more than 25 student chapters by fall. National plans for program and staff expansion continued to be hampered by lack of funds, however, as few locals were meeting their promised levels of financial support. Financed by loans, SANE could increase its staff to the still-modest number of 7 full-time administrative and 5 support positions shared by national and New York SANE.[24]

SANE's second annual national conference in late October 1959 was attended by eighty-five representatives of locals from ten states. In accordance with a 1958 agreement, this body continued to play only a consultative role. The executive committee, now reconstituted as a board of directors, remained the top policy-making body, with one-third of its members now elected by local representatives. Speakers noted that SANE had expanded in both scope and structure far beyond its initial plans.[25] Instead of a few local affiliates designated as informal working groups of representatives from established organizations, there were dozens of active chapters run by new activists. And although leaders welcomed this expansion, they again quietly raised concerns over whether some of these local activists were Communists. They believed that Communists were manipulative and disruptive, and feared that SANE could be tarred as a Soviet front should the public learn of Communist participation in the organization. Although Senator McCarthy had been discredited, anticommunism was still strong. SANE had started a program to charter local chapters that allowed national leaders to screen local leaders but had set no deadline for its completion. National leaders also expressed concern that many local activists lacked organizing and political experience, and recognized the need for members of the national office to conduct fieldwork. Because SANE had no organizers, in 1960 top staff took turns traveling around the country, meeting with and assisting local activists.

The national officers reported that income was derived mainly from small contributions responding to ads and mail solicitations and that few locals had met their pledges. Meeting later as the Council of Local Committees, delegates agreed to try to fulfill their pledges but rejected a plan to impose quotas based on a percentage of net local income. Agreeing that the impact of testing was beginning to fade with the moratorium in place and talks dragging on, delegates approved an expanded focus, still centering on a test ban but including disarmament down to police levels. Most chapters emphasized public education, but Gilmore urged greater attention to electoral work as the 1960 campaign season approached.

In the fall of 1959, the test ban again became an issue in presidential politics. Nelson Rockefeller, a candidate for the 1960 Republican nomination, advocated resumption of underground testing. Other presidential contenders, including Republican Richard Nixon and Democrats Hubert Humphrey and John F. Kennedy, argued for a continued moratorium. The failure of the Geneva parties to reach agreement at a technical conference on verification increased the pressure for testing. Frustrated by this failure and responding to domestic critics, President Eisenhower on December 29 declared that American observation of the moratorium would be "day-by-day."

According to Divine (1978), for top policy makers at least, this marked the end of the quest for a comprehensive test ban.[26] Instead, the United States early in 1960 proposed a threshold treaty, barring all atmospheric, underwater, and outer-space tests, and underground tests above a certain size. Eisenhower even agreed to a Soviet proposal to observe a moratorium on tests below the threshold, but he attempted to impose a two-year limit on this provision. Although France, which was not a party to the moratorium, exploded its first atomic bomb in February in the atmosphere above the Sahara, it seemed that progress was being made toward an agreement. Sentiment for a ban within the Eisenhower administration was bolstered by a growing consensus that a test ban would leave the United States with a substantial lead in nuclear weapons.

SANE's 1960 strategy called for continued support of the talks and for a focus on the fall elections in an attempt to influence presidential candidates and platforms in both major parties, and for a secondary emphasis on selected congressional races. In February, SANE opened a Washington, D.C., office and hired Sanford Gottlieb as political action director.[27] Early in the year he helped to form the "1960 Campaign for Disarmament," a coalition including several peace and religious groups, funded and staffed by SANE to pursue a coordinated electoral strategy, an important strategic turn for a movement long estranged from electoral politics. Local chapters, however, were not skilled in electoral work or coalition building. National SANE devoted most of its resources in the first half of the year to electoral efforts. Local committees, in consultation with the national office, endorsed several candidates for Congress; a few were elected, mostly as Democrats. The 1960 Campaign for Disarmament worked at both national and community levels, talking with candidates and their staffs, preparing testimony for party platform hearings, helping local activity, and sponsoring an eleven-state student caravan for disarmament.

The test ban campaign seemed to be picking up momentum in the winter and spring of 1960, as did the student and civil rights movements. In February, the antisegregation sit-in movement began in Greensboro, North Carolina, and quickly spread throughout the South. FOR and other pacifist groups had helped shape and teach the Gandhian philosophy and techniques that inspired these actions. The Student Peace Union grew to 5,000 members and 12,000 newsletter subscribers; its May peace petition gathered 10,000 signatures. On campuses on both coasts, there were well-attended speeches and rallies for disarmament and for civil liberties. The growing momentum was derailed, however, by international and organizational crises. In May 1960, tensions resulting from the downing of an American U-2 spy plane over Soviet territory broke up a Paris superpower summit. SANE went ahead with a rally planned to support the summit, and on May 19, 20,000 turned out at New York's Madison Square Garden to hear speakers, including Eleanor Roosevelt. This proved to be SANE's last major action before it became embroiled in a public crisis over Communist participation in the organization.

In the summer of 1958, Norman Cousins had asked the FBI to help in identifying any "subversives" in the New York or other chapters. The FBI turned him down on legal grounds. Norman Thomas, a staunchly anti-Communist Socialist, had expressed to SANE's leadership his fears that failure to confront concerns over Communists active in SANE chapters would open the organization to crippling attacks from outside (Katz 1986, 4).

Senator Thomas Dodd, chair of the Senate Internal Security Subcommittee and ironically a friend and neighbor of Cousins and a fellow UWF member, launched the strongest attack by subpoenaing SANE leaders and members and claiming Communist "infiltration" of local SANE chapters. Dodd was an advocate of unrestrained nuclear testing, and many within SANE saw his attacks as an attempt to kill the chances for a test ban.

Some SANE leaders, particularly pacifists and students, argued for a strong response along the lines of recent student demonstrations protesting continued McCarthy-style investigations by the House Un-American Activities Committee (HUAC). Cousins, however, dismissed one New York leader who had refused to testify before Dodd or to explain himself to Cousins's satisfaction beyond assurances that he was not under any party discipline. SANE's board did denounce the Senate committee's action, but they also disinvited Communists from participation in SANE, required local chapters to become chartered, and reorganized the Greater New York committee.

The actions of Cousins and the board split SANE and the test ban campaign. Half the New York chapters, comprising one-quarter of all SANE locals, refused to apply for charters and were expelled. Walter Lear, acting chair of the Greater New York committee, observed that some activists in these local chapters were indeed former Communist party members who had hoped "to make SANE their new religion" (Katz 1986, 55–56).[28] He thought the loss of the New York chapters deprived SANE of some of its more committed and politically astute activists.

When Dodd continued to subpoena SANE members and supporters, including Linus Pauling, many peace activists inside and out-side SANE felt Cousins and the SANE board again failed to protest strongly enough. They argued that this was the time to make a clear break with McCarthyism, and that a strong stand by SANE would galvanize public support. Cousins and much of the liberal leadership of SANE were less optimistic. They believed that they must tread softly lest the movement be critically damaged. The debates went on into the fall of 1960 and led to the resignation of some key pacifist leaders, including Gilmore, who according to Norman Thomas had been SANE's "guiding hand and brain" (Katz 1986, 57). Both Linus Pau-ling, the focus of one Dodd subcommittee controversy, and Bertrand Russell resigned as sponsors of SANE. Relations between the liberal leadership of SANE and more radical movement groups turned sour. Pacifists, including A. J. Muste and Barbara Deming, argued that the actions of SANE's leaders would keep the movement from achiev-ing historic scope and influence (see Deming 1960, Muste 1960). Al-though they did not advocate united front work with Communists, these leaders believed that SANE must more firmly denounce the ac-tions and motives of Dodd, who in their eyes represented a greater danger to the movement than did the Communists and former party members in SANE.

Most members of SANE's Board of Directors, however, believed that the participation of Communists and others unwilling to criti-cize Soviet policy was the major threat to SANE's integrity and public image. The board replaced Donald Keys with Homer Jack as Execu-tive Director, a position he would keep until 1964. Jack had been ac-tive in Chicago in the 1940s and 1950s with civil rights and civil liberties groups that had struggled with issues of Communist partici-pation. He reflected the dominant view on the board that while civil liberties must be protected, organizations had the right to exclude Communists, who tended to manipulate non-Communist groups for their own ends. The board hoped that Jack's experienced leadership would help resolve the issue of Communist participation in SANE, but by the time he took over, the liberal-radical split had occurred (Jack interview). Although it is impossible to measure the damage from this episode or to say what would have happened had SANE followed the advice of Muste and others, clearly SANE and the test ban campaign lost much support and momentum in the latter part of 1960. A proposal from one local leader to organize a new, inclu-sive organization was rejected by other local activists, however, and SANE continued its electoral and other work.

Meanwhile, CNVA was moving toward a greater emphasis on

what some of its younger members saw as more radical Gandhian strategies and tactics. Beginning in September, several CNVA activists participated in an ongoing "Polaris Action" in New London, Connecticut, combining attempts to board the Polaris submarines under construction there with discussions with workers at the boatyards. Although many workers and townspeople responded positively, some CNVA founders had by this time become alienated by what they saw as younger members' fascination with direct action for its own sake. Several left the organization. This growing radicalism, as well as the liberal-pacifist split precipitated by the Dodd crisis, left the pacifists farther outside the mainstream of the test ban campaign. Although CNVA activists continued to work on disarmament through 1963, the hopes for a close relationship with SANE, and greater access to the public for pacifists through a Left-Center coalition, faded in the spring of 1960.

SANE's leaders attempted to move forward with renewed emphasis on the 1960 elections. The summer Democratic and Republican conventions were disappointing: John F. Kennedy defeated Hubert Humphrey, the strongest pro-test-ban candidate, for the Democratic nomination; and Richard Nixon captured the Republican nomination. Although both opposed a resumption of testing by the United States, both also took many hawkish positions on foreign policy and superpower relations. SANE found little to recommend in one or the other, although by the fall Kennedy was judged marginally the better candidate.

In mid-October 1960, SANE held its third national conference in Chicago. Seventy-one voting delegates represented more than twenty states. Half the delegates came from the New York metropolitan region and Chicago, reflecting the continued regional imbalance of the organization. The conference reaffirmed SANE's basic goal of a test ban as a first step toward disarmament and endorsed the goal of "economic conversion," the move from a military-based to a civilian economy.

Although education and lobbying remained the main strategies, Sanford Gottlieb argued for a greater emphasis on electoral work. He warned that to be effective in this arena, local chapters had to form coalitions with religious, labor, student, and business groups, and that SANE would have to develop a strong presence in one major party. To support this and other work, SANE's leaders announced that despite financial problems they would make a "leap of faith" and expand the executive staff from two to four, hoping that increased fund raising would pay more staff, support more visits by them to local chapters, and allow more mailings.[29] For the first time, a national membership program was discussed.

A hotly debated one-vote endorsement of the board's response to Dodd, however, opened old wounds and threw into question SANE's ability to move in new directions. Many Student SANE members resigned and joined more radical groups, either the SPU or the newly formed Students for a Democratic Society (SDS). SANE worked to address the organizational and political shortcomings identified at the conference that remained serious problems throughout the test ban campaign.

President Kennedy and the Limited Test Ban, 1961–1963

When the Kennedy administration took power in 1961, the Geneva test ban talks were still stalled, but both sides continued to honor the moratorium on testing begun in November 1959. The Right, including the military and the AEC, renewed its push to resume testing. SANE's leadership believed that this pressure would keep Kennedy from moving as fast and as far toward a total ban as they would like, but that the pro-test-ban forces could nonetheless influence the new administration, which probably would use its first few months in office to evaluate policy options (Jack 1961).

Throughout the Kennedy years, SANE would often find itself encouraged by hopeful signs and speeches from the president, yet frustrated by the administration's continued cold war militarism. Some, including Cousins, would argue that Kennedy agreed with the goals of the disarmament movement. They recommended a shift from public criticism of the administration to quieter lobbying. Most SANE leaders would become more skeptical toward the president and more vocal in their criticism.

SANE's intitial strategy toward the Kennedy administration included both low-key and pressure tactics. SANE circulated a petition calling on Kennedy, Khrushchev, and Prime Minister Harold MacMillan to continue the Geneva talks until they achieved a test ban agreement. SANE also lobbied for the creation of a separate government agency to research and formulate disarmament policy and to serve as a counterweight to the AEC and the Pentagon.

On April 1, 25,000 people marched for peace in several cities in the largest peace demonstration since World War II. SANE modeled this event on a series of large Easter marches in Great Britain, sponsored by the Campaign for Nuclear Disarmament (CND, founded in 1958).

Any optimism this turnout generated was short-lived, however. On April 17, an American-sponsored invasion of the Bay of Pigs in Cuba began, and fifteen hundred Cuban exiles went ashore to overthrow Fidel Castro. The failed invasion led to increased cold war tensions. In June, Khrushchev escalated simmering tensions over West Berlin by reimposing a six-month deadline for the departure of American troops. SANE's national board held a special meeting to consider shifting from a test ban to an international relations focus. Some, including Gottlieb and future cochair H. Stuart Hughes, argued that Cuba and Berlin showed the need to emphasize the development of peaceful international relations and a less militaristic foreign policy.

Others, including Donald Keys and Homer Jack, wanted SANE to continue focusing on atomic weapons and to keep disarmament and international relations a secondary theme. They cautioned against diluting SANE's work by making it one more full-fledged foreign policy advocacy group and suggested that SANE treat crises as "teachable moments" to bring home to the public and policy makers the connections between foreign policy and the chances of nuclear war. Although no firm decisions were made, future SANE actions followed the policy advocated by Keys and Jack.[30]

The board reaffirmed its commitment to move SANE from an ad hoc short-term campaign to a more formal organization, with stronger financial ties between a national office and local chapters and a program of chapter development. Sanford Gottlieb argued that to become a political force of consequence, SANE had to expand its geographic base beyond the seventeen states where it had strong locals and become a truly mass organization with a membership larger than its current 26,000 and with participation in local coalitions.[31] All this, he noted, required even more fieldwork from the national office and therefore more money. Deficits, though, were again mounting (they were to reach $30,000 by October 1961), as support by locals, large gifts, and small contributions lagged behind projections. Fiscal and other problems would continue to limit SANE's growth and impact, but the expanded fieldwork effort begun in 1960 was maintained for the next several years, and SANE was able to exert some important pro-test-ban pressure at both the national and grassroots levels.

As SANE was assessing its progress and planning for the future, the Geneva talks remained stalemated, primarily because of continued disputes over the scope and nature of onsite inspections. SANE ran ads reflecting the belief of most of its leaders that the Soviet Union was the more intransigent of the two powers and that Kennedy was sincerely working for a test ban. But they also criticized those within and outside the administration whom they saw as insisting on unnecessarily strict verification procedures as a way of scuttling any treaty.[32]

The international situation deteriorated over the summer of 1961. Tensions in Germany worsened, and on August 13 the Berlin wall was built. On September 1, the Soviet Union resumed atmospheric testing. This move may have been a response by a politically insecure Khrushchev to pressure from Soviet hard-liners, and a reaction to French atmospheric tests, which had not stopped during the moratorium observed by the three Geneva parties. Cousins (1972) believed that Khrushchev may have misread press reports of escalating pressure on the United States government to renew tests as evidence that the administration had decided to do so. In any case the moratorium, which had lasted two months short of three years — the last two years day-by-day since Eisenhower's December 1959 announcement — was over. Despite pleas from SANE and other groups, the United States resumed underground testing September 15 (and began testing in the atmosphere again in April 1962).

Also in September, Congress passed legislation authorizing the establishment of the Arms Control and Disarmament Agency (ACDA). Although given a broad mandate to negotiate treaties and to research and formulate policy, the agency soon showed that it would not become anything like the peace agency SANE and others had hoped for. Instead, the ACDA at best served as a base for advocates of the sorts of limited arms control measures seen by many peace activists as weak substitutes for meaningful arms reductions.

Despite the renewal of atmospheric testing, the 183 delegates attending the October 1961 national conference of SANE found signs of continued movement health and took hope from a softening of administration rhetoric. Although his policies had not changed perceptibly, Kennedy had challenged the Soviet Union to a "peace race," adopting (deliberately or not) a phrase introduced that spring by Seymour Melman, SANE board member and leading advocate of economic conversion. The conference endorsed the policy and structure decisions reached by the June special board meeting.[33]

At the monthly board meeting later in October, Homer Jack summed up what he saw as SANE's assets and liabilities. On the plus side, he noted SANE's national and international visibility, a list of prestigious sponsors, some active national board members, 125 local chapters "in varied states of activity," a Washington office and a U.N. observer's office (in addition to the main national office in New York), a flow of action bulletins from Washington to the locals, a list of 3,500 individuals contributing $40,000 yearly, and the end of the "ideological problems" plaguing SANE the year before. Also, despite difficulty in obtaining ongoing major sponsorship, he acknowledged the receipt of $70,000 the previous year in major gifts for special projects and debt retirement.[34] He listed as liabilities a program over extended for the size of the budget, a $30,000 deficit, and an inability to develop specific projects to maintain and increase national visibility.

In November, a series of highly publicized demonstrations in several cities was carried out by a new group, Women Strike for Peace (WSP). WSP was a loose network put together by activists, some of whom had been SANE members unhappy over the organization's handling of the Dodd affair.[35] The original intent of WSP was to sponsor a nationwide strike for peace. The strike did not come off, although as many as 30,000 women eventually participated in WSP-sponsored rallies and demonstrations, providing the movement with renewed energy and visibility. After the demonstrations, WSP focused almost exclusively on education about fallout dangers from atmospheric testing. It faded from the national scene after the ratification of the 1963 limited test ban.

In late 1961, SANE participated in the formation of Turn Toward Peace (TTP), an organization designed to serve as a national clearinghouse of information, to establish selected local clearinghouses, and to help transcend divisions within the campaign by promoting shared goals where possible. Modeled on a three-year-old San Francisco Bay Area coalition headed by Robert Pickus, TTP, under the leadership of Pickus and Sanford Gottlieb, drew in around thirty groups and promoted some useful interchanges. Pickus, however, proved to be a divisive figure, with what some saw as an anti-Communist obsession. Some SANE leaders were also concerned that the TTP "local peace centers" were becoming membership chapters rather than clearinghouses and that the organization was focusing on these instead of on its primary goal of holding together a loose national coalition.[36] TTP was dissolved in 1963.

The year ended with pessimism over international developments and uncertainty about the course of the Kennedy administration. Ironically, however, the worsening world scene also produced new momentum for the test ban campaign. At a November board meeting, Donald

Keys reported that a Midwest tour of local chapters had convinced him that not only was there renewed concern over fallout from testing but people were "stirred up for the first time about the possibility of nuclear war."[37]

In the first part of 1962, SANE and other groups tried to capitalize on these renewed fears to mobilize pressure and dissuade the Kennedy administration from resuming nuclear tests in the atmosphere. SANE's role included running more newspaper ads and lobbying the administration. Kennedy, however, announced on March 2 his intention to start atmospheric tests.

SANE responded with a series of protests and vigils and a stepped-up educational campaign on the dangers of fallout from tests. One of the most famous of SANE's newspaper ads was published on April 16. Captioned "Dr. Spock Is Worried," the ad was dominated by a photograph of Dr. Benjamin Spock, the noted pediatrician and author, looking down with paternal concern at a small girl standing in front of him. The brief text stressed the health and moral issues of testing.[38] Despite these efforts, Kennedy's decision stood and American atmospheric tests resumed in the Pacific on April 25.

With the moratorium completely over, SANE pushed for progress in the Geneva talks, which had broken off in January and reconvened in March, and began working with local chapters on the November congressional elections. Its work was again disrupted, however, by the issue of Communist participation, this time in Student SANE. A January 1962 staff report claimed that a small "hard core," close to the Communist party in outlook, had come to dominate the student group, and a special SANE committee recommended the termination of agreements between SANE and Student SANE and the invalidation of the most recent student board election.[39] In February, the national board of Student SANE resigned, and once again many student activists left to join the more radical SPU and other groups, including the young SDS, which was to break with its parent group, the socialist League for Industrial Democracy, partly over issues of exclusionism. Clearly, SANE leaders had been wrong in thinking that the end of the Dodd affair marked the end of divisions over Communist participation.[40]

The idea of a limited test ban treaty had been dismissed by both American activists and the Soviets when suggested by the Eisenhower administration. In the summer of 1962, with progress toward a comprehensive ban blocked, the United States again proposed a ban on testing in the atmosphere, the oceans, and outer space; however, underground testing could continue. Khrushchev had rejected a limited test ban because the United States possessed a substantial lead in the technology for conducting underground tests and because such a ban would reduce public fears and pressure for a comprehensive ban without slowing the arms race.[41] Although he still had these concerns in 1962, Khrushchev was under great pressure to achieve tangible results from his policy of peaceful coexistence with the West. Both China and hardliners at home opposed this policy and threatened to undermine Khrushchev domestically and to erode Soviet prestige in the Third World. Beginning late in 1962, a series of contacts between Khrushchev, Pope John, and President Kennedy, mediated by Norman Cousins, had raised the Soviet leader's hopes for some settlement to strengthen his position.[42]

Before any progress toward a limited test ban was made, however, the Cuban missile crisis brought the world to the brink of nuclear war. On October 22, 1962, President Kennedy announced that American intelligence had discovered in Cuba Soviet nuclear missiles capable of launching an attack against the American mainland. He issued a quarantine on all "offensive military equipment" shipped to Cuba, and ordered the navy to blockade the island and intercept any ships, including Soviet freighters. Finally, he announced that American nuclear forces would be placed under full alert, and appealed to Khrushchev to remove the missiles under U.N. supervision. Meanwhile, the U.S. Navy moved to intercept sixteen Soviet ships heading across the Atlantic toward Cuba.

For four days, the world held its breath while the outcome of the showdown was in doubt. During the crisis, SANE published an ad condemning both sides, the Soviets for establishing missile bases and the United States for unilaterally establishing a naval blockade, which under international law constituted an act of war. The ad called for a settlement under U.N. auspices, reflecting SANE's policy of support for strengthening the U.N.'s role in world affairs. SANE also helped to organize a rally of 10,000 in New York to show support for a peaceful resolution. This was the largest outdoor peace rally to that time in New York City history (Katz 1986, 80), but many inside and outside the peace movement saw the missile crisis as exposing the impotence of the movement in the face of the nuclear threat. On October 28, on the verge of a planned American air strike on the installations, Khrushchev agreed to remove the missiles in exchange for an American pledge not to invade Cuba.[43]

The missile crisis temporarily ended progress in the test ban negotiations, but the accompanying worldwide fright may have prompted the two sides to work harder for some start to arms control. In the United States, the domestic political impact was unclear. After the drama of the crisis, the peace forces made only a small showing in the November elections. H. Stuart Hughes, running as an independent candidate for a U.S. Senate seat from Massachusetts, received less than 3 percent of the vote. Around the country, some twenty candidates supported by SANE and other groups ran for Congress, but only a few were elected, all running on major party tickets.[44]

In November, SANE held a fifth anniversary celebration with its fifth national conference. Year-end staff reports continued to depict an organization that had not escaped its financial weaknesses or relative political impotence, although, with the resumption of atmospheric testing and the Cuban missile crisis, nuclear issues had never seemed so important.[45] New chapters had been added at a rate of about three per month, but total membership held at around 25,000. Few chapters had become proficient at organization building and achieving high levels of community acceptance.[46] A deficit of $28,000 remained, despite increased fund raising and expanded program budgets. At board meetings in November, the integrated national-local fund raising plan adopted in 1960 was dropped as a failure. Instead, less formal arrangements were pursued: locals would send mailing lists and monthly donations to the national; the national would share its lists of donors and sponsor joint fund-raising events.[47]

In summing up the events of 1962, SANE's leaders admitted that the organization had failed to take full political advantage of heightened fears of nuclear testing and nuclear war. They could not celebrate an end to testing, but they took pride in having fought two elements of what they saw as a plan by the Kennedy administration to move from a policy of nuclear deterrence to one of fighting nuclear war. SANE had helped to defeat in Congress the administration's proposals for an expanded civil defense program. It had helped to expose the administration's counterforce nuclear policy, which called for the development of a capacity to destroy Soviet bombers and missiles before they could strike. Although both civil defense and counterforce could be seen as defensive, SANE and other critics argued that they would lead policymakers to think that a nuclear war could be fought and won, thereby making one more likely.[48] The conference concluded with a pledge to spend the next two years building political strength for the 1964 elections.

However realistic these plans may have been, the campaign for a comprehensive test ban was soon short-circuited by the negotiation and signing of a limited test ban in July 1963. The treaty would take away the campaign's key organizing tool, the immediate fear of fallout, although nonsignatories, including France and later China and India, tested above ground beyond this date.

During the first part of 1963, SANE continued pushing for a comprehensive ban, hoping to move the superpowers off a continued impasse over verification of underground testing. Misunderstandings between the two sides were eroding trust, however, and there were continued disagreements over the scope of negotiations. Khrushchev had been pressing for additional measures, included a NATO–Warsaw Pact nonaggression treaty, and the United States refused to go beyond discussions of a test ban.[49]

Frustrated by the failure to move ahead in Geneva, even some of those who had opposed the limited ban as "barbaric" began to back the idea as a first step toward a comprehensive ban. SANE found itself in this camp, partly because of Norman Cousins's close ties to Kennedy and his role in superpower talks (Jack interview). In May, Senator Humphrey, along with Senator Dodd (who did not favor a comprehensive ban) and thirty-two cosponsors, introduced a Senate resolution urging the administration to try to negotiate a limited ban.

As it became clear that progress toward a limited test ban was being made, SANE and other groups organized a campaign urging Americans to write to Washington in support of a settlement. The campaign produced at least 18,000 letters to the Senate and the White House. Disappointed in this number, noting that the peace groups had sent out 100,000 letters to members asking them to write, SANE also observed that the results constituted the largest pro-arms-control public communication with policy makers to date.[50]

The limited test ban treaty, pledging the three powers (and those later joining the treaty) to refrain from nuclear testing in the atmosphere, the oceans, and outer space, was signed on July 25. SANE and other groups then faced the task of generating pressure on the Senate for the needed two-thirds ratification vote, which was by no means seen as certain. Only fifty of the necessary sixty-seven votes were considered definite at the time of signing. Public opinion was perhaps even on the issue, but congressional mail and visits had been running between ten-to-one and twenty-to-one against a treaty (Cousins 1972, Katz 1986).

Beyond mobilizing public opinion, the President had to court the Joint Chiefs of Staff to prevent their opposition, which almost certainly would have scuttled the treaty. He therefore issued a series of guarantees, which, I. F. Stone (1970) observed, "read like a meticulously spelled out treaty between the military and the Kennedy administration, an agreement between two bureaucratic superpowers." The most important promise was that the United States would move ahead with a vigorous program of underground testing. Given the American lead in the technology of underground testing, this amounted to promising to widen the lead the United States already possessed in nuclear weapons technology. Military spending also reached a new peacetime high at the same time that the treaty was being considered.

With substantial guidance from the White House, Norman Cousins took a leading role in forming the Citizens' Committee for a Nuclear Test Ban, an expanded and more active version of the high-level Ad Hoc Committee for a Nuclear Test Ban that Kennedy had previously assembled to lobby other elites to support the treaty negotiations. The citizens' committee included leading figures from labor, religious groups, business, and other constituencies, some hand-picked and recruited by the president.

SANE worked with the committee to ensure Senate ratification, taking out newspaper ads and lobbying key senators. The combination of high-level debate and lobbying, orchestrated by the citizens' committee, and local work by SANE and other groups paid off as public support for the treaty increased and mail to Congress shifted in favor of ratification. On September 24, 1963, the limited test ban treaty was ratified by a vote of 80-19.

After the Treaty

Although the limited test ban treaty did ease the immediate fall-out danger, it did not soon lead to other measures slowing the arms race and easing superpower tensions. In fact, I. F. Stone (1970) argued that Khrushchev's inability to obtain such agreements led to his downfall in 1964 and strengthened Moscow hard-liners who had opposed his overtures to the West. Kennedy fulfilled his promises to the Joint Chiefs; the buildup of nuclear weapons continued unabated, and testing went underground.

Domestically, the treaty took the urgency out of the campaign for a comprehensive test ban. Norman Cousins went so far as to advocate the dissolution of SANE, arguing that its mission was largely accomplished. Most other leaders, recognizing the shortcomings of the treaty (although probably not anticipating the high level of testing in the years to come) recommended that the organization search for ways to maintain public mobilization for its goals of "general and complete disarmament with adequate inspection and control, down to levels needed to maintain order within nations, under a strengthened U.N. to keep the peace and promote world development." The board endorsed the latter position, but members expressed concern that SANE might be reduced "to a level of other peace organizations with a broad, distant goal without dramatic public appeal."[51]

On the other hand, it was argued that SANE's role in the passage of the treaty (which Homer Jack cautioned was only a modest one) might lend the organization substantial prestige. SANE's national and local leaders searched for ways to maintain the momentum generated by the test ban campaign. Their new short-term goals of reductions in nuclear arsenals and opposition to expanded civil defense, however, lacked broad public appeal. Their long-term goals of reducing cold war tensions and of economic conversion did not translate into an effective program.

Homer Jack, in an internal document, offered a sober assessment of the state of the peace movement.[52] There were dozens of national organizations and hundreds of local groups, but the peace movement was neither coherent nor large. Combined membership, excluding overlaps, probably numbered no more than 150,000 families; and the total budget reached at most several million dollars. The influence and effectiveness of these groups was modest, whether measured by access to policy makers and influential figures or by substantive impact. Jack recommended unification of all the secular, action-oriented organizations, including SANE. Beyond this point, a bolder and ultimately more effective movement for peace and justice, he claimed, could be formed by further merging these groups with organizations working on domestic issues, including civil rights.

Despite the appeal of this vision, Jack offered a caution that proved prophetic: mergers that look logical may fail because of vested interests and personality conflicts. SANE and the UWF had been discussing merger since 1961, and the plan had gained momentum in the past year, partly out of concern over declining strength in both groups after the treaty ratification. SANE's board approved and the 1964 national conference ratified the merger, but the UWF board rejected the plan. The merger ultimately fell through in 1965 largely because old-guard members of the UWF board regarded SANE as too radical, ironic given SANE's rocky relations with groups and individuals to its left.[53]

SANE's hopes for a continued strong movement for a comprehensive test ban and nuclear arms reductions also were not realized. Donald Keys (who took over again in 1964 as SANE's executive director) observed that the history of SANE had been one of crisis and response, and that "the fact that SANE was dealing in a direct, pragmatic, and political way with immediate issues guaranteed a membership of concerned, awake, and active people. The same fact has also meant, however, periodic exhaustion of energies, interest, and funds after one crisis and then another" (Keys 1964).

Keys saw the post-treaty period as one of détente in which SANE's work was harder because better superpower relations took the urgency out of the peace movement. Echoing Cousins's 1960 remarks, Keys argued that SANE should turn from protest to advocacy in the more accommodating political climate. Although Keys may have been too optimistic about the state of the cold war (as Cousins may have been after Kennedy's election), this perception, undoubtedly common, contributed along with the limited test ban to the end of this phase of the test ban campaign, typified and dominated by the work of SANE.

Although CNVA activists had turned increasingly to civil rights work before the treaty, they had continued to protest nuclear weapons and were affected by the treaty and its aftermath. According to Neil Katz (1973, 186), "There seemed to be a pervasive feeling of frustration and despair with the results and potential of the peace movement — there was general agreement among the radical pacifists that the nuclear testing issue had been co-opted by the [treaty], and that the more inclusive anti-war issues such as opposition to ICBMs had failed to attract a wider public."

According to historian Paul Boyer (1984, 1985), the treaty was one of several factors that not only deflated the test ban campaign but also led to a prolonged period of "nuclear apathy"—a dramatic decline in public notice and attention to the nuclear threat during the "Era of the Big Sleep" (1963 to the late 1970s) similar to a decline that occurred after the initial flurry of post–World War II activism and concern. The political and cultural factors Boyer enumerates include:

1. An illusion of diminished risk of nuclear war, due to the treaty and apparent détente.

2. A loss of immediacy, as nuclear arsenals once out of the spotlight seemed increasingly unreal and a sanitized strategic vocabulary emerged.

3. Heavy government promotion of "the peaceful atom" in the form of atomic power plants.

4. The complexity and comfort of deterrence theory.

5. The growing American role in Vietnam, which began to absorb almost all the energy of the peace movement.

As the war in Vietnam escalated, the peace movement again expanded into an antiwar movement, and organizations, including SANE, were reinvigorated as domestic opposition increased. SANE played a key role in consolidating and expressing liberal opposition to the war, but the organization was again torn by ideological disputes over cooperation with more radical groups. CNVA merged in 1967 with the WRL.

SANE survived this period, only to decline with the end of the war, almost folding in 1976. In the early 1980s, however, the nuclear freeze campaign once more roused the nation from its nuclear apathy, and gave SANE and other groups renewed life. Under the leadership of David Cortwright, a Vietnam-era draftee and founder of GIs United Against the War in Vietnam, SANE developed a professionalized structure with a strong national office supported by small contributions from isolated adherents and a handful of active chapters, some holdovers from the test ban campaign. In 1986 SANE began merger talks with the NWFC, which then resembled in many ways the SANE of the early 1960s—a financially shaky national office linked with a vigorous grassroots base. The two organizations merged in 1987, in the hope that their complementary strengths would enable the merged organization to reach its avowed goal of creating an ongoing, mass peace organization for the first time in American history.

The Impact of the Test Ban Campaign

The test ban campaign was the first significant peace effort after World War II. Struggling against the cold war tide, the campaign had a modest impact in several areas. According to some scholars, the test ban campaign helped to raise the salience of the testing issue and to arouse public fears of atomic fallout (Divine 1978, Seaborg 1981, Rosi 1965, Kriesberg 1985). Presidents Eisenhower and Kennedy, however, consistently shaped opinion on what specific steps should be taken to address these problems.[54] Rosi (1965) found the administrations influenced both "attentive" and "mass" publics—those who followed the issue closely and the majority who did not. Although the peace movement did not build consistent support for a comprehensive test ban, it contributed to the consensus that atmospheric testing had to be stopped, a domestic and international consensus that no doubt pressured both sides to work toward some kind of test ban.

The test ban campaign failed to achieve its major goal, a comprehensive test ban. Whether the limited test ban was a key step toward the campaign's underlying goal — reducing the prospects for atomic warfare — is harder to judge. Some see any superpower talks and agreements as reducing cold war tensions. On the other hand, by driving testing underground, the limited test ban treaty may have contributed to the ensuing "big sleep" on the issues of a comprehensive ban and a halt to the buildup of superpower arsenals, as well as to the proliferation of atomic weapons to other nations. The quid pro quo extracted from Kennedy by the Joint Chiefs, in fact, meant an increase in testing and superpower buildups.

In the interest of mobilizing a public consensus in a short time, the test ban campaign limited most of its attention to the issue of atomic weapons and atomic testing. Nevertheless, many sympathetic critics argued that without alteration of the cold war system itself changes in nuclear policy alone would not fundamentally reduce the risk of atomic war. The campaign did not lead to any real change in cold war policies; its impact on public and elite opinion about the need to change these policies is not clear.

The campaign legitimized public participation in the formulation of nuclear weapons policy, and the establishment of ACDA in response to pressure from the campaign and pro-test-ban scientists helped reduce the dominance of the military in nuclear policy making. Ironically, in the long term, the ACDA may have helped undermine public participation. As Boyer (1984, 1985) and others have suggested, by developing reassuring language and strategic formulations, the arms control establishment helped quiet fears about atomic policy. The development of an atomic "priesthood" provided symbolic reassurance that professionals were in charge, and excluded those without expert credentials.

Because SANE and most of the campaign activity had such a narrow focus, much of the public was not touched by more than an anti-testing message, and a fear-based one at that. In broadening public understanding of and sympathy for either liberal or pacifist tendencies, the campaign probably had little impact.

Ongoing peace groups were not substantially strengthened by the campaign, as most of the activism was channeled through the new organizations. Many of these did not last much beyond the end of the campaign: the SPU folded in 1964, and the CNVA merged with the WRL in 1967. SANE, however, did survive as both a national office and a handful of local chapters and went on to play a role in the anti-

Vietnam protests and to provide a small base for antimilitary and anti-nuclear activity before and during the nuclear freeze campaign.

Overall, however, the test ban campaign did not break the cycle of activism that characterized the modern American peace movement, nor did it significantly broaden the peace movement beyond its traditional middle-class base. The test ban campaign was a precursor to the outburst of movement activity in the 1960s. Because the campaign brought new people into the peace movement, it provided education and training that may have played a role in the early stages of the movement against the Vietnam war. SANE's response to Senator Dodd failed to confront and perhaps force a break with McCarthyism, but the incident radicalized many students and other activists, shaping their perceptions and actions throughout the following decade and beyond.

Organizational Tensions in the Test Ban Campaign

The test ban campaign involved and produced several groups, but it centered on the two main organizations created in 1957. CNVA remained a small pacifist group, sponsoring direct actions that at first gained surprisingly widespread, favorable publicity, but later were largely ignored outside the movement. The heart of the public campaign was SANE.

SANE moved from an ad hoc coalition of professionals operating at the national level to a more formal organization with federated local chapters and significant grassroots participation. The transition was unforeseen and rapid, putting severe strains on the organization. SANE coped with these tensions, managing for seven years to spearhead the public campaign for an end to atomic testing, but organizational weaknesses limited SANE's capacity to consolidate and extend the momentum generated by the initial wave of public concern over atomic testing and hampered its ability to turn public fear into sustained pressure for a comprehensive test ban and a reduction in cold war militarism.

Like the EPC, the test ban campaign involved both the formation and the maintenance of a coalition and the establishment of new organizations. Both aspects of the campaign opened new possibilities for the peace movement, and both created tensions within the campaign. The political environment in the mid-1950s was different from that of the mid-1930s. The EPC had been a Center-Left coalition, with the Left, both pacifist and nonpacifist, relatively strong and highly mobilized, and the Center enjoying significant access to policy elites.

The test ban campaign emerged at a time when McCarthyism and the rise of the national security state had moved the center of gravity of politics to the right. Liberals were for the most part in the cold war liberal camp; those who rejected cold war politics were marginalized and repressed. The pacifist movement had shrunk from its peak size and influence in the mid-1930s down to a small embattled core. The test ban campaign was therefore a coalition of a minority of "peace liberals," cut off from the mainstream of cold war liberalism, plus a marginalized Left—seemingly a much less potent combination than the EPC's base of dissident but influential liberals and centrists, plus a vigorous Left.

Another key difference in the nature of these coalitions worked in favor of the test ban campaign. The EPC was torn almost from the outset by disagreements over the key issue of neutrality. Although the pacifists in control of the campaign held the coalition together enough to present a common front, the EPC in a sense represented less than its public face because of significant discomfort with neutrality. On the other hand, the test ban campaign represented much more than its manifest content: it contained several varieties of confined dissent. SANE provided a "retreat bunker for liberals who couldn't find a place to take a stand in the structure of political parties" (Katz 1986, xi). The same might be said for most of the non-Communist Left; to disillusioned Communists, SANE offered an outlet for political dissent and perhaps a new secular religion, as some critics maintained. For pacifists, the campaign provided a means to move in from the margins. As a protest vehicle, the test ban campaign gained momentum as it, along with the civil rights and student movements, helped to relegitimize dissent. The coalition united the peace movement and launched a broader campaign that expanded the reach and impact of the existing groups. It did so through a structure different from that of the EPC. Instead of uniting liberals and pacifists in one organization, the test ban campaign established separate organizations. I have found no evidence that this decision resulted from any conscious reflection on the history of the EPC, although some founders of the test ban campaign were active in the earlier effort.

The two-organization structure did, for a time, permit the campaign to follow simultaneously two basic strategies and employ a range of tactics, and it gave pacifists a wider platform for their unique ideas. It also kept infighting to a minimum, as each group had its own organization. When the coalition split after the Dodd affair, both organizations carried on, whereas the EPC had collapsed with the end of its sponsoring coalition. On the other hand, neither SANE nor CNVA transcended the limitation of the two approaches — the timidity of liberalism and the marginalism of pacifism. SANE knuckled under to Senator Dodd; and although direct actions sponsored by CNVA at first raised the testing issue, they did not seem to increase the popular understanding of or support for pacifism.

The relationship between the split over Dodd and the two-organization structure is complex, and the key questions — would a single organization have responded differently, and with what impact internally and externally — are impossible to answer. A greater pacifist presence within SANE might have changed the key decisions or the decision-making process, but no one can say whether this would have led to more or less conflict and with what consequences. Clearly, the bitter aftermath of the Dodd affair weakened the movement and SANE, driving off many supporters into other endeavors. Whether the movement had the transformative potential that some of its critics accused it of squandering, however, is also impossible to tell.

Beyond the two core organizations, the coalition expanded in size and diversity as new organizations proliferated. The one effort to bring these groups and the original coalition members into tighter coordination, the formation of TTP, failed because of organizational rivalries and conflicts between leaders.

Even before 1960 and the split over the Dodd affair, SANE was well on its way toward becoming an independent organization — within a coalition. As SANE moved toward independence, there was little or no resistance from established peace groups. The EPC had met resistance. In another contrast to the 1930s, the grassroots response to the start of the campaign provided a "pull" toward a long-term structure.

At the start of the test ban campaign, the peace groups were much smaller and less effective than in 1936 when they launched the EPC.[55] They could neither continue to sponsor SANE nor block it from emerging as an independent organization with a larger chapter structure than any of the established groups. They could, however, perform some key functions of movement halfway houses, providing the core national leaders and important ideas as the campaign began. SANE's transition from a coalition umbrella group to an independent organization was not completely smooth. Beyond national-local tensions were important tensions between the coalitional and organizational aspects of the campaign. For example, SANE responded to Senator Dodd as an organization and not as the leading member of a coalition; SANE's leaders did not consult with other groups in formulating its policy. By acting as an organization, SANE jeopardized the coalition. Despite these tensions, from 1957 to 1963 the coalition members continued to work toward a test ban.

CNVA, almost entirely grassroots in structure and strategy, still had no ongoing, indigenous presence in cities and towns. The Polaris action drew some CNVA activists to New London for an extended period, but this was a very different enterprise from establishing local organizations and chapters. CNVA was a national-level grassroots organization. It could use small groups of committed activists to mobilize quickly for dramatic actions, but it had a limited ability to use other tactics. In the early 1960s, CORE faced a similar situation. Members of the pacifist FOR had established CORE in Chicago in 1942 as an organization using nonviolent direct action to end segregation. CORE had developed chapters in several northern cities, but none in the South. In 1961, CORE organized "freedom rides," sending integrated groups on commercial interstate buses into the deep South. Freedom riders showed extraordinary courage in facing violent white mobs. The federal government eventually intervened to protect them, establishing a pattern that became important throughout the civil rights movement. Without an indigenous base in the South, however, CORE could not generate the sustained local campaigns that proved effective in cities like Montgomery. Unlike CNVA, however, CORE later began to develop more of an indigenous base in some communities.

SANE began as a mostly professionalized national-level organization, but the rapid proliferation of local chapters led to the establishment of a federated structure with a strong local presence. SANE's founders had planned to develop a few local chapters in the form of coalitions of local peace leaders. The organization that emerged after 1957 greatly outstripped their expectations in size, and it differed in form. Much of the organizational history of SANE revolved around efforts to turn an awkward dual structure — unplanned local chapters were added to a small national office — into an integrated federated organization.

At first SANE's program depended on the work of full-time paid staff. In comparison with the early EPC, it was a very modest professional organization with a much smaller staff, a much lower budget, and a lower-profile effort to educate and mobilize the public.[56] As the campaign and the organization grew, SANE added a Washington office to coordinate lobbying, increased the size of its staff and the amount of money it raised, and provided hands-on training for local leaders. Still, the national office remained small, with a maximum of four full-time executive staff and a peak budget of $216,000 in 1963.[57] In 1984 dollars, SANE's 1960 budget was $758,000; the EPC's budget was $2 million annually.[58]

Local chapters formed quickly and for the most part without the direct intervention of the national office. Most chapters were started by people outside the peace movement, some of whom had been active in Left-liberal organizations such as the American Civil Liberties Union. Often one or two people who had seen an early national SANE advertisement recruited others through personal networks or by taking out ads in local papers or writing letters to the editor and including contact instructions.[59] The exceptions were New York, where the leaders of the metropolitan organization included many peace activists, and Chicago, where the chapter was established after a visit by Norman Cousins.[60] By May 1958, SANE had seventy chapters, and by the end of that summer there were about 130. Although the intensity of SANE activism fluctuated during the campaign, the number of chapters and chapter members did not change much after the fall of 1959, when they reached about 150 regular and twenty-five student chapters and about twenty-five thousand members.[61] These groups were typical of local chapters of SMOs during a period of intense mobilization, with a core group of between five and fifteen volunteers, a larger circle of up to forty or so who would take on specific intermittent tasks, and a wider mailing list of people who would contribute such things as small amounts of money and time, attend rallies, and write letters to Congress.[62]

The local chapters changed the nature of SANE and the campaign, giving it an activist tone instead of the air of quiet lobbying some founders had planned. According to SANE's national staff, however, few chapters effectively established a power base in their communities or built strong local coalitions.[63] Plans to hire a field organizer to help local leaders develop political and organizing skills were never implemented because of a lack of funds, although the national executive staff visited locals when possible.

As a federated, or federating, organization, SANE developed tensions between the local and national levels over governance, local autonomy, and finance. The governance issue emerged quickly, as local activists demanded a voice in national policy making, which many believed had been dominated by a few top leaders in New York. Local leaders were given one-third of the seats on the national board of directors. These arrangements preserved local autonomy, but SANE's failure to resolve internally the issue of Communists in local chapters contributed to the harm done by the Dodd affair.

Money remained a problem. In return for national leadership and support, the local chapters had pledged to help fund the national office. These small pledges were never substantially fulfilled, nor was any other effective form of income sharing between levels developed. In 1960, for example, pledges from locals made up less than a quarter of the budget. Probably no more than half and perhaps as few as one-third of the dollars pledged were ever received by the national office.[64] Despite increased pressure from the national office and further resolutions by the locals to meet their pledged contributions, the situation never greatly improved throughout the test ban campaign.

Why did the locals not provide more financial support to the national? First, most chapters probably did little fund raising. Very few chapters had any paid staff and therefore any need to do regular fund raising.[65] Second, any money raised locally went first to meet local needs and concerns. As Sanford Gottlieb remarked, it is difficult to get members to feel ownership of both local and national organizations (Gottlieb interview), especially when local chapters are started by what appears to be local initiative — that is, without direct, hands-on assistance from a national office. This history plus the failure to establish formal arrangements quickly, the endemic problems of policing a voluntary organization and of sustaining more than one level of organization on member dues led to the low level of local financial support of the national office.[66]

SANE's program and organizational development suffered because the national office was usually short of funds. Advertising campaigns were limited. National staff members consistently noted a lack of skills at local levels, but they lacked time and numbers to do much about it. SANE never resolved the problems of federation that emerged early in the campaign. As a result, the organization, less effective than it might have been, declined with popular attention and enthusiasm at the end of the test ban campaign. If SANE did not overcome these problems, it did manage the national-local tensions. As a federated organization, SANE from 1957 through 1963 mounted pressure at both national and local levels for a test ban. National SANE and a few local chapters survived the end of the test ban campaign and played important roles in the peace and antiwar movements of the 1960s and 1970s.

The test ban campaign had less professional activity and more of a grassroots component than did the EPC. Although paid staff from established peace groups were instrumental in starting the campaign, neither SANE nor any other group could match what the EPC and the established peace groups of the 1930s had done in mounting a staff-based program of publicity and lobbying. On the other hand, inside and outside SANE and CNVA, thousands of volunteers gave the test ban campaign a significant grassroots presence that the earlier campaign had lacked.

CNVA was entirely a grassroots group — small, but visible, like larger grassroots-based organizations such as WSP. SANE had both a professional operation in the national office and a significant grassroots component within the local chapters. As a professional operation, SANE was small in both staff and fund raising, resembling the peace movement organizations of the time. Paid staff peaked at four executive staff members, plus a handful of support staff, in contrast with the EPC's 150 staff members.[67] Most of the money SANE raised came from small donations, not major donors, as happened in the EPC, or member and chapter dues, as in some federated organizations.

Although few, SANE's top staff and leaders were well-known both within and outside the organization and the movement. People like Norman Cousins and Norman Thomas had great stature in liberal and Left circles, and Robert Gilmore was a highly respected pacifist. These people provided SANE with strong (if at times autocratic or divided leadership.

The grassroots part of SANE was a surprise to the early leaders. Although SANE's membership of 25,000 consisted mostly of paper members, between one and two thousand activists became core members of local chapters, and another three to five thousand took part in occasional activity.[68]

This grassroots base proliferated rapidly because the issue was considered important. As Boyer (1985) shows, awareness of the atomic threat declined after 1950, but it did not disappear. Once the issue had been raised again by fallout from atmospheric tests, the campaign's simple appeal to fear of atomic fallout catalyzed many people into action.

Both the test ban campaign and the earlier neutrality campaign presented narrow and ideologically neutral messages appealing to fear, producing broad but shallow public support for campaign goals. The test ban appeal galvanized action, first because harm was already being done by fallout, whereas in 1936 war was just a possibility. Second, the testing issue seemed less "political" than neutrality because of its health and scientific dimensions — although neutrality often appealed to a not-very-political isolationism.

Another reason for greater grassroots response in the test ban campaign is that during the 1930s much of the Left was already mobilized in the labor movement, the movement of the unemployed, Socialist electoral politics, and other efforts; in 1957, the Left was just starting to recover from McCarthyism. Both campaigns pitched to the political middle, but it was the Left that provided the activist core. In the late 1950s, SANE was one of the few channels for the expression of political dissent by the Left which was not just quieter, but was smaller than in the 1930s. Leaders of both the labor movement and the white middle-class church were more conservative than they had been in the 1930s (or would be in the 1980s, during the freeze campaign), and so the test ban campaign did not have access to the networks these insitutions could provide. The grassroots response was limited to a few tens of thousands.

The campaign did not pull strongly toward either the professional or the grassroots side, nor was there much debate over which way to move it, beyond very early discussions over whether to involve the public at all. The tensions around federation did involve differences between the grassroots chapters and the professional national office, but these did not concern the campaign's professional or grassroots direction. The two sides of the campaign strengthened each other in a relationship structured by connections between the national office and the local chapters. The grassroots base gave the professional staff political leverage, while the staff provided leadership and some services to local volunteer activists. The problems of federation, though, limited this reinforcement. The lack of field organizers restricted the development of volunteer activism in skill if not size, and rank-and-file members did not provide much financial support to the professional part of the campaign.

Given the political constraints of the post-McCarthy era and the difficulties of organizing around transient fears of nuclear testing, the test ban campaign achieved some remarkable breakthroughs, even if it fell far short of achieving its main goal. The campaign left a small but important legacy of activists, ideas, and organizations.

Although each set of organizational tensions was managed well enough to permit SANE to carry on, each also caused problems. As SANE emerged as an organization, the broad coalition broke apart. This was not a simple cause-and-effect relationship, and most members of the coalition continued working on common goals; it proved difficult both to hold together a coalition and to build a campaign organization. SANE never became a well-integrated federation of national and local elements, nor did it go beyond a modest effort toward either professionalism or grassroots activism. These limitations reflect both the original vision of the campaign's leaders and the difficulty of adapting political and organizational strategies for a short-term pressure campaign to those for a long-term movement organization. The ad hoc coalition that promoted the test ban did a good job of catalyzing a movement and encouraging local, grassroots initiative. It could not develop structures to keep the momentum building for a comprehensive test ban and a shift away from cold war militarism. SANE did change, but the changes were difficult and incomplete. Slightly more than twenty years later, the central organization of the next major wave of antinuclear activism, the NWFC, would face similar problems of organizational transition.

6

The Nuclear Weapons Freeze Campaign

The nuclear weapons freeze campaign[1] was the second wave of mass antinuclear activism in the United States and the largest grassroots peace campaign of the modern American peace movement. As part of widespread international protest against a new generation of nuclear weapons and the escalation of cold war tensions, the freeze again raised the threat of nuclear war to the top of the public agenda.[2]

Starting with a few referenda in western Massachusetts in 1980, the public campaign for a halt to new nuclear weapons spread rapidly at the local level and reached national prominence in 1983 when Congress approved a nonbinding freeze resolution. Confronted with an unexpected grassroots movement, the Reagan administration moderated its aggressive anti-Soviet rhetoric and reopened arms control talks.

Like the test ban campaign some twenty years earlier, the freeze movement declined without having achieved its main goal, a mutual superpower halt to testing, production, and deployment of new nuclear weapons. It is too soon to evaluate fully the impact of the freeze campaign. So far, it has left a larger legacy than its predecessor in dozens of active local peace groups, peace and conflict-resolution curricula at many colleges and other schools, and Congress's stronger role in arms control. Some credit the nuclear freeze campaign and associated international protests with helping to cause the "end of the Cold War," challenging the conventional view that the hard-line policies of the Reagan administration were responsible for this dramatic development (Cortright 1991, Marullo 1992, Meyer 1990A).[3]

Historical Context

Three key developments led to the freeze campaign: post-Vietnam local organizing by peace, environmental, and community-economic organizations; a turn to the right in national politics; and resurgent cold war militarism. In the early 1970s, many peace leaders felt that the Vietnam protests had exposed both the penetration of the military-industrial complex into all facets of political life and civil society and the weakness of the peace movement. Without strong roots in local communities, the movement could not hope to reverse the increasing militarization of the American political, economic, and social systems. Inspired by New Left values of participatory democracy, as the war wound down they began to emphasize local organizing.

Two campaigns against weapons systems seen as costly and dangerous helped establish the movement's new local presence. Starting in 1969 SANE and Clergy and Laity Concerned (CALC), a religious group formed originally as Clergy and Laity Against the [Vietnam] War, ran a locally based campaign opposing the development of an ABM system essentially outlawed by the SALT I and ABM treaties of 1972. In 1982, CALC and the AFSC began a campaign against the B-1 bomber, which they saw as a costly and militarily unnecessary weapon that exemplified the power and waste of the military-industrial complex. More than 40 national organizations and 160 local groups, including environmental, feminist, labor, and religious organizations, joined the campaign (Meyer 1988, 289). The combination of vigorous grassroots lobbying and a weapons system that was hard to justify—in addition to the expense, it appeared that the B-1 would be technologically obsolete shortly after planned deployment—led Congress in 1976 to delay appropriations beyond the presidential election. President Jimmy Carter canceled the program the following year.[4] One AFSC staff member saw the broad base and perceived success of the campaign as "a breakthrough in terms of grassroots work."[5]

Another local network developed when the AFSC and the FOR sponsored local opposition to nuclear weapons facilities and helped form organizations such as the Rocky Flats Action Group, which led a campaign to close a plutonium trigger plant in Colorado. In 1978, activists formed the Nuclear Weapons Facilities Task Force (NWFTF), a loose network of more than sixty local peace and environmental groups. Many local religious congregations set up peace and justice committees, forming another network that would later help spread the freeze campaign and the Central America solidarity movement.

As the local base of the peace movement grew, leaders looked for a way to unify the movement and redevelop a national presence. In 1977, they created the Mobilization for Survival (MFS) as a coalition with a broad agenda, including demands for nuclear disarmament, an end to civilian nuclear power plants, and increased social spending. The coalition grew to include more than 40 national and 280 local and state-level organizations. In 1978, it sponsored a demonstration that drew between 15,000 and 20,000 to support the United Nations's first special session on disarmament. With no real focus and no galvanizing issue, however, the coalition stagnated. MFS continued as a small independent organization through the efforts of a few paid staff members.

The 1979 Three Mile Island accident raised public fears of fallout and helped overcome differences between the peace groups and a network of local environmental groups fighting nuclear power plants. With a strong and more unified local base, leaders soon seized on the idea of the nuclear freeze as the means to recapture national attention and influence.

At the start of the freeze campaign in 1980, the peace movement included several components with the new local groups. Established peace groups had continued to maintain pacifist and internationalist traditions. The AFSC included a national office and more than 30 regional offices working on conflict resolution and social justice issues and the antimilitary campaigns.[6] The FOR, with 30,000 members nationally, was working with the AFSC on economic conversion. Liberal-internationalist and antinuclear organizations included SANE, which had almost collapsed after Vietnam and was slowly making the transition to an organization with a large base of paper members, a few local chapters, and a full-time paid national staff working primarily on antinuclear issues.

The rise of many new groups in the 1960s and 1970s that did not identify with either tradition meant that the movement was no longer so clearly divided into two camps. CALC was one of several religion-based organizations. An interfaith network, by 1983 it would grow to include forty-two local chapters and 30,000 members. Pax Christi, an international organization of Catholic clergy and laypeople, was founded in 1949 in France. The American branch was established in 1973, and by 1983 had grown to a membership of seven thousand, including 20 percent of American bishops. The established leaders of many religious denominations started speaking out against the nuclear arms race, encouraging the growth of local church-based activism.

The WILPF remained the most visible feminist peace organization. It would grow to include 15,000 members and several local affiliates by 1983. Physicians for Social Responsibility (PSR) was revived from a dormant state in 1979 through the work of Dr. Helen Caldicott, whose speeches galvanized many into action in the early stages of the freeze.[7] PSR provided a model for many new professionally based antinuclear organizations started during the early part of the freeze campaign.

And there were research and lobby groups and arms control organizations. With the growth of nuclear weapons and the increasing elaboration of nuclear strategy, and with arms control negotiations continuing after the 1963 test ban, a large arms control establishment developed inside the government, in agencies including the Arms Control and Disarmament Agency and outside government, in universities such as MIT, Harvard, and Stanford, and private research and lobbying organizations. Some, including the Union of Concerned Scientists (UCS) and the Council for a Livable World (CLW), constituted a liberal wing that at times cooperated with the peace movement; groups such as the Arms Control Association were more moderate and establishment-oriented. These national and local organizations and networks provided the foundation for the rapid growth of the nuclear freeze campaign as a grassroots movement. Like the civil rights movement of the 1960s, the campaign was built on institutions widely ignored by contemporary observers and later analysts.

Conventional political wisdom holds that the election of Ronald Reagan and a Republican Senate in 1980 represented a turning point in American politics. The decline of Democratic liberalism and the rise of Republican conservatism had begun earlier, however. In the 1960s, American corporations, facing a drop in profitability and international competitiveness, began an ideological and political assault on the welfare state and labor unions (Ferguson and Rogers 1986A, Tilly 1990). Along with popular reaction against the civil rights and antiwar movements, the growing intervention of conservative corporate elites into the political arena contributed to the election of Richard Nixon in 1968 and 1972 and to the outcome of the 1980 election.[8]

This right turn influenced politics in many ways. It was felt most strongly in foreign and military policy, not just in the Republican administrations but also during the Carter years. From the middle of his presidency, Carter began to increase military spending and aggressive rhetoric. He was responding to a general shift to the Right among elites and in public sentiment and to pressure from groups like the Committee on the Present Danger (CPD).

In the 1970s, conservative policy makers feared that two trends were eroding American military dominance. Public disillusionment with the Vietnam War was turning into a "Vietnam syndrome" that would make future military intervention in the Third World difficult if not impossible: the burden of proof would be on the government to show that the next war would not be so costly.[9] Second, the Soviet Union had continued to build up its nuclear arsenal since the Cuban missile crisis and had reached rough parity with the United States by the mid-1970s.

In 1976, the CPD was reconstituted to lobby for greater military spending on strategic forces and greater capacity and resolve for overseas intervention. The original CPD had been formed in the 1950s as a right-wing group to promote cold war militarism as a response to what members saw as a Soviet threat to American global hegemony. In 1976, some early members reformed the organization, enlisting top policy makers and former policy makers to promote the view that the Soviet Union had gained or would soon gain a potentially decisive edge in strategic nuclear forces and that American security was soon to be profoundly threatened.

Reagan gave many top posts in the Pentagon and national security agencies to CPD members. Earlier, the CPD's offensive had an impact on Carter's policies. His 1977 cancellation of the B-1 bomber had left him open to charges of caving in to the peace movement and becoming "soft on defense." In 1979, the Iran hostage crisis, the Soviet invasion of Afghanistan, and the overthrow of American-backed Nicaraguan dictator Somoza by a Left-Center revolt helped the CPD make its case that American power was on the decline as the Soviet threat was rising. Carter took steps designed to show his "resolve" in military matters (Meyer 1988, 1990A; Solo 1988). He announced his support for two new nuclear missile systems with multiple warheads and sufficient accuracy (presumably) to destroy Soviet missiles in their hardened underground silos: the MX, based on land, and the Trident II, based on submarines. Although the administration insisted these were merely a response to a new generation of larger Soviet "silo-busting" missiles, critics in the arms control community and the peace movement argued that the MX and Trident II were part of a larger strategy designed to give the United States a "first-strike" capacity, the ability to launch a nuclear attack without fear of complete annihilation in return. This capacity would undermine deterrence, the unstated policy that neither side would launch a nuclear attack because both sides knew that would be suicide.[10] A first-strike capacity also meant an incentive to strike first — a devastating prospect in a world with more than fifty thousand nuclear weapons.

An apparent change in official doctrine added to the new fears of nuclear war. After a year's secret discussions, in July 1980, Carter signed Presidential Directive no. 59 (PD59), which seemed to commit the United States to a "nuclear warfighting" policy in which nuclear weapons would be used not just to retaliate against a nuclear attack but also in other circumstances that were not spelled out but presumably included interventions in the Third World and conventional war in Europe.[11] The new "Carter Doctrine" declared the Persian Gulf an area of "vital interest." Some took this as a signal that the "nuclear umbrella" would extend to the Gulf. The "rapid deployment force" was created to speed troops to this and other areas, and the 1979 and 1980 military budgets both called for increases in real spending of 5 percent.[12] Opinion polls showed public support for greater military spending for the first time since the middle of the Vietnam War. Carter also announced a boycott of the 1980 Olympics to be held in Moscow.

In December 1979, NATO announced a decision to deploy new intermediate-range nuclear weapons in several European countries. NATO claimed that cruise and Pershing II "Euromissiles" were merely a response to new Soviet missiles targeting Europe, but critics saw these as part of a western first-strike strategy. Activists resolved to block the deployment.[13] After the Soviet invasion of Afghanistan at the end of 1979, Carter withdrew the SALT (Strategic Arms Limitations Talks) II treaty from Senate consideration. In 1972, the superpowers had signed SALT I, limiting the number of strategic weapons but allowing the development of MIRVs: multiple-warhead missiles, widely seen as threatening to deterrence and stability because of the alleged silo-busting capacity of these warheads and because the relatively few launchers provided prime targets for preemptive strikes. The SALT II talks addressed this problem. In 1979, Jimmy Carter and Leonid Brezhnev signed a treaty capping MIRVs and placing other new limits on weapons. Right-wing pressure had kept the Senate from approving the treaty until Carter withdrew it.

Peace leaders and arms control moderates reacted to these ominous developments. Critical arms control experts were overwhelmed by the CPD-generated pressure, however. After Reagan's election they would be shut out of official policy-making bodies. Some would break with tradition, speaking out publicly against the new policies and in support of the revived antinuclear movement. In the United States, peace groups, including SANE and the NWFTF, organized opposition to the MX missile in several western states the government had targeted as sites for a "racetrack" system of MX rail-based deployment.

Basing missiles on mobile rail cars would, in theory, prevent Soviet preemptive strikes. It would also use up land and make nuclear weapons more visible and frightening. Even conservative Utah rebelled.

The planned Euromissile deployments led to widespread protest in the NATO nations. Major opposition parties including Labour in Britain and the West German Social Democrats adopted antideployment positions. These protests did not succeed; conservative parties won several key elections — but a large grassroots movement began in many Western European nations. Whatever their domestic impact, the protests inspired activists in the United States who were planning the freeze campaign.

Origins of the Freeze Campaign

Like the approach of war in the 1930s and the spread of fallout in the 1950s, nuclear war-fighting plans and rhetoric in the late 1970s were a threat that provided the peace movement with an opportunity for organizing. The movement again responded by developing a campaign around a simple but important goal. The notion of a freeze on nuclear weapons was not new. Looking to gain political or military advantages or both, the United States and the Soviet Union had made public and private proposals for some kind of freeze since the early 1960s (Solo 1988, Meyer 1990A, Meyer and Kleidman 1991). Peace groups, including MFS, had been circulating petitions calling for a unilateral American nuclear moratorium, but the idea did not catch on. A variation on it soon did.

When Randall Forsberg, an arms control expert outside the mainstream arms control groups, proposed to the December 1979 annual convention of the MFS that a bilateral nuclear freeze should be the centerpiece of a new antinuclear campaign, the peace movement embraced the idea with enthusiasm. Forsberg with a handful of staff members from the AFSC and other peace groups had developed a "Call to Halt the Arms Race" that was more specific than earlier moratorium ideas and was bilateral, demanding that both superpowers stop the testing, production, and deployment of new nuclear weapons. The bilateral and specific nature of the call would, its authors thought, appeal to moderate arms control experts and politicians and would allow activists to discuss the nuclear arms race without assessing blame or confronting the anti-Soviet sentiments deeply entrenched in American politics. The simplicity of demanding an end to new weapons would draw support from a public generally shut out of nuclear policy making. As a first step toward arms reduction and other means of ending the cold war it would gain support from the Left within and outside the peace movement, despite the overt apolitical tone of the call.

Forsberg's background as a researcher and writer for the Stockholm International Peace Research Institute (SIPRI) and a graduate student of military policy and arms control at MIT had given her insight into the arms control process. She believed it would not move toward major reductions in nuclear weapons without outside pressure. No activist or an organizer, she was not sure how to catalyze this pressure. A first step was to lobby the leaders of the major peace groups at the MFS convention to unite behind her plans for a national campaign for a nuclear freeze. Most of them, won over, encouraged her to continue refining the call.

In February 1980, Carol Jensen of CALC convened a meeting of staff from AFSC, CALC, and FOR to form an "Ad Hoc Task Force for a Nuclear Weapons Freeze Campaign." The task force met throughout the spring. When the call was ready in April, the AFSC printed and distributed five thousand copies as a four-page pamphlet. It demanded that the United States and the USSR both adopt a freeze as "an essential, verifiable first step toward lessening the risk of nuclear war and reducing the nuclear arsenals." Less moralistic than SANE's newspaper advertisement that launched the test ban campaign, the call emphasized the alleged dangers that a new generation of nuclear weapons presented and the technical importance and practicality of a freeze. It also mentioned economic benefits that might stem from reducing spending on nuclear weapons.

The freeze proposal quickly gained support from peace and religious groups and grassroots Democratic party activists. It was rejected by party leaders and the arms control establishment. In the spring of 1980, a consultation of churches on disarmament of the National Council of Churches endorsed the freeze, throwing the support of many Protestant denominations behind the campaign. During the summer, the AFSC organized lobbying at the presidential nominating conventions. Forty percent of the Democratic delegates endorsed the freeze proposal but neither Carter nor his chief rival Senator Edward Kennedy did. The annual conferences of CALC and FOR endorsed the freeze, as did the national board of the AFSC. All three made their local networks available for organizing. Other peace, religious, and environmental groups also made the freeze a top priority. A few liberal arms control experts endorsed the call but no major arms control groups did. Some objected to the call on technical grounds, others, considering Forsberg as an outsider, saw no reason to put aside their own agenda for hers (Leavitt 1983A, 18). The rejection of the freeze by political elites and most of the arms control establishment reinforced the campaign's turn to the grassroots.

Forsberg had hoped that the freeze proposal "would survive or fall on the basis of its innate attractiveness to people, not on the basis of [the campaign's] structure; that if it was a good enough idea it would simply spread and motivate people (Forsberg, quoted in Leavitt 1983A, 20). Peace activists convinced her of the need for grassroots organizing and started planning a founding conference involving local leaders. Forsberg was afraid that the peace groups would try to control the campaign, imposing their "pacifist-vegetarian anti-corporate value system" and alienating centrist supporters whom she saw as vital to a mainstream campaign (Leavitt 1983A, 23). She insisted that the invitation list to the founding conference be expanded beyond the existing peace network to include a variety of local activists and potential supporters and that the peace groups must turn the campaign over to leaders who emerged in its early stages.

Forsberg had leverage because she wrote the call and she controlled the Ad Hoc Committee's funding, a grant of more than five thousand dollars given her by Alan Kay, a Boston area businessperson and fellow arms control student at MIT. The peace leaders accepted her ideas — with resistance. Jan Orr-Harter, a committee member who was not a peace movement insider, observed that "Most of these people were involved in this from the point of view of the peace movement [in which they had participated] for a long time. They thought that the peace movement would lead the way to a nuclear freeze, and that they could do that. I think it was hard for them to realize that their job was to get it going, and then throw it out to the country; that other people would then come in and take the leadership . . . . So there was a sort of crisis for the committee as they came to realize that it wasn't business as usual. It wasn't like the B-1 campaign, it wasn't like the Vietnam war campaign. It wasn't in the same ballpark with those things. They did come to realize that, but it didn't happen overnight" (Leavitt 1983A, 24).

The initial plans for the nuclear freeze campaign therefore differed from the earlier peace campaigns by emphasizing grassroots organizing, local leadership, and a broader coalition extending beyond peace groups. Tensions within the early coalition were not just between Forsberg and the peace groups. There were also "turf battles" between the groups that Solo (1988) argues contributed to a lack of strong leadership and clear, efficient decision-making structures and procedures.[14]

While the task force was planning for the first national conference of what was to become the NWFC, Randall Kehler and his colleagues at the Traprock Peace Center in Deerfield, Massachusetts, were organizing an independent effort to put nuclear freeze referenda on the November ballots of small towns throughout western Massachusetts. Kehler had been a draft resister and antiwar activist in the 1960s, and had turned down the executive directorship of the War Resisters' League to pursue local organizing. In 1979, he helped form Traprock as a center focusing on global issues, but, according to Leavitt (1983A, 20), "the staff quickly realized that local organizing around particular issues held more promise for immediate gain than did the original idea of focusing on the development of international ties and on general training sessions in non-violent conflict resolution."

Kehler seized upon the idea of the freeze, which he had heard about in its pre-call form through Sojourners, a pacifist Christian community. If he turned the freeze into a simple ballot referendum, he had the local angle Traprock had been looking for. The use of a conventional political device, the ballot, in an unconventional manner, addressing issues of nuclear strategy, turned out to be the central tactic for the first two years of the freeze campaign. It had an immediate populist appeal; the newly formed Western Massachusetts Referendum Organizing Committee made it explicit by arguing for public participation in military and foreign policy. They also discussed the negative impact of military spending on local economies, the consequences of nuclear war, and ethical reasons for disarmament.

Although national figures such as Daniel Ellsberg were brought in to speak to college and other audiences, the campaign was locally run and locally financed through small contributions totaling $15,000, which helped pay for ads in print and broadcast media. The referendum gained endorsements from hundreds of local elites, including business and professional people, and elected officials, including Republican Silvio Conte, the moderate congressperson from the district. The campaign brought out hundreds of volunteers. This was exactly the scenario that those planning the national freeze campaign were envisioning for communities around the country.

On November 4, 1980, the freeze referendum passed in fifty-nine of sixty-two towns, with a total vote of 94,000 for and 65,000 against. It was the only good news that the national freeze organizers received the same day Ronald Reagan was elected. In the campaign, he and Carter both talked tough about the Soviets and promised greater military spending. The Republican party gained control of the Senate for the first time since 1952, and the Democratic majority in the House was reduced.

The message delivered by the voters in western Massachusetts was mixed. A clear majority voted for the freeze referendum, but most also voted for Reagan, the more hawkish of the two major candidates. This too set a pattern that would continue: public support for a freeze developed quickly but did not translate easily into the hard political currency of votes for candidates. This pattern soon encouraged centrist policy makers to pay lip service to the freeze while pursuing military strategy as usual. The national media would treat public support for a freeze as an expression of fear and not as an endorsement of a serious policy proposal. During 1981 and 1982, however, the freeze campaign avoided these problems by building local strength and ignoring the national media and policy makers.

Rise of the Freeze Campaign

Starting with the November 1980 local referenda and the election of Reagan, the freeze became the fastest-growing peace campaign and one of the largest grassroots movements in American history. The Massachusetts referenda provided a much-needed victory for the peace movement and a concrete model for local organizing. The Reagan administration quickly produced rhetoric, staffing decisions, and policies that alarmed not just the peace movement but also moderate arms controllers and a good segment of the European and American publics.

Upon taking office, Reagan replaced moderates in the military planning and arms control establishments with conservatives and ultra-conservatives. Some stated publicly that the United States could fight and win a nuclear war and that the American government should use this capacity to pressure the Soviets into changing their political and economic systems. These remarks and Reagan's own aggressive rhetoric against the Soviet "evil empire" raised public fears of nuclear war and pushed moderate arms control and military experts into the freeze camp. Some did not fully support the freeze proposal but saw the campaign as a vehicle to help them push policy back to the center.

Although the new administration did not have much impact on policy until the fall of 1981, freeze organizing went forward immediately after the 1980 election. Forsberg's Institute for Defense and Disarmament Studies (IDDS) served as the campaign clearinghouse, spreading the word through existing circles and organizing the founding national conference. The effort was run on a shoestring: one full-time staffer had been hired in September 1980; funding came from the five-thousand-dollar Kay grant to Forsberg and a handful of contributions from national and local peace groups totaling another few thousand dollars.[15]

On March 20–22, 1981, more than three hundred peace, religious, environmental, and community activists met at Georgetown University in the first national conference of the NWFC to plan the campaign's basic strategy and structure. The Ad Hoc Committee and others had formed a wide but fragile consensus around the freeze proposal. Beyond that, there was no agreement on what if anything should follow a freeze or on whether and how to bring in other issues, although Forsberg and the other founders saw the freeze idea as only a first step toward ending the arms race and redirecting foreign and domestic policies.

There were vigorous debates over whether and how to link the freeze proposal to issues such as economic conversion and how to broaden the base of the campaign beyond the peace movement's usual white middle-class base. The conference decided to endorse a single-issue, moderate message, with no statements about accompanying or following steps. This decision was not surprising given the diversity of the freeze coalition. Solo (1988) believes it also reflected the turf battles within the Ad Hoc Committee, which had hindered leadership and strategic and organization planning. The conference did not spend enough time developing a more comprehensive campaign plan (Solo 1988). After the conference decision, some groups, including MFS and the WRL, left the campaign in favor of continued work on an integrated, multi-issue agenda, although the WRL later endorsed the freeze proposal and many local affiliates worked with the freeze campaign.

Tensions between a broad- and a narrow-issue focus were to continue throughout the campaign. The NWFC, under Kehler's leadership, most often chose to keep the "strategic" focus narrow — taking public stands on few other issues and directing energies toward achieving a nuclear freeze but "educating" broadly — providing materials and information on a range of issues. Some see this as a strength of the campaign because it kept the freeze a "broad front door" that brought many new people into the peace and justice movement without imposing a long list of issues on them. Also it allowed local activists to find those linked issues that motivated them and that "worked" in their communities (Senturia interview). Others argue that by failing to connect the freeze consistently to other issues and further steps the campaign left itself open to political incorporation (Solo 1988).[16]

The conference endorsed a four-step strategy proposed by the Ad Hoc Committee. The strategy called for a four- to five-year effort in four basic stages: demonstrate the potential of the freeze proposal for stopping the arms race, build broad and visible public support, focus pressure on policy makers and make the freeze a matter of national policy debate, and win the debate and have the freeze adopted as national policy. Significantly, the first two stages called for a focus on local work including education, working to gain endorsements from local elites and policy makers, and running ballot referenda campaigns. The local emphasis was a core part of the grassroots strategy of the freeze. Throughout the campaign, in fact, both local activists and national leaders explicitly used the term "grassroots" to characterize their vision of a movement based on mass participation.

The organization established was to consist of a network of local groups held together by a national clearinghouse. The local groups were to be vital organizations that would establish a "permanent peace constituency throughout the country" (Solo 1988, 6). The campaign would not be relying on isolated adherents to generate political pressure. Some delegates pushed for a structure ensuring efficient national coordination of the campaign; many were suspicious of any form of centralized control. As a compromise, an annual national conference was established, allowing for equal voting representation from each congressional district, and entrusted with final authority over policy and other matters (at this first conference, all who showed up had a vote). In addition, both a national committee and a smaller executive committee were created to oversee implementation and make interim decisions. The original national committee consisted mostly of representatives from those peace groups taking an active role in the campaign. By late 1983, they would be supplanted by representatives of local and state NWFC groups, marking a transition by the NWFC from coalition to independent organization.

The name and functions of the clearinghouse reflected the decentralized structure and grassroots strategy of the campaign. The clearinghouse would coordinate the work of local groups, assemble a series of ad hoc national task forces responsible for organizing specific projects, publish a national newsletter and provide other information, but it would not be a national headquarters with control over local groups. No plans were made for formal chartering of chapters, a national membership system, or funding of the clearinghouse by local chapters.

Some at the conference felt that because the AFSC was the largest and best-funded of the peace groups, the clearinghouse should be located in the AFSC's national office in Philadelphia. This course had been taken by the EPC forty-five years earlier. The conference decided instead to select a location in the center of the country, away from the influence of the East Coast's established peace groups, away from the influence of the national media in New York and the national political establishment in Washington, D.C. The strategy was to pressure the establishment from the outside. The "heartland" location of the clearinghouse would better serve this strategy. It would symbolize the grassroots nature of the campaign. After temporary housing in Forsberg's IDDS, the clearinghouse was set up in St. Louis in December 1981.

The freeze campaign emerged from the founding conference with a strategy and a structure well-suited to starting a widespread antinuclear campaign. The central goal of the campaign was simple enough to be widely understood, important enough to motivate people to act, and politically feasible enough to raise hopes of victory. The tactic of the local referendum provided a focus for local organizing and the possibility of small but significant early victories. Local peace, environmental, religious, and other groups gave the freeze a larger local network than those available to the previous peace campaigns. Most of the peace movement remained in the freeze coalition. Groups such as the AFSC provided critical early support for the national clearinghouse; the campaign's structure provided a framework for coordinating local work and allowing the campaign to grow beyond the established peace movement.

The political context was more favorable than most observers thought, despite the 1980 elections. The national scene was quiet, but it was not the quiet of the 1950s: the movements of the 1960s had opened up the political system and helped legitimize protest. They had left behind a generation of activists ready to respond to the call.

Throughout most of 1981, the freeze campaign operated out of the national limelight. The national clearinghouse was small and money was tight; this first year's budget would total less than $50,000.[17] If the national effort was slow to get off the ground, local organizing spread rapidly. This was according to plan. On the Traprock model, which the clearinghouse helped publicize through a quarterly newsletter, local activists spoke to community organizations, including religious congregations, labor unions, business associations, senior citizens, community, and minority groups, and energy and environmental organizations.[18] They gained endorsements from many of these groups and from local politicians and other elites and received mostly favorable publicity from local mass media. The clearinghouse printed and distributed information on the arms race, manuals for organizers and other material, and helped to organize workshops and training for activists.

Early organizing was concentrated on both coasts, with some work also in the upper Midwest and plains states. The early tactical focus was on local and state legislative resolutions and ballot referenda. In June 1981, the Massachusetts and Oregon state legislatures passed freeze resolutions, and three other states and eight city councils joined them by the end of the year. Freeze activists gained endorsements from religious, occupational, civic, and trade union groups, adding to the local networks available to the campaign and to the list of prominent national supporters.

PSR formally endorsed the freeze proposal in the summer of 1981, and new occupation-based peace groups began to spring up. These included Educators for Social Responsibility, Communicators for Nuclear Disarmament, and similar groups for nurses, lawyers, computer professionals, and business executives. By the end of 1981, PSR, the most active and visible of these groups, had grown from a few hundred members in the Boston area to a national membership of more than 10,000. The number of local chapters and members would double in 1982, reaching 125 chapters and 20,000 members.

The local activists who gave the freeze campaign such a strong start came, first, from the network of people active in peace, environmental, religious, community, and other groups. Among this group were volunteers and paid staff, people affiliated with national organizations, and those working strictly at the local level. This primary network quickly mobilized a second wave of local volunteers who brought a missionary spirit to the campaigns. Many early activists remarked on how easy organizing was in 1981 and 1982: one had merely to distribute or post a few leaflets and dozens of people would show up for a meeting, ready to go out and work. Although the evidence is only suggestive, it appears that many of the primary and secondary group were members of the 1960s generation, born during the ten years following the end of World War II, and politically mature during the 1960s.[19] Most of this early growth in the movement took the organizational form of new local groups, especially local NWFC organizations, but existing groups also grew substantially.[20]

Local organizing remained the focus of the campaign, but the freeze was percolating up onto the national agenda. A July 1981 Gallup poll found 72-percent support for the freeze. The national media began to notice the movement after a series of huge demonstrations in Europe in the fall. In August, the Reagan administration had announced plans to produce the neutron bomb, a controversial "enhanced-radiation" weapon designed to maximize human destruction and minimize property damage. European antinuclear activists protested the contemplated stockpiling of the bomb by NATO and the proposed deployment of the Euromissiles. In early October, 300,000 people demonstrated in Bonn at a rally sponsored by more than nine hundred West German organizations. Adding fuel to the fire, shortly thereafter President Reagan remarked at a press conference that he thought that a limited nuclear war could be fought in Europe without escalation to a full-scale superpower conflict. Although this was longstanding NATO doctrine, the president's statement raised fears and prompted a round of demonstrations in cities, including London, where 150,000 people turned out, and in Rome, where 200,000 demonstrated.

In the United States, both the NWFC and other organizations continued to grow. The October issue of the national *Freeze Newsletter* claimed that "so much is happening so fast that it has been impossible for the Clearinghouse to monitor all activities. We do know that Freeze work is being done in 40 states and that there are coordinated petition campaigns in 21." These petitions had together gathered more than 250,000 signatures. In addition, forty national organizations and nineteen members of Congress had endorsed the freeze proposal. In November, the UCS held a Veteran's Day convocation on the threat of nuclear war, and 100,000 people participated in 151 campus-based teach-ins, leading to the 1982 formation of United Campuses Against Nuclear War (UCAM).

At the end of 1981, the NWFC was in the midst of an enormous growth spurt. From a group of three hundred at the March conference, the campaign had mobilized a network of as many as 20,000 activists, mostly volunteers, covering much of the nation.[21] In December, the clearinghouse was formally moved to St. Louis, and Randall Kehler was hired as national coordinator. Both choices reflected and further encouraged the freeze campaign's emphasis on local grassroots organizing.

The campaign was primarily a loose-knit coalition. The NWFC was moving toward establishing itself as an independent organization — it had a formal structure and now a national office with a top executive — but the committees and task forces that provided ideas and leadership were dominated by staff and volunteers from established peace groups. The local NWFC groups that were springing up were mostly informal, volunteer-run efforts. They received leadership and information from the clearinghouse but had no formal role in the structure of the campaign organization.

Peak of the Freeze Campaign, 1982–1984

Five hundred people met in Denver on February 20–21, 1982, for the second national conference of the NWFC. Added to the members of the founding coalition were local activists from almost every state. The conference gave voting privileges to the representatives of established peace groups and to one delegate from each congressional district. Local activists chose their delegates, and the campaign did not get involved in approving credentials or chartering local chapters. The open structure of this and later conferences reflected the campaign's goal of maximizing participation as well as the antiexclusionary values held by many activists.[22] Likewise, at this stage the lack of a national membership program was not seen as a problem. Indeed, many leaders and local activists saw it as a virtue, permitting wide participation in the campaign.

The conference set strategic goals of broadening the base of support for the freeze, linking it to key economic issues, extending activity to every congressional district, and gaining the support of at least 150 U.S. representatives and 35 senators. Delegates also voted to support a rally planned for June 12 in New York during the U.N.'s second special session on disarmament.

The major tactical focus for 1982 would be a series of state and local freeze referenda to be voted on in the fall. The freeze also began to move onto the national political agenda. Just before the conference, Representative Edward Markey of Massachusetts, a state with extensive freeze organizing, had introduced a freeze resolution in the House. On March 10, Senators Edward Kennedy and Mark Hatfield placed a similar measure before the Senate. Hatfield was a Republican from Oregon who had been on the board of the pacifist group Sojourners, and who, in 1979, had introduced a freeze amendment to the SALT II treaty that was later withdrawn by President Carter. Kennedy, like Markey from Massachusetts, had been Carter's chief rival for the Democratic presidential nomination in 1980 and appeared to be the front-runner for the 1984 nomination. Some viewed his embrace of the freeze proposal and campaign as an attempt to enhance his political prospects by identifying with the only widespread anti-administration movement of the time.

Along with congressional interest in the **freeze** proposal, media attention to the campaign continued to grow. Starting in February, in a series of three powerful articles written for the *New Yorker,* Jonathan Schell explored the potential effects of nuclear war, concluding that the extinction of human life was a real possibility. Some compared the impact of these articles — soon turned into a best-selling book, *The Fate of the Earth* — to Rachel Carson's *Silent Sspring,* which in the 1960s helped put environmentalism on the public agenda. Schell was joined by a slew of authors writing on nuclear war and nuclear policy, publishing in books, magazines, and daily newspapers.

By March, the campaign claimed 20,000 volunteers working for a freeze through 149 offices in 47 states, encompassing 75 percent of the nation's congressional districts (Solo 1988, 8). On March 2, 157 Vermont town meetings endorsed the freeze, again demonstrating its popular, and populist, appeal. A second round of European demonstrations was larger than the first, drawing 200,000 in Athens, 250,000 in Bonn, 350,000 in Amsterdam, and 400,000 in Madrid.

As the freeze continued to mobilize thousands of volunteers, the growth in national attention led to a large increase in funding by foundations and major donors, many close to the Democratic party. The campaign had projected a 1982 budget of $350,000–$375,000,[23] almost a seven-fold increase over the previous year. Fund raising actually outstripped expectations, totaling (for the national clearinghouse) $450,000.[24] Of this, $337,000 came from foundations and major individual donors contributing more than $2,000 each; initial projections had been for only $55,000 from foundations. Another $75,000 came from large donations ranging from $500 to $2,000, and only $5,000 represented small contributions from "grassroots support." The persistent tension between the grassroots nature of the movement and the national clearinghouse's financial reliance on major outside funding would have different effects at different stages of the campaign.

During the spring of 1982, the campaign continued to emphasize public education. Ground Zero, an organization founded by former Carter NSA member Roger Molander, sponsored educational events in 750 communities and on 450 college campuses during "Ground Zero Week" in April.[25] During this week, 133 of the nation's 280 Catholic bishops endorsed the freeze proposal. The campaign was becoming a force with mainstream visibility, respectability, and political potential. Recognizing this, the Reagan administration responded with a three-fold attack.

The first tactic was red-baiting. Administration members implied or flatly stated that freeze activists were helping the Soviet Union, knowingly or not, by working to limit the United States's nuclear buildup. This did not work nearly as well as had the attacks on SANE in the test ban era by Senator Dodd and others. The political climate had changed, and the NWFC had gathered endorsements of the freeze idea from many mainstream leaders, including former heads of the Pentagon and the CIA. The smear campaign did put freeze campaign leaders on the defensive: the peace movement and the Left had not overcome the ability of the promilitary right to capture the symbols and rhetoric of patriotism. Along with the move to Congress, this defensiveness helped move the campaign toward the political center. The rhetoric narrowed, emphasizing technological arguments or conservative-sounding "national security" rationales for a freeze. NWFC leaders became more wary of demanding that the United States take unilateral initiatives that would further the disarmament process.

Second, top State Department officials and other high-ranking figures were sent out to communities around the nation to debate NWFC spokespersons, who were often amazed to find themselves sharing platforms with deputy secretaries. The impact of this tactic seems to have been slight, given the great success of freeze referenda and the continuing high levels of support for a freeze in public opinion polls.

The third tactic proved more successful. The administration toned down its war fighting and anti-Soviet rhetoric, and on May 9 announced its proposals for new superpower arms control negotiations.[26] The new Strategic Arms Reductions Talks (START) would take the place of the Strategic Arms Limitations Talks (SALT), which the administration had ended upon taking office. These new negotiations, Reagan claimed, would seek to reduce the nuclear stockpiles, thereby going beyond the goals of both the SALT talks and the freeze proposal.

Freeze campaign leaders and other critics charged that the talks were designed to calm public fears of superpower confrontation while the administration continued its buildup.[27] Military spending, in fact, would increase by 50 percent from 1980 through 1985. In 1982, the previous peacetime peak was surpassed, and by 1986 military spending was higher than during the Vietnam and Korean wars (Meyer 1988).

The administration's change of strategy and tone if not policy was too late to stop the freeze campaign. These changes, providing symbolic reassurance that the administration wanted peace, eventually helped slow the movement. In the spring of 1982, however, this impact was slight, and the campaign was still growing.

The June 12 New York rally during the U.N.'s second special session on disarmament drew between 750,000 and 1 million people in support of freezing and reversing the arms race and redirecting resources from military spending to human needs. Many peace and social change groups had (with much debate and friction) organized the rally. They called it the largest political demonstration in American history. The mass media tended to give the credit to the NWFC and not to the other groups (Meyer 1990A, Solo 1988).

On June 23, the House Foreign Affairs Committee passed a freeze resolution by a vote of 26 to 11, sending it onto the floor for debate. In July, the freeze campaign opened an office in Washington, D.C., and hired a full-time lobbyist to work with other groups in getting the resolution passed.

The campaign had a double focus that summer — on the congressional resolution, and on state and local referenda. The House vote on the resolution came in August, and the measure was defeated when a substitute motion passed 204 to 202. This vote was generally reported as a victory for the administration, but the congressional managers of the resolution and the campaign leaders saw the outcome as positive: a change in one vote would have meant passage for the freeze resolution, a fact used to inspire activists to elect a "pro freeze" House that fall.

Meanwhile, the ballot campaigns received a big boost in September, when Wisconsin voters passed the first statewide freeze referendum by a three-to-one margin. The November results were impressive: nine of the ten statewide referenda passed, as did thirty-four of the thirty-seven local ones. Because almost one-third of the American electorate had the opportunity to vote on these measures, NWFC leaders claimed victory in what amounted to a national referendum.[28]

The freeze did well in November 1982, not just in ballot referenda but also in electoral politics. Of forty-seven congressional races in which Representative Markey's office considered the freeze was a campaign issue, profreeze candidates won thirty-eight and lost only nine. Overall, NWFC leaders figured that they had netted a gain of twenty to thirty supporters in the House. Democrats, also helped by a severe economic recession, increased their House majority by twenty-six seats. According to Douglas Waller, Markey's legislative director, both Republicans and Democrats in Congress expected the freeze idea to become a key national issue (Waller 1987). Journalist William Greider thought that the freeze might have enough appeal to "change the face of American politics" (quoted in Waller 1987, 161).

The success of the movement was reflected in the optimistic theme of the third national conference of the NWFC, "From Popular Mandate to Public Policy." Six hundred local NWFC activists and representatives of other peace and disarmament groups met in St. Louis February 4–6 to decide how to increase and direct the movement's momentum. Strategy would center on passing the congressional resolution rejected by a two-vote margin in 1982. The key debate was whether the resolution would be advisory, simply calling upon both superpowers to enact a nuclear freeze, or binding, cutting off funds for testing, production, and deployment of nuclear weapons. Some argued for making the resolution binding because the administration was unlikely to negotiate a freeze. Waller and other congressional aides argued at the conference that the administration could block passage of the binding resolution, that this would hurt the chances of passing a nonbinding measure, and that the media would then proclaim that the freeze movement was in decline. As a compromise, the conference voted to press for the nonbinding resolution while allowing the option of working for binding measures should the opportunity arise.

A second key debate involved the politically sensitive issue of unilateralism. Congressional sponsors and some freeze activists considered it necessary to avoid the appearance of promoting unilateral American initiatives, even if they decided that these would not put the United States in any military jeopardy. They argued that if a congressional funding cutoff were not tied to the Soviets' also adopting a nuclear freeze, the freeze movement would be branded by opponents and the mass media as unilateralists ready to give the Soviets a nuclear advantage. Others contended that unilateral initiatives were the most likely means toward achieving a freeze and that the movement should not fear red-baiting. The conference adopted language that mostly favored the bilateral position.[29]

Unilateralism surfaced most strongly in the debate over the imminent deployment of Euromissiles. Those who favored unilateral initiatives claimed Euromissiles presented the most immediate threat of destabilizing the nuclear balance of terror. They argued that opposition to the Euromissiles should be absolute rather than contingent on Soviet concessions. They also stressed the importance of solidarity with European peace activists. The conference again adopted a compromise version that called for a ban on NATO deployment, for reduc-

tions in Soviet intermediate-range missiles, and for a one-year unilateral delay by NATO to allow time to negotiate these measures. Solo
(1988) contends that these decisions, especially the choice of the nonbinding resolution, reflected the growing influence of congressional
sponsors, the lack of political experience among NWFC leaders, and
a poor strategy-making process within the campaign.[30] The motives
of legislators included various mixtures of opportunism and sincere
support, but they were Washington insiders who understood legislation, not movement building. Solo sees the campaign's decision to back
away from binding measures as the first step in handing over effective
leadership of the movement to outsiders and abandoning the grassroots strategy in favor of a political insider's game with no chance of
achieving fundamental reform. She and other critics also claim that
there was a drift toward narrowing the issue focus of the campaign.
As passing a congressional resolution became a possibility, NWFC
leaders feared risking political respectability by taking on the aboli-
tion of nuclear weapons and opposition to military interventionism
and the influence of the military-industrial complex. Before the conference, campaign leaders had decided to retain a narrow focus on
a bilateral freeze.[31]

In addition to the congressional freeze resolution and opposition
to the Euromissiles, the conference agreed with the leadership's plans
to start work on the 1984 elections. More money would be needed
for lobbying, working with the mass media, and helping local groups
generate grassroots pressure. The conference voted to make fund raising
a higher priority at national, state, and local levels and to integrate
it into educational and political work.[32] In 1983, the NWFC was to
raise $1.3 million at the national level (vs. $50,000 in 1981 and $450,000
in 1982). Foundation grants would almost double from 1982 to
$500,000, but the biggest jump would be in direct-mail contributions,
from a loss of $8,000 to a gain of $375,000.[33] Contributions from local
NWFC groups would add only $17,000.

This increase in funding allowed the national office to hire more
staff in 1983. In 1982, the national staff had grown to include the national coordinator and coordinators for labor outreach, publications,
field organizing, education and general outreach, and political education. Also on staff were several office and support workers and a lobbyist and news director in Washington, D.C. In 1983, the campaign would
add a fund raiser, a special events coordinator, a second lobbyist, and
two minority outreach staff.[34] Freeze leaders had been discussing an
expansion of the field program, and the conference voted to instruct

the national staff to initiate a field project as soon as possible.[35] By the end of 1983, four staff members were working full time on coordinating the efforts of local groups and providing hands-on training.[36]

After the conference, the major focus was on passing the congressional resolution. On March 7–9, during the "Citizen's Lobby" in Washington, 5,000 local activists took to their senators and representatives petitions with more than 800,000 signatures. The House Foreign Affairs Committee again reported a nonbinding freeze resolution to the floor of the House by a vote.

That month conservative, prodeployment governments were elected in Britain and West Germany. On March 23, President Reagan went on the offensive with his "Star Wars" speech. He took advantage of the fears of nuclear war generated by his own administration and amplified by the freeze, and presented to the nation his plans for a world safe from nuclear weapons. This safety would come not from the tricky arena of multilateral negotiations, but through the unilateral development of a series of weapons designed to shoot down ballistic missiles. Although critics denounced the Strategic Defense Initiative (SDI), as the program was called, as a smokescreen, a technological impossibility, and even another component of a first-strike capacity, this speech seemed to restore to the administration some initiative, especially when coupled with the START negotiations begun in 1982.[37]

Meanwhile, the congressional resolution was moving toward what looked like a favorable vote on the House floor, and opponents were maneuvering to amend it. The key amendment that passed was an ambiguous one, interpreted by freeze opponents to mean that any freeze not followed by reductions would end after two years. Although this seemed innocuous, it lent credence to administration claims that a freeze would prevent the achievement of the real goal of reductions by preventing further development of American "bargaining chips" like SDI and the MX. Freeze opponents cheered the passage of this amendment. It allowed many moderates to vote for the amended nonbinding referendum, which passed on May 4 by a vote of 278–149 (Waller 1987).

Both sides claimed victory, but, according to Waller, "the almost universal conclusion in the press was that the administration had lost a serious vote of confidence" (Waller 1987, 290). Congress quickly turned, though, and on May 24 approved money for further production of the MX missile. In 1982, the House had voted against administration production plans in a move hailed by freeze leaders as a stand for arms control. This time, many legislators claimed to be swayed when a bilateral commission appointed by the administration argued that approval of the MX would give the United States an important bargaining chip in the START talks. Many also saw the MX vote as a chance to "balance" their vote for a freeze, and were undeterred by the apparent contradiction of voting for both.[38] The mass media declared the freeze a paper tiger.

This result strengthened those in the campaign who had been advocating greater electoral efforts. In June, local activists and national staff formed Freeze Voter, a political action committee they hoped would build political muscle for the movement. Despite these plans, the campaign suffered organizational problems during the summer. Many local activists believed that the national leadership had failed to develop programs that could generate the excitement of the referenda and the congressional resolution. This strategic drift was aggravated by a lack of communication among the national staff, now spread out through four offices around the country.[39] In August, the NWFC did conduct a political training institute for local activists from thirty-five states. Thousands of freeze campaign activists attended the twentieth anniversary Martin Luther King March in Washington for Jobs, Peace, and Justice.

In the fall, the NWFC tried to implement its goal of integrating fund raising with educational and political efforts by holding "Freeze Walks" in more than two hundred cities and towns on October 1. These walks became an important way for local groups to raise issues and funds. At the end of October, the NWFC held a series of rallies against the Euromissiles, but in November the British Parliament and the West German Bundestag voted to proceed with deployment. The first Euromissiles were deployed by the end of the month, and the Soviets shortly withdrew from the Intermediate Nuclear Forces (INF) talks. On October 31, the Senate tabled the Kennedy-Hatfield freeze resolution (similar to the House version) by a 59–40 vote. Although this represented a gain in support in the Republican-controlled Senate, it showed that the campaign still had a long way to go, reinforcing the decision to make the 1984 campaign theme "create a pro freeze government."

As 1984 approached, freeze activists and the rest of the nation began anticipating the presidential election as a mandate on Reagan's policies. To allow time to organize, the NWFC moved up the date of its fourth national conference from February 1984 to December 1983. Six hundred activists attended the conference in St. Louis December 2–3. The focus was on legislation. Because Congress in 1983 had passed both the nonbinding freeze resolution and funding for the MX, NWFC leaders decided to introduce binding legislation that would mandate a freeze. The question was what form the bill would take. Some arms control lobbyists argued that Congress could not be convinced that a production halt could be verified and that the campaign should limit the proposed legislation to testing and deployment. The conference voted to accept this more limited "quick freeze," despite the objections of some delegates who saw this as capitulation to politicians.

The issue of "direct action" (nonviolent civil disobedience) surfaced, as some in the campaign argued that resistance from the political establishment demanded more militant tactics. Others argued that direct action would endanger the freeze's mainstream appeal. The issue was debated for two years within the NWFC until the December 1985 national conference narrowly voted against engaging in direct action as an organization.[40] A few members angrily left the organization after this vote to establish a new group, the American Peace Test (APT), which sponsored actions at the Nevada underground test sites and elsewhere. Eventually, APT and NWFC leaders and members established a close working relationship similar to that between SANE and CNVA in the first few years of the test ban campaign.

At this December 1983 conference the relationship of interest was between the NWFC and Freeze Voter, now an independent political action committee (PAC) headed by Executive Director Bill Curry. As a non profit organization, the NWFC was prevented from working on elections. Like many such organizations it set up a PAC to do so. Although the NWFC could have formed and run directly an internal PAC, this would have been limited by federal election law to soliciting money and time from members of the parent organization. Because the NWFC had no formal membership program at the national level Freeze Voter was set up as a nominally independent organization.[41] At the time of the December 1983 conference, the two groups were still cooperating well. During 1984, however, relations often became strained over administrative issues, strategy, and competition for volunteers and donors (Solo 1988). Communication between the NWFC and Freeze Voter suffered.[42]

Problems between the NWFC organization and the freeze coalition members were already surfacing by the time of the conference. Local freeze activists had been demanding more of a voice in national decision making, and the campaign leadership had responded by changing the composition of the national committee from mostly representatives of peace groups to a majority of local- and state-level activists.

This change and what some saw as a narrowing of the campaign's agenda left several peace groups feeling pushed out of the campaign — which exacerbated tensions over funding and visibility.

Local activists on the decision-making bodies and at the conference pressed the national leadership to develop a strategy and devise projects that would provide a basis for reenergizing the grassroots. In response, the national leaders presented to the conference a set of three "citizen pressure directives" related to the national legislative and electoral goals. These directives involved grassroots lobbying of members of Congress, mobilizing volunteers for electoral work through local and state PACs, and additional actions including locally based, nationally coordinated demonstrations.

Some local activists shared with members of the freeze coalition the concern that the focus on legislation and elections was contributing to a narrowing of the campaign's scope. The conference voted to "continue [the campaign's] policy of keeping its strategic focus sharp — that is, on the Freeze itself—and its educational focus broad—that is, showing the conections between the Freeze and related economic and foreign policy issues."[43] Both the legislative and the electoral strategies encountered problems in 1984. In February, conflicts developed over the legislative strategy. The national campaign had decided on the quick freeze, which would be introduced in the House in May. Massachusetts Freeze activists asked the national committee to approve their plans to continue lobbying for a comprehensive freeze. Turned down, they persisted. The introduction of such legislation by a Massachusetts representative divided the campaign. Congress and the press began to view the NWFC as an organization incapable of managing its own agenda. Neither bill did well, although, in October, Congress did place some restrictions on administration requests for funding of the MX missile and antisatellite weapons.

Early in 1984, it had become clear that Reagan would be difficult to beat. He held a large lead in the polls over Walter Mondale, his likely Democratic opponent. The economy was beginning to recover from recession: unemployment had dropped from over 10 percent in late 1982 to 8 percent at the start of 1984.[44] Reagan also moved to take the peace issue away from the Democrats. In January, he proclaimed 1984 a "year of peace." Claiming that the United States could now bargain from strength, he invited the Soviets to rejoin the arms talks they had walked out on after the Euromissile deployment. At first the Soviets refused, partly to avoid giving Reagan the one issue on which he seemed vulnerable.[45] By midyear, however, their strategy changed. They began a series of public proposals and private discussions, including a September 1984 meeting between Reagan and the Soviet foreign minister.[46]

Despite his attempt to change image, Freeze Voter and the NWFC had no interest in Reagan. More difficult was the decision about what to do in the Democratic race. Bill Curry of Freeze Voter was a strong Mondale supporter; but both organizations were divided among supporters of several candidates, all of whom had pledged support for a freeze. Freeze Voter decided not to endorse before the primary; instead, it raised funds for the general election and worked with state groups on voter registration and education. This failure to endorse, Solo (1988) claims, disempowered national Freeze Voter, as candidates worked on gaining endorsements from state-level peace PACs, including several affiliated with or set up by state NWFC organizations.

Before and after the summer primaries, state and local freeze PACs with PACs set up by other peace groups, notably SANE and Women's Action for Nuclear Disarmament (WAND), recruited and trained thousands of volunteers to work for candidates. They also raised more than $5 million, an impressive figure far surpassed by PACs related to military contractors and conservative organizations.[47] These efforts marked the most serious involvement of the American peace movement in electoral politics. In congressional elections, four of the eight senatorial candidates and twenty-four of the thirty-seven candidates for House seats supported by peace groups did win, but the Reagan landslide buried the peace groups and other progressive forces and hastened the decline of the freeze campaign.

Decline and Merger, 1985–1987

The results of the 1984 elections completed the disappearance of the freeze movement from the national mass media that began after the 1983 House votes on the freeze and MX. According to journalist Mark Hertsgaard (1985), mainstream media generally cover a grassroots movement only when it produces a clear political effect. Although the Democratic presidential candidates had courted the freeze vote, only Senator Alan Cranston closely identified himself with the movement, and his candidacy had not gone very far.[48] In early 1985, the NWFC had more life than the media recognized. Despite the onset of national decline, state and local groups continued to increase in number and paid staff, although many seemed to be losing volunteer activism.[49] According to the campaign's own figures, the number of state and local freeze organizations increased from 1,333 in October 1984 to 1,481 in December 1985 to 1,824 in August 1986.[50]

Aware of their base but stung by their failure to change national politics, activists gathered again in St. Louis in December 1984, for the fifth national conference of the NWFC. The proposed strategy called for a turn inward and downward: inward, to build a "mature, nationally-organized movement that has the long-term staying power, goals, and commitment to achieve a Freeze" (Kehler, quoted in Marullo [forthcoming]); downward, as reflected in the conference theme "re-focus on the grassroots, re-localize the Freeze," in an effort to return to the original strength of the movement. Some believed that the NWFC had squandered this strength in a premature attempt to become a national force. Although they understood that the embrace of politicians like Kennedy had helped short-circuit the original strategy of slowly building local strength, they thought that leaders had too eagerly accepted this embrace and too willingly let politicians take public leadership of the movement.

It proved impossible to recapture the original momentum. Activists were discouraged, the national media and politicians saw the movement as declining if not dead, and funders were pulling back. The open and loose structure of the NWFC that had made it easy for grass-roots activists to build a movement now made it difficult to create the kind of long-lasting organization Kehler and others wanted. This was clearest in terms of funding. In 1984, the NWFC had experienced its first decline in funding, from the 1983 peak of $1.33 million to $1.23 million. More important than this slight decrease were warnings from the big foundations providing almost half this amount, and from some major donors, that they would begin to cut their support. They were responding to a perceived lack of national coordination within the campaign and following a policy common in foundation giving: providing seed money for an organization to establish itself rather than giving continuing support.[51]

Cesar Chavez, a keynote speaker at the conference, told how he had refused outside money from foundations when he organized the United Farmworkers Union (UFW). Instead, he had insisted that each member, no matter how poor, pay $3.50 per month in dues.[52] What he did not say—but it was clear to many—was that the NWFC had not only taken foundation money but had failed to use it to develop a long-term funding base, whether from member dues, contributions from local and state organizations, small donations from isolated supporters, or from other sponsors.

The conference also addressed problems in the campaign's decision-making process. Although the national conference and the national committee gave local activists the major say in national policy, many felt shut out of national decision making (Marullo [forthcoming]). On the other hand, national staff members thought that some decisions made at national conferences restricted their latitude and ability to exercise judgment. These two views were not necessarily contradictory. Both reflected the campaign's cumbersome decision-making structure. National conferences spent far too much time on details of strategy and implementation. There were no effective mechanisms for adjusting strategy between conferences or for developing long-term strategy.[53]

The conference heard a report from a structure task force appointed in 1984 and approved a more streamlined process that retained the final authority of the national conference but gave more power to the national committee and the executive committee.[54] The composition of the national committee was changed: to help rebuild the freeze coalition and broaden its base, seats were given to delegates from the national peace groups and to members of "underrepresented groups." Reflecting the growth in the state-level groups, each state was given representation. The report also called for the development of a membership program. Some still opposed this as excluding participants by erecting formal barriers and charging money, but most had come to agree with the report that a membership program would strengthen accountability and fund raising in what had become a formal organization. The conference instructed the national committee to develop a membership program, but it was not until 1986 that a pilot program would be started in eleven states.

Both conference and campaign were paying more attention to structural issues, but political strategy remained a key concern. Randall Forsberg, the author of the original Call to Halt, urged the campaign to adopt a broader agenda including opposition to military intervention.[55] This strategy also fit in the larger plan to rebuild the NWFC for the long term. The more mainstream politics responded to the movement, the more leaders and activists had been willing to narrow their demands to pass legislation and to elect politicians. Facing what some had argued all along was an intractable political system, the campaign returned to a wider focus, longer-term goals, and a renewed commitment to establishing a local grassroots base. The key goals for 1985 adopted at the conference included "teach the Freeze, activate supporters, and strengthen the organization."

Unfortunately for the national campaign, the turn to organizational matters came in a time of decline. State and local groups, although stronger than the national NWFC, could not replace foundation funding, which by 1987 dropped to $79,000 (from a 1983 peak of $571,000). Other sources did not increase enough to compensate for this loss. The total 1987 budget was only $8,000 more than the 1983 foundation funding.[56] This financial downturn required layoffs of staff—the national NWFC went from twenty-five national program staff in 1985 to twelve by June of 1986—and meant great difficulty maintaining any program. What saved the national office, ironically, was a merger with SANE. SANE had gone through a cycle during the test ban campaign similar to what the NWFC experienced in the 1980s. It too was left with a national office and no local funding base. SANE, however recovered from near-collapse in 1977 to build a large paper membership to complement its small chapter structure. As a result it had a relatively efficient and well-funded national office and more than $4 million in 1987 revenues vs. the NWFC's $570,000.[57] During the 1980s, SANE like other peace groups benefited from the new mobilization and adding to its membership and fund-raising base. Because SANE did not have an extensive grassroots network, the merger seemed to fit together two organizations with complementary strengths.

Until the merger was accomplished in 1987 (talks began in 1985 and plans were approved in December 1986), the NWFC was an organization in trouble. Retrenchment began in late 1984, when rumors hit the national conference that national offices would be consolidated in Washington, D.C. This measure was promoted by foundations and major donors who believed that having more than one national office increased communication problems and duplication of effort. The December 1984 national conference passed a resolution opposing the move, fearing that it would further separate local groups from the national campaign and end the NWFC's commitment to building a grassroots-based organization. Only a last-minute appeal from Randall Kehler led to the revocation of this resolution. The move itself, in early 1985, left many national staff and local activists unhappy. Most of the St. Louis–based staff members chose not to make the move.

Kehler's resignation as national coordinator, also announced in early 1985, allowed the campaign to close the Massachusetts office and consolidate the national staff in Washington. Although major funders had pushed for consolidation, Kehler's departure led to a further decline in foundation funding. As national spokesperson for the campaign since 1982, he had developed good relations with funders. His replacement, Jane Gruenebaum, could not match his fund-raising skills and resigned under pressure from the executive committee in 1986 after financial crises and further layoffs that included staff members who had been with the NWFC since it began.

Meanwhile, the NWFC struggled to hold together a program and to devise a long-term strategy in a context of international developments and change. In March 1985, Mikhail Gorbachev took power in the Soviet Union. He offered sweeping proposals to move the stalled arms control talks forward. In August, on the fortieth anniversary of the atomic bombing of Hiroshima, he began a unilateral moratorium on underground testing in an attempt to get the United States to agree to a comprehensive test ban (CTB). The United States maintained the position it had established in the early 1960s, opposing the ban on technical grounds, and refused to move despite improvements in monitoring technology and greater Soviet openness to on-site inspections.

The NWFC could not move into the space opened by Soviet initiatives. Media coverage had disappeared. After the 1984 elections, the freeze had virtually vanished from Capitol Hill. According to Waller (1987, 299) "Senators and congressmen marveled at the near silence compared to [1983] when their offices were flooded with antinuclear petitions and activists." This silence reflected the organizational weaknesses of the NWFC and the fading public appeal of its issues. Although the Soviets canceled their moratorium in early 1987 when the American position did not change, in October 1986, Reagan and Gorbachev, meeting in Reykjavik, Iceland, had discussed in general terms the goal of nuclear disarmament by the year 2000. Although spokespersons for the American government quickly backed away from this goal, the very discussion seemed to change the public perception of what was possible. Peace activists grew bolder about proclaiming more extensive goals in nuclear and conventional disarmament.

This changing context facilitated the merger between SANE and the NWFC. Although SANE had cooperated with the NWFC in lobbying and electoral work, it had maintained throughout the 1980s an agenda broader than that of the NWFC, dealing with the cold war, military intervention, and the transition to a peace economy.[58] With short-term prospects for a freeze still bleak, but with more extensive changes appearing as real possibilities, most NWFC leaders and activists embraced the broader agenda. In the December 1986 national conference, NWFC activists approved the merger by a nine-to-one ratio and adopted "common security" as the central policy goal for the new organization. Common security, an internationalist outlook, encompasses military, economic, and ecological issues, stressing the need for international cooperation in all these areas and greater equity among nations. The merger was also approved by the SANE board of directors at the end of 1986. Their agreement with this general goal was symbolized by the 1989 adoption of the new name for the organization: SANE/FREEZE, Campaign for Global Security.

The merger has had its tensions. SANE had built a national staff of thirty plus regionally based canvass staff. It was a professionalized organization. Most of its 140,000 members contributed money, not time, although there were some fifty local chapters (*Freeze Focus,* Winter 1987, 3). What many NWFC activists found significant was that SANE had been raising 90 percent of its budget in dues and additional contributions from this membership base.

The NWFC, on the other hand, still had not established a membership program. National fund raising and staff had declined. Despite declines in grassroots activism, it had maintained a network of more than one thousand local and state chapters. Of these, roughly forty had paid staff. Most remained volunteer-run. Freeze activists insisted that the new organization commit itself to maintaining and strengthening local grassroots organizing. The political impact of both SANE and the NWFC had declined in recent years. Both had gone through organizational crises. According to journalist John Judis (1987), during the peak of the freeze movement, it was SANE that had developed "the most respected and feared arms control lobby on Capitol Hill," relying on its isolated membership for letters to Congress and for the funding that paid for lobbyists, two full time and one half time. Interpersonal conflicts and disagreements over strategy among staff and leaders led to a loss of some staff and an uncertainty in direction. The lobbying effort flagged and lost respect. Judis commented that "people in the Washington arms control community believe that SANE's principal activity has become raising money for itself." SANE leaders answered that their electoral and lobbying work were still strong—but clearly they saw the merger as a chance to reinvigorate these efforts.[59]

The merger caused a clash of organizational cultures.[60] Many SANE leaders had been active in the organization for a long time, some since its inception. Their perspective linked critiques of militarism, capitalism, and other issues. They saw the NWFC as too narrow and technologically focused. Many freeze activists viewed SANE's structure as too centralized, and SANE's leaders as not strongly committed to grassroots organizing and participation. The organizations managed these tensions well enough to keep the process on track, although not without false starts and problems. Local activists who felt shut out of initial plans made their feelings known to the national staff and leadership.[61] During 1987, staff and leaders of both the NWFC and SANE traveled the country in a "listening project" to hear what local and state leaders and staff members had to say. They heard widespread support for the merger, but concerns as well. Freeze activists were especially emphatic about maintaining the grassroots focus of their organization. Where chapters of both groups existed (state or local or both) there were conflicts over whether and how to merge.

These and other concerns dragged the merger process out over 1987. A transition team of staff and leaders from both groups met throughout the year. They developed a structure combining those of the two organizations: SANE/FREEZE would have an annual meeting (the national congress) where representatives elected by congressional district would vote on key issues. A board of directors would exercise substantial authority and guide less chaotic, more informed policy formulation and decision making. The board would include representatives of statewide chapters who would elect a second group of at-large members to broaden the base of the organization and make room for former leaders.

In November 1987, one thousand activists attended the first national congress of SANE/FREEZE in Cleveland. They approved this structure and four political goals to guide the organization through to the year 2000: a nuclear freeze and eventual nuclear disarmament, with reductions in conventional weapons; changing foreign and military policies to end intervention, protect human rights, and promote social and economic development; cutting military spending and promoting economic reconstruction through conversion to a civilian economy; and improving international relations. The strategy would remain focused on electoral work, lobbying, and education. Freeze Voter remained a separate organization; SANE/FREEZE incorporated SANE's PAC. The new organization would be, like SANE, a membership-based organization, making this internal PAC more effective.[62]

After local and state chapters merged and after some initial erosion, SANE/FREEZE had more than 170,000 members in more than 270 state and local groups and 30 state affiliates. Problems in management and fund-raising soon led to large deficits and the layoff of al-

most one-fourth of the national staff. By the fall of 1990, SANE/
FREEZE was down to 250 state and local affiliates and 130,000 mem-
bers. The national staff had been cut that year alone from 24 to 16
(*Nuclear Times,* Autumn 1990, 7). By early 1993, according the SANE/
FREEZE national office, the organization had further declined in size
to about 100,000 members in 200 state and local affiliates.

These problems have kept the campaign from adequately managing its political programs and serving state and local groups. Formally
affiliating state groups continued to be difficult. Some groups were
reluctant to affiliate once they saw a dropoff in national services; the
varying structures of state groups continued to complicate plans for
joint membership programs and revenue sharing. Nevertheless, SANE/
FREEZE opened its first regional office in Atlanta, in an attempt to
establish a southern base and build ties to the southern African-
American community. It also established a small international office
in an attempt to overcome an insularity typical of the moderate wing
of the American peace movement, including the NWFC.

The political program has evolved along with the dramatic changes
in world events, including the breakup of the Warsaw Pact and the
fragmentation of the Soviet Union. SANE/FREEZE has continued
to emphasize the danger of nuclear weapons and of nuclear proliferation, despite public perceptions that the end of the cold war has
eliminated the arms race. With more nations on the verge of developing nuclear weapons, SANE/FREEZE has focused on achieving a
comprehensive test ban, a measure more modest but more politically
acceptable to American politicians than a full-fledged freeze. Some
argue that until the superpowers halt testing and developing new
weapons, nonnuclear powers will be less inclined to continue to observe
their end of the nonproliferation Treaty, in which they pledged to refrain
from developing nuclear weapons. The Bush administration resisted
growing congressional and international pressure to negotiate a CTB.

A lower priority has been opposition to nonnuclear military intervention abroad. Since Vietnam, the United States has shifted its
intervention policy in two directions. First, by fighting proxy wars in
what some have called "low-intensity conflicts," using groups such as
the Nicaraguan contras to continue to impose American policies on
Third World nations. Second, by limited direct intervention in fights
that could be won quickly, such as Grenada, Panama, and the Persian
Gulf War. SANE/FREEZE and other peace groups have found these
wars harder to oppose because they kill and injure far fewer American troops than do wars like Korea and Vietnam, although they are

devastating to the nations where they are fought. Nevertheless, local chapters of SANE/FREEZE and other groups provided a core of opposition to the Gulf War that formed much more quickly than had opposition to the Vietnam War.

Working for a peace economy has emerged as the organization's major goal and central organizing tool.[63] During the 1980s, military spending had soared while social programs were slashed. Many cities and regions fell into severe economic decline, and the American economy became less competitive internationally. Many see economic conversion as the key to reversing these trends, a goal that will allow the peace movement to build coalitions with organizations representing those most hurt by the loss of jobs and social programs, including civil rights, labor, and women's groups, and small business.

SANE/FREEZE has made organization building a priority from the start, something neither parent organization did, but it is a priority in a time of decline. Initially, the organization envisioned growing to include 1 million members by 1997, with chapters in every congressional district and affiliates in every state, and a strong national office with a vigorous field program operating from regional offices. It now finds itself struggling to integrate the existing chapters into a smaller but effective national structure and to develop a political strategy capable of keeping current activists working and attracting new ones.

Impact of the Freeze Campaign

Many polls and observers have concluded that the freeze campaign managed to raise awareness of the threat of nuclear war and to raise and maintain strong (60 percent and above) support for a mutual freeze on nuclear weapons (WAND 1986, Americans Talk Security 1988). During the rise of the freeze, campaign pollsters remarked on the rapid movement of the nuclear issue to the top of the list of social problems and on the strong desire of Americans to move toward arms control and reductions. In 1984, Daniel Yankelovich reported that 61 percent of the public favored a six-month unilateral freeze to see if the Soviets would respond (Hertsgaard 1985,44).

The campaign's net impact on public opinion is probably similar to its effect on policy: it helped move both back toward the middle. Since 1945, there has been consistent support for arms control talks on the one hand and the maintenance of deterrent forces and parity in nuclear forces on the other. The freeze campaign's ability to draw on both positions and to paint Reagan as opposed to them helps explain its great popularity (Waller 1987, 32). It also explains some limitations of the campaign. The freeze built on fears that war fighting was replacing deterrence and that the end of arms control talks signaled an escalation in superpower hostility. Once Reagan resumed the talks and talked peace rather than war, fear rapidly declined.

As Daniel Ellsberg and others have noted, the freeze did not convince many that the arms race itself presented an urgent and imminent threat. The movement helped persuade the public that nuclear war could not be won, but it did not make the point that it should not be threatened (Peck 1985). Therefore, support for developing new weapons systems remains high, as does support for at least some SDI research (Americans Talk Security, no. 12). Fear of war has been reduced to the point where it does not make top-ten lists of perceived social problems, and confidence in deterrence remains.

Critics of the freeze campaign who, with the campaign's leaders, had hoped for more profound change, argue that the narrow message and scare tactics of the freeze contributed to the lack of deeper changes and the transience of the issue (Sandman and Valenti 1986, Solo 1988). Others point to the extensive use of polling and the sophisticated packaging of messages practiced by the Reagan administration (WAND 1986). Polls have shown a big shift in views on the military budget, from support for more spending to support for major reductions. This shift began in the late 1980s and accelerated with the breakup of the Soviet Union in 1992.

There has been substantial progress in arms control since the end of the nuclear freeze campaign. In 1987, the United States and the Soviet Union signed the INF treaty, which removed both the Euromissiles and the Soviet intermediate-range missiles targeting Western Europe. The 1991 START Treaty eliminated thousands of strategic warheads from American and Soviet arsenals. In January 1993, President George Bush and Russian President Boris Yeltsin signed a START 2 Treaty that would reduce the superpower strategic arsenals by two-thirds.

Political changes in the Soviet Union and its successor states helped bring about both these treaties and the end of the cold war. The Gorbachev-led reforms of the Soviet Union greatly eased superpower tensions, which were virtually ended with the breakup of the Soviet Union. Conservatives credit the Reagan and Bush administrations' hard-line policies for pressuring the Soviet Union into reform and political collapse. Others such as Meyer (1990B) argue that the Western peace movement of the 1980s, including the nuclear freeze campaign, had more to do with the end of the cold war. They claim that this movement prevented further escalation of the arms race in the early 1980s, helped push the United States to the bargaining table, and encouraged reformers in the East.

Despite these gains, the remaining superpower arsenals retain their devastating power, and political instability in the former Soviet Union has raised concerns about control of nuclear weapons. Proliferation of nuclear weapons continues, as post–Gulf War discoveries about Iraq's nuclear program dramatized. Wars in Eastern Europe and the Third World show that the end of the cold war does not mean peace. War grows ever more deadly, as the major powers continue to increase their arms sales around the world.

Whatever its role in promoting the progress that has been made, the freeze did not achieve its main policy goal. Its greatest direct impact on the arms race has been to encourage congressional action to limit administration plans for new weapons and SDI, and to block attempts to break away from past treaty limits.[64] Since the mid-1980s, Congress consistently has cut back on proposed military budgets. These actions are significant by themselves and as indicators of a change in the policy-making process. The nuclear freeze campaign helped embolden Congress to take a more active role, although one still subordinate to that of the executive branch.[65] Congress as a whole has not sought radical cuts in military spending or weapons, nuclear or conventional, but it was a moderating force on the Reagan and Bush administrations.

More than any previous peace campaign, the freeze has changed the American peace movement. The freeze campaign peaked in the mid-1980s with as many as 10 million participants in 6,000 organizations, both peace groups and other groups cooperating with the campaign. After that, activism declined but organizations continued to proliferate; by 1990, there were still a half-million activists in 7,500 groups with a primary or secondary focus on peace (Lofland, Colwell, and Johnson 1990). More than 5,000 of these organizations were established in the years from 1980 to 1988. Most were small local groups with budgets of less than $30,000 (Colwell 1989). New national organizations formed and old ones revived, and many of these also continue. Organizations such as PSR have lost members and funding since the peak of the campaign, but they still maintain memberships and political activity far above 1980 levels: PSR in 1987 claimed a national membership of 70,000, whereas in 1979 there were only a few hundred members.

The peace movement has become institutionalized in several contexts, including in curricula at all levels of education (Wehr 1986). Many colleges and universities began peace studies programs and added courses in war, peace, and international relations. Funding for peace research has dropped since the mid-1980s peak, but it too seems to have undergone a ratchet effect and is more substantial than a decade ago. Many religious congregations have maintained their focus on peace and justice, with Central America often replacing the freeze as a main concern. The established peace groups, both those closely involved with the NWFC and those that distanced themselves, continue to maintain the traditions of the modern peace movement and to support organizing on a range of issues and in a variety of contexts. The impact of the freeze campaign on these groups is unclear but should be investigated. The campaign, deliberately creating a "broad front door" by keeping the issue simple, brought into the movement people who gained experience and skills and are now using them in other organizations and on other issues.[66]

It is harder to assess the effect of the freeze on the peace movement outside its organizations. Many thousands of people who worked on the freeze are no longer members of organized peace groups. Some may be active in other social change organizations; most probably are not. Nevertheless, their participation in the freeze may have long-lasting effects on their beliefs about nuclear weapons, American foreign policy, and politics. Having been part of a vital grassroots movement, they may be more likely to join another one in the future, and the experience and skills they gained during the freeze may prove important.

Organizational Tensions

Although the nuclear freeze campaign differed in many critical ways from the previous two peace campaigns, it shared the same set of organizational tensions that greatly affected its course and outcome. The freeze campaign began as a coalition of peace groups that very quickly and deliberately expanded to include local activists inside and outside the peace movement. Although the peace groups were not as clearly divided into two camps as in earlier times, there was a wide range of perspectives among them and important differences between their views and those of arms control expert Randall Forsberg. Despite these differences, the peace groups and the many local activists they brought in cooperated in starting and running the campaign.

Tensions within the early coalition centered on ideological and organizational issues. Although there was consensus that the freeze was the single issue that could unite the coalition and motivate public action, there were disagreements over how to promote it. A fairly narrow appeal prevailed, based on arms control language rather than deeper analyses of the cold war and internationalism, and limiting or excluding discussions of issues such as economic conversion. This was partly a strategic decision to keep the appeal simple. It also seems to reflect a tendency in short-term coalitions to seek the least common denominator in rhetoric and goals. Some Left-leaning peace groups, not satisfied with this solution, distanced themselves from the freeze campaign.

The campaign's structural plans differed from those of previous campaigns, but, like them, reflected a short-term orientation and tensions between established groups: the EPC was envisioned as a sponsored organization, and SANE was to be a small ad hoc coalition with few organizational trappings, while the freeze was intended to become a large, mostly independent campaign. Unlike the EPC sponsors, the peace groups in 1980 could not provide a large national presence. Unlike the founders of the test ban campaign, most of those who started the freeze campaign believed that they would have to mobilize grassroots activism to achieve their goals.

Tensions over leadership and organizational turf similar to those in the earlier campaigns were present in the freeze coalition. Together with a post-1960s distrust of centralization, they led to the establishment of a loose network for the NWFC, an absence of strong national leadership, and a failure to develop a strategy for organization building. The failure to build was also influenced by the optimistic belief that a freeze could be won in five years.[67] As the campaign went on, the nature of the coalition changed. The growing appeal of the freeze, both as an issue and as a vehicle to express opposition to the Reagan administration, brought in new groups and constituencies. The embrace of the liberal establishment and the early departure of the more radical peace groups shifted the center of gravity of the coalition to the Center.

The early success of the freeze and the move to Congress kept the coalition together and focused, although some peace groups felt eclipsed in terms of attention and fund raising. Even as the NWFC developed more independence as an organization, the coalition continued outside the formal structure of the NWFC, as many groups cooperated on lobbying and other tasks. Once the campaign began to decline in visibility, impact, and fund raising, the centrifugal forces typical of coalitions had greater effect, and the peace movement lost its central focus. Groups returned to business as usual or found new projects.

For the NWFC itself, the transition from coalition to independent organization was not blocked, as in the EPC, by strong peace groups, or disrupted, as in the test ban campaign, by a major split among wings of the peace movement. Within three years of its beginning, the campaign was independent of the peace groups and still growing, with a large base of local and state NWFC groups. As an independent organization, the NWFC had important strengths and key weaknesses. Its greatest strength was what the founders had planned, local grass-roots activism. When the campaign hit political obstacles, however, it became clear that the organizational structure was better-suited to mobilizing this activism than it was to sustaining it or integrating it with professional and national work.

Tensions between the freeze-as-coalition and freeze-as-organization became clear during this transition process, as local activists gradually replaced peace group representatives from the governing structure of the NWFC. The energies and attention of the national staff turned to fostering local groups rather than maintaining the coalition. Competition for resources and visibility also increased. At first all groups had seemed to benefit from the growth in participation and funding that accompanied the rise of the freeze.[68] Over time, though, some in the peace groups found themselves overshadowed by the freeze organization that they had helped create. Fearing that the campaign had become the movement in the eyes of the public and potential donors, they anticipated a loss of identity and fund-raising ability.

Kehler addressed the organization-coalition problem in a June 1984 article, "We Need A Common Voice," in *Nuclear Times*.[69] He argued that "We are not, in fact, a disarmament movement. We are a collection of disarmament organizations." He acknowledged some responsibility on the part of the NWFC for the collapse of the coalition. The NWFC had expended most of its energy on encouraging the growth of local groups, and had neglected the hard work of holding together a national coalition. Strategically, he acknowledged that many groups had been unhappy with the NWFC's overwhelming emphasis on passing a nonbinding resolution, and that their criticism of this strategy may have been correct. Kehler argued that the freeze was still the key to ending the arms race and urged peace and arms control groups to suspend their "institutional egos" and re-create the freeze coalition by cooperating strategically and organizationally in fieldwork and fund-raising programs. *Nuclear Times* polled a cross-section of national and local leaders, who agreed by a two-to-one margin on the need to re-create a larger coalition or federation. Most favored a broad "peace and justice" platform (*Nuclear Times*, Oct./Nov. 1984). This did not come about, however, as the movement declined and competition for funding, members, and other resources increased. Each organization needed, as Kehler put it, "to carve out its own niche in the disarmament field" (Kehler 1984).

The freeze campaign departed from earlier peace campaigns by emphasizing local organizing and by succeeding in this arena. It built on the work of post-Vietnam organizers for the peace movement and other movements, who had established a network of local peace activists, some affiliated with the established peace groups, some with new groups including the NWFTF, and some independent. The founders of the NWFC reached out to these groups and other local organizers, bringing them into the planning and initial work of the campaign. Through local referenda and resolutions, and such things as town meetings, these organizers extended this base quickly and established more than one thousand NWFC chapters.[70]

The local work drew on more than the freeze issue. It developed a populist appeal based on the notion that ordinary people should have some say in nuclear policy. Another strategic advantage to local work was that local elites and local media were, in most places, more sympathetic to the freeze than were national elites caught up in the military-industrial complex. The local groups mobilized an unprecedented number of activists, and many of these groups found ways to institutionalize themselves after the decline of the initial wave of grassroots enthusiasm. After the passage of referenda and the House resolution, however, most felt cast adrift in terms of strategy, unable to come up with ways to maintain local programs capable of attracting and retaining volunteers. This problem was partly structural; arms control is a nationally decided issue, and the NWFC had limited itself to an arms control focus. The referenda were a clever way of localizing a national issue, but they had run their course. Only after the merger, when SANE/FREEZE made economic issues central, did the organization establish a strong foundation for renewed local activism.

The national clearinghouse began as a small office in St. Louis that did a good job of catalyzing local activism by providing organizing ideas and resources while holding together the freeze coalition. As the campaign grew, the national office had to manage the congressional lobbying effort while continuing the coalition work and the job of servicing a rapidly expanding set of local chapters. The increase in outside resources that accompanied the campaign's rise allowed the national office(s) to add staff to do all these jobs, but none was done well. The NWFC's leaders and staff lacked political and lobbying experience, the coalition was neglected, and the local chapters complained of a lack of national leadership, although the small field program helped some local chapters.

Relations between the national office and local chapters also changed over time. Foundation and major donor funding allowed the clearinghouse to develop without direct support from the locals, which benefited from national leadership and assistance but did not have to support it financially through dues sharing or other contributions. This situation proved fragile. As outside resources declined, other support, including that from the locals, did not rise enough to maintain national staff and program.

SANE had discovered during the test ban campaign that it was impossible to squeeze enough money out of local chapters to support the national office. The NWFC, like SANE, did try to increase local contributions. The February 1983 national conference approved a measure "encouraging" local groups to contribute 5 percent of their income to the national campaign, but these contributions actually fell in 1984 to below the 1983 figure of $15,000. They never accounted for more than 10 percent of the national budget.[71] In 1985, the NWFC attempted to formalize revenue sharing by establishing a national membership program in which members of local or state organizations, or both, also became national members. This plan did not go very far, partly because of variations in local and state groups. Some had paid staff, large paper memberships, and few active chapters; others were more grassroots in composition. No one plan could satisfy all groups, especially when fund raising was falling and money was tight.[72] Yet, negotiating dozens of separate agreements seemed impossible. Cesar Chavez's speech at the 1985 national conference may have been a pointed message to local and state groups to increase their contributions to the national NWFC to make up for the anticipated decline in outside funding, but it was a difficult message to accept and implement.

Local and state groups failed to provide adequate financial support to the national office for several reasons. The local strategy of the NWFC meant that national leaders were inclined to encourage local activists to keep the resources they raised for local work. The national office for some years did not need local support. Local chapters established themselves without hands-on help from the national office. The loose structure of the organization did not include any rules for local contributions and had no mechanisms to enforce guidelines. The Freeze had established state-level organizations and developed local- or state-level professionalism. The early use of state referenda as an organizing tool and the focus in some states on U.S. Senate races led to the formation of many state-level freeze organizations. Some were loose networks, but others became formal organizations. Many hired staff members, as did some local chapters. By the end of 1984, there were thirty-six state and local NWFC offices with paid staff members.[73] Local and state groups that hired staff thereby committed money to their salaries, leaving less money for contributions to the national office.

Local-national relations changed in governance as well as funding. Local organizers were involved with the NWFC from the start, and the authority of the national conference gave local activists an important role in decision making. As the campaign evolved, local chapters began to demand and to get a major role in the other national policy-making bodies, while the peace groups lost influence. Throughout the campaign local and state organizations had complete autonomy in setting their own programs.

Overall, the history of local-national developments, relations, and tensions within the NWFC was similar to that of SANE. A loose network structure, useful for the early stages of a campaign, gave way to a more formal federated organization that was more successful in integrating local organizations into the governance structure than it was in building a local financial base for the national office. Nevertheless, the NWFC combined vigorous local organizing with occasionally strong national political work. The interaction between the two levels, though strained, often benefited both. Even with the decline experienced by the NWFC and SANE/FREEZE, beyond the merged national organization there is a legacy of more than two hundred local chapters and state chapters in most states.

The most striking feature of the freeze campaign was the extent and intensity of grassroots participation. Unfortunately, there are no good figures available to document how many people went to meetings, lobbied local and national elites, attended rallies, held house meetings, put up posters, signed up petitioners, or did any of the other tasks that typified the early freeze movement. The 20,000 claimed by the NWFC campaign in 1983 at the peak of this activism is more than likely an underestimate. First, within the NWFC, there were 1,800 chapters. The NWFC's count of 20,000 therefore included only ten or so core activists per chapter. Based on my observations of the organization and on the usual composition of highly mobilized SMOs, I will assume that each chapter had another fifteen to twenty occasional activists, which would bring the total number of activists within the NWFC to between 45,000 and 72,000. This is a large increase over SANE's total of 175 chapters and 4,000 to 7,000 activists during the test ban campaign. Also, the NWFC's own count includes those affiliated with local NWFC groups but omits people working on the freeze through religious congregations and other local organizations and networks. Lofland, Colwell, and Johnson (1990) estimate that 10 million people in 6,000 organizations — peace movement groups and other organizations with an interest in peace — participated in the freeze campaign.

The grassroots proliferation of the freeze occurred because the campaign had planned a grassroots strategy from the start, using networks built by peace, environmental, and community organizers. Activism spread quickly through these and other networks, especially religious congregations. Many, possibly most, local groups were started by people with no previous social movement experience, but in many places veterans of the movements of the 1960s and 1970s played an important role. The issue was framed to have immediate appeal, and the movement provided a means for expressing opposition to the right turn of national politics. The NWFC proclaimed itself a grassroots-based movement, and many leaders and activists saw it in this light, consciously opposing this to what they saw as its antithesis, a professionalized organization. Nevertheless, the NWFC from the start used paid staff to coordinate grassroots organizing. When the freeze issue went national, the huge influx of outside funds allowed the campaign to hire more staff to do lobbying and publicity and to coordinate the growing number of local chapters and activists.

The success of the NWFC in catalyzing grassroots activism was not matched by success in the external and internal tasks associated with formal, professionalized organization. Both lobbying and public relations suffered from inexperience and lack of strategic planning (Meyer 1990A, Solo 1988, Waller 1987, WAND 1986). Like the peace groups from which it emerged, the NWFC tended to have staff who were better at organizing than at working with Congress or the national media. The overall strategic planning process was often weak, management was inconsistent, and communication between different leaders, offices, and organizations (such as the NWFC and Freeze Voter) was frequently poor.[74]

The professional and grassroots aspects of the NWFC coexisted uneasily. The national office did devote most of its staff time early on, and a substantial amount later, to nurturing the grassroots proliferation of the movement. Most activists looked to the national staff for leadership and resources and, at the same time, insisted that the campaign be run by and for the grassroots. Sometimes this became a strongly antileadership attitude that saw almost any aspect of formalism and professionalism as threatening the grassroots campaign. This attitude contributed to the campaign's failure to develop a national membership program and to problems in efficient planning and administration.[75]

Professionalism did at times conflict with grassroots activism. There were tendencies within the national leadership toward oligarchy, at least in the form of top-down planning that slighted the needs and wishes of local leaders. More critically, the NWFC did turn away from an emphasis on local grassroots organizing in 1983, when strategy focused on passing a congressional resolution. National and local leaders developed grassroots lobbying tactics, but the success or failure of the NWFC now depended on the actions of a national elite rather than on local campaigns. The 1983 congressional votes and the 1984 elections, on which the campaign had placed so much emphasis, led to grassroots disillusionment and disempowerment.[76]

Although some see the NWFC as simply a case of political incorporation and cooptation in which liberal foundations bought off the movement, the relations between funding, strategy, and the course of the campaign were not simple. It is true that major foundations became key sponsors of the NWFC in 1982. From 1983 through 1986 foundations funded almost half the national campaign budget.[77] There were probably several motives behind this increase, including some sincere desire for reform. Those most critical of the foundations that supported the freeze see in them an East Coast liberal establishment tied to real estate and multinational business and seeking a vehicle to oppose Reagan administration policies harmful to these interests.[78] Others argue that major funders like to be where the political action is, to maintain their influence (Senturia interview). In this view, foundations follow rather than lead, although their impact may be large.

NWFC leaders did not simply take foundation and major donor money and use it to hire lobbyists and publicists, ignoring grassroots activists. In fact, some of this money was used to develop a field program based in St. Louis, while the Washington office in 1983 had only three full-time staff members involved in legislative and media work.[79] The embrace of the NWFC by some national elites, both funders and politicians, did encourage the shift in strategy that moved the campaign away from a grassroots focus. More direct was the influence of funders who insisted that national offices be consolidated in Washington in 1985. Many local leaders saw this move creating an unbridgeable gulf between national leaders and grassroots activists.[80] Professionalism therefore was part of a complicated process that hurt the grassroots base of the movement and narrowed strategy. No one knows how long grassroots activism could have been sustained, but most observers believe that its decline was hastened by the processes and decisions described.

Once the campaign was in decline, formalization and professionalism assisted the survival of many local and state organizations, as former volunteers became staff whose pay, though small, was enough to keep them working on the freeze and related issues long after national publicity died and volunteer activism greatly decreased. The relations between professionalism and grassroots mobilization probably vary across these locals. In some cases, staff may encourage and help sustain volunteer activism; in others, they may replace and discourage it.

Like SANE during the test ban campaign, the NWFC developed a strategy and a structure that catalyzed widespread mobilization and raised the issue of nuclear war to the forefront of public debate. Both campaigns were driven by popular enthusiasm for a simple goal, and both became vehicles for the expression of general political dissent. They peaked in three years then declined as a combination of political obstacles and questionable decisions slowed the initial momentum of the campaign, and the key organization had difficulty in establishing a structure that could fight an extended battle.

The early structures were loose confederations between a network of local chapters and a small national office, with a strong coalition of peace and other groups cooperating at both levels. Over the course of the campaigns, each coalition broke apart and the central organization became more independent and more of a formal federation. Tensions between local organizing and national coordination were expressed as problems in federating. For the NWFC, which had developed a much larger grassroots component, tensions between professionalism and grassroots organizing also increased. Like SANE, the NWFC survived as a smaller organization after the campaign. As the central goals of a comprehensive test ban and a freeze receded, the organizations focused on broader issues.

The three sets of organizational tensions interacted most clearly in conflicts between achieving short-term mobilization and sustaining activism over the long term. The NWFC's strategy, structure, and main tactics proved almost ideal for the short run. The key goal of a nuclear freeze was simple and compelling, and the appeal was kept simple and almost ideologically neutral, giving the freeze a broad front door. The loose confederation gave local activists the initiative, and the national office developed supporting materials and organizing ideas (at no cost to local leaders). The referenda gave local activists an immediate goal that generated excitement and publicity and that could be won.

This strategy and structure held up well during the rise of the NWFC, but problems were papered over by a great increase in outside funding and ignored during a brief honeymoon between the campaign and national political figures and the mass media. The turning point came in 1983 when the attention of these national leaders and institutions preempted the campaign's strategy of local base building by raising the freeze to the top of the national agenda. In this test of the campaign's leaders, strategy, and structure, all came up short.

The NWFC leadership lost, or gave up, much of the control of the campaign both strategically and organizationally by placing so much emphasis on the congressional resolution and by allowing congressional leaders to define the terms of debate. Clearly, the NWFC faced a dilemma, as Congress was going ahead no matter what. In retrospect, most Freeze leaders agree that they rushed in too quickly without enough political sophistication (Ferguson 1987). Not just the congressional strategy but totally focusing on the freeze proved a problem in the longer term. The emphasis on a freeze, framed in narrow and often technical terms, made it easy for the Reagan administration to counter with a combination of conciliatory language, symbolic reassurance by restarting arms control talks, and visions of strategic defense. Key structural problems involved each of the three sets of organizational tensions I have discussed. Political setbacks starting in 1983 exposed these problems.

As the NWFC became an independent organization, the coalition members were displaced from their leadership positions. Resentment over this and over the monopoly the NWFC had gained on national publicity was held in check by the popularity of the freeze and the focus on the congressional resolution. After the MX vote, tensions within the coalition were more freely expressed, and many peace groups turned to other issues. The national office had become dependent on outside funding that started to decline after 1983, and the organization did not find substitutes. Despite appeals and efforts, local chapters did not support the national office.

Freeze leaders and activists had not solved the problem of integrating professional work into an organization committed to grassroots organizing. Some argue that the issue had not even been addressed and debated.[81] After the heady days of national attention had passed, the campaign found that grassroots activism was in decline, and that it had no plan for relocalizing the NWFC and reenergizing activists. The underlying problems of the NWFC were not caused simply by poor decisions made in 1983 or at the start of the campaign. Tensions within the initial coalition made it more likely that the campaign would emerge with a narrow focus to keep the coalition broad, and a short-term structure, because an organization is not likely to create a long-term rival. Also, tensions and rivalries may have prevented the emergence of leaders and a decision-making process oriented toward a long-term view.

Although the failure to solve organizational tensions contributed to the NWFC's political failures, the campaign managed the tensions well enough to generate an important movement and leave a legacy whose impact is yet to be determined. The most important organizational legacy may be at the local level, reflecting the NWFC's emphasis on local grassroots activism.

The Organizational Dynamics of Modern American Peace Campaigns

The EPC, the test ban campaign and SANE, and the NWFC all succeeded in uniting a fractious peace movement behind one or two key goals, in presenting a strong case for those goals, in mobilizing significant support, and in affecting foreign and military policy. None, however, achieved its key goal or goals. Political factors were critical in establishing the conditions for mobilization and the limits of success, but given these conditions and limits, the ways in which the campaigns organized themselves had a critical impact on their course and outcomes. Especially important was how the campaigns managed the organizational tensions inherent in their efforts.

These tensions were presented as sets of two potentially incompatible tasks: managing a coalition while building an independent organization, working at both local and national levels, and mobilizing both professional expertise and grassroots activism. All three campaigns managed these tensions well enough to start and sustain a major mobilization. At times the campaigns even found ways to make two tasks complementary rather than conflictual. Eventually, however, organizational tensions contributed to the decline and end of the campaigns. These similarities and key differences between the campaigns provide the basis for a better understanding of them and for a deeper exploration of the nature of the organizational tensions and of social movement campaigns. They also allow for the clarification of key concepts such as professionalism, and the identification of any significant trends over time.

Coalition-Organization

The campaigns were started by coalitions of peace organizations, including the major organizations started during and just after World War I, such as the AFSC. The campaigns were a top priority for these groups, and they devoted much of their time and energy to forming a coalition that could launch a major campaign. Many coalitions are not the central focus of all or even some of their member organizations, and their dynamics may differ from those that are.

All the coalitions succeeded in increasing the size and impact of the peace movement. During the EPC and possibly during the NWFC (in lobbying), the campaign organization duplicated some of the efforts of the existing groups; the gains were not simply from a better division of labor. Rather, the combined groups concentrated their forces at a key moment, bringing to the movement new attention and, during the antinuclear campaigns, new resources.

Against these advantages for the organizations were several threats, including loss of visibility and perhaps supporters and resources, loss of control over political goals and strategies, and disproportionate contributions to the coalition. Politically, the tensions were managed by focusing on one or two shared goals and by using institutional strategies, not just to appeal to the public but also to keep the more moderate groups in the coalition. Organizationally, the coalition members managed these tensions in different ways. The EPC began with a time limit of two years. The test ban campaign created a second, more radical organization. The freeze campaign created a loose network, freeing the member groups of the need to coordinate the campaign tightly.

Over time the coalition members drifted or split apart. The split between pacifists and liberals during the EPC ended the campaign. The test ban coalition was torn by the Dodd affair but survived in a weakened state. The freeze coalition slowly disintegrated as the political prospects for the campaign dimmed. Both antinuclear campaigns tried to reforge a coalition but failed. These experiences illustrate the power of the centrifugal forces within coalitions and suggest that organizations are more likely to form coalitions at a time of threat and opportunity than at a time of movement decline. A more common response to movement downturn and the loss of resources may be merger: SANE tried to merge with the UWF at the end of the test ban campaign, and the NWFC did merge with SANE.

There were important differences in the composition and meaning of the coalitions. The peace groups were more sharply divided into two or three camps at the start of the EPC, and the campaign was dominated by the more radical wing made up of pacifist groups and those close to pacifism. They kept neutrality a major demand, despite the internationalists' misgivings, which deepened over time. The EPC therefore represented less than its public face, because the campaign masked disagreement over a key goal. There was also disagreement within the antinuclear coalitions, but not because any partners disagreed with their main goals. Rather, the disputes were over how far to link these goals with more long-term goals and with a broader analysis of the underlying problems. These campaigns represented more than their public face, serving as vehicles for dissent at times when other movements were quiet. The symbolic meaning of movements may be as important as their manifest goals.

Like many coalitions, the peace campaigns created umbrella organizations to coordinate activism. The EPC was the closest to a pure coalition manager; SANE, CNVA, and the NWFC became independent organizations. Their histories reinforce the belief that umbrella organizations tend toward independence, and they help explain why. Staff, volunteers, and contributors are attracted by the goals and tactics of the campaign, and in affiliating with the new organization develop political, social, and sometimes career interests in maintaining it. The EPC is the exception that proves the rule, as it took deliberate plans and continuing vigilance by the peace groups to check tendencies toward independence.

Both the EPC and the NWFC were given the job of managing the campaign; the test ban campaign created two organizations. SANE was most like the EPC and the NWFC, as it was the major campaign organization. CNVA began and remained a small group whose members engaged in direct actions. The early ones helped the campaign gain public attention and support; the later ones seemed to have little impact. The two-organization structure did affect the internal dynamics of the campaign. It was intended to give the campaign more diversity in tactics without making this diversity a source of additional tensions. Nevertheless, differences between radical pacifists and the moderate leaders of SANE surfaced, more over how to deal with Senator Dodd and the Communist issue than over tactics. These differences led to estrangement between the organizations and to splits within SANE.

Beyond both the conflicts inherent in coalitions and the difficulties experienced by umbrella organizations there are tensions between the coalitions and the organizations they create. Umbrella organizations heighten the concerns that accompany a coalition. Because they are founded on the most publicly attractive goals and strategies, they may bring new activists and other resources into the peace movement. They may also eclipse existing groups by monopolizing public attention and support. The peace groups recognized the threat posed by the umbrella organizations and took steps to deal with them.

The founders of the EPC not only imposed a time limit on the campaign, but they prevented the campaign from forming its own local chapters. They also kept the EPC dependent on the peace groups for staff and funding. This sponsorship of the EPC may have been a sound strategy for quickly generating an emergency mobilization. It may have been necessary in a Depression economy when outside resources were scarce and during a time when potential activists were involved in labor and other struggles. It also served to keep the EPC from moving too far toward independence. Even so, some pacifist leaders feared the campaign as an organizational rival, and expressed relief when it ended.

The antinuclear campaigns were formed when the peace groups were weak and the social movement scene was quiet. Most of the peace leaders were mainly interested in finding a way to build an effective movement; but they also looked to protect the interests of their organizations, and were therefore concerned over the creation of a new organization. They hoped that the campaigns would mobilize potential leaders, activists, and money, and help the peace groups grow along with the umbrella groups.

The founders of the test ban campaign did not expect to create a large new organization. They thought, correctly, that CNVA would be a small but visible group of volunteer activists. Their plans for SANE to remain a small ad hoc organization serving mainly to coordinate the work of peace groups and a few new activists did not materialize. A strong grassroots response to the call for a test ban brought more than one hundred local chapters into SANE. There is no evidence that the peace groups fought SANE's growth. In any case, it was out of their control because it was based on the support of new activists and sponsors. The few staff members SANE had were independent of the sponsoring groups. Their main concern became managing the new organization and promoting a test ban, not protecting the groups from which they had come. The key tensions between SANE and other organizations, including CNVA, involved dealing with the issue of Communist participation.

Tensions between the NWFC and the coalition members were

more obvious. These groups had declined after Vietnam, but they were not in the cold war doldrums as the test ban sponsors had been; therefore, they had more to lose. By some accounts, turf battles at the founding of the campaign created a leadership vacuum, which was compounded by the antileadership ethos prevalent in the NWFC. These conflicts also inhibited the development of a thought-out organizational strategy. Although the coalition achieved great success in starting a campaign, tensions within it spilled over into the structure of the NWFC. The rise of the NWFC at first strengthened the coalition by bringing in new supporters, money, and attention, but soon the problems of managing the organization began to monopolize the attention of the leaders. They neglected the concerns of coalition members, many of whom fell away in 1983 and 1984. This process accelerated when local activists replaced coalition members on the governing bodies of the NWFC.

Initial sponsorship by peace organizations was crucial in getting the EPC, SANE, and the NWFC off to a strong start. Despite important differences in how coalition-organization tensions were managed, however, origins within coalitions inscribed important structural weaknesses within the umbrella organizations. These became apparent over the course of the campaign. Even with SANE, which met little overt resistance from established groups, failure to plan for the development of an independent organization with local chapters led to important problems in managing local-national tensions. This failure had many causes, including the impossibility of predicting grassroots response, but it was probably increased by the reluctance of existing organizations to create a rival with a structure made for the long term. Neither the sponsoring coalitions nor the umbrella organizations could manage the campaigns well for more than three years.

For the peace movement, cycles of mobilization and decline are also cycles of coalition formation and dissolution. At both ends of the cycle, coalitions magnified trends in timing and magnitude: upsurges happened faster and went farther because of the participation of established groups, but the fracturing of coalitions accelerated and exacerbated the declines. This pattern undoubtedly occurs in other movements and campaigns. There are probably other patterns. Established organizations may ignore or resist new mobilizations for organizational and political reasons, for example.

The tensions inherent in coalitions can be mitigated by early success and by outside funding and other new resources, including activists, but they are not resolved. They may not be resolvable. They influence the campaign both directly and indirectly through their impact on the umbrella organizations.

National-Local

The campaigns worked to develop local support and action. They worked at the national level to coordinate these efforts and to pressure and influence key institutions, including the government and the mass media.

The EPC was run by top national staff members of the pacifist organizations, working out of a national office. Decision making was concentrated in the hands of the campaign staff and leaders of the peace groups who made up the EPC's governing bodies. Extensive local work was planned from the top, with local contacts used to implement the details and organize meetings and other events. The leaders of the EPC rejected any thoughts of developing local chapters, both to avoid competing with the peace groups and to move as quickly as possible to influence national policy.

The NWFC contrasted sharply with the EPC in strategy and structure. Building on extensive local networks, it set out to develop slowly local chapters that would be fairly autonomous in planning and implementing strategies and tactics. Although urgency was part of the freeze message and that of the test ban campaign, there was nothing like the imminence of war that motivated the EPC.

SANE started as a nationally focused organization. An unexpected grassroots response gave it a modest but important local component. CNVA was a purely grassroots group that sponsored direct actions in several locations, without chapters based in local communities.

Several factors caused these differences. First, the initial state of the peace groups varied from strong at the national level in the 1930s to strong locally in the 1980s to modest at both levels in the 1950s. Second, the campaigns deliberately built upon existing strengths. Third, the antinuclear campaigns generated a grassroots upsurge.

At the national level, the EPC was by far the largest organization, measured by staff size and budget. At its peak it employed 150 national staff, including 91 in area offices. This was not a sustainable level, because many were on loan from peace groups or were working at subsistence wages as their contribution to an emergency mobilization, but it gave the campaign a large national office and several area offices that served to implement national programs. This national campaign was run on a budget of $4 million (in 1984 dollars) over its two years of operation. SANE had no more than a dozen staff members at its national offices in New York and Washington, with a peak annual budget of $750,000.[1] The national NWFC employed 25 national staff members at its peak in 1985, and state and local groups had more than 66 staff.[2] Its largest annual budget was $1.3 million.

The NWFC developed the largest and most vigorous local component, with more than 1,800 local groups and between 45,000 and 72,000 volunteers. SANE had 175 local chapters, with between 4,000 and 7,000 volunteers. The EPC established 1,200 local committees, but these were typically one or two people working directly with the national office to organize meetings or implement meetings planned by the national and area offices.

The NWFC also developed state organizations in most states as a result of state-level referenda and elections on which the campaign worked. Like the EPC's regional offices, they served to bridge the large gap between a national office and local activists and chapters. Unlike these offices, the state NWFC groups were created from the bottom up and tended to be closely related to the local organizations. Some even managed the kind of federated structure that the NWFC was unable to create nationally.

These regional and state offices show that the distinction between national and local work is not a true dichotomy. Not only may organizations work at both levels, they also may develop intermediate structures. The campaigns integrated national and local work differently. The social movement literature deals with two main forms of integration. Isolated structures connect individuals directly to a national office by mail, phone, and the mass media. Federated structures connect local chapters with a national office. The EPC was somewhere between these two forms. There were local activists who were more than paper members but less than chapter members. They helped organize meetings and other events, but they did not recruit new activists or develop autonomous programs. Like the difference between national and local organization, the federation-isolation contrast is not as sharp as some theoretical discussions suggest. The varieties and consequences of intermediate forms should be further explored.

One consequence that has been debated is the impact of federation on organizational stability. Federated organizations have been judged more stable than isolated ones because the face-to-face interaction of chapter members produces a sense of solidarity lacking in isolated organizations. Both SANE and the NWFC quickly developed local chapters and became federated organizations. They did survive far longer than did the EPC, which although not strictly isolated did not create the interpersonal relations that generate solidarity.

SANE and the NWFC show that federation is a diverse and complex form, involving issues of governance, local autonomy, and resources. They also show that to understand these organizations it is necessary to examine the process of federating. In both cases the local chapters pushed for and gained a role in governance of the national organization. With SANE, this role was at first limited to one-third of the seats on the main governing body and was then increased to one-half. In the NWFC, local activists gained more power. The NWFC's decision-making national conferences were dominated by local activists, who were given one vote per electoral district. The smaller national committee and executive committee came to include a majority of local and state representatives.

These differences were related to eventual differences in local autonomy. With the NWFC, local autonomy was almost complete because of the organization's commitment to decentralization and grassroots empowerment and because most locals were started without hands-on help from the national. The NWFC did not develop formal affiliation processes until well after the peak of the campaign. SANE chapters also were mostly self-forming and enjoyed great autonomy until the Dodd affair. After it, the national organization took over the Greater New York chapter and required other chapters to take out formal charters.

Although local chapters were integrated into the governance of the campaign organizations, neither found a way to convince or coerce them to support the national organization financially. There were specific reasons for this: the chapters were self-starting, the campaign organizations were loosely structured, and organization building was not a priority. During the existence of the NWFC especially, the national office was able to grow on outside support. It also seems inherently difficult to support more than one level of administration on member dues and contributions and volunteer labor power. Whether and how this problem can be overcome should be addressed by a larger comparative study of federated organizations that also would help clarify other important issues, including the advantages and disadvantages of various forms of federation.

Within the federated organizations, the tensions between local and national work became clear through conflicts over governance, autonomy, and resources. The EPC did not have active chapters and therefore did not develop this overt conflict. Instead, tensions were resolved by limiting the local component of the campaign. This eliminated both a source of tension and a potential source of strength and eventual stability.

Across the campaigns, there was a clear trend toward local organizing. A possible reason for this trend was the focus by the peace movement and other movements on local organizing in the 1970s. Without further research, it is impossible to tell how many movements turned to local work and with what success or to generalize about trends in local organizing from the 1930s to the 1980s, within the peace movement and in other movements. However, Tilly (1984) and others stress that during this century social movements have tended to become more national in scope to keep pace with the concentration of power in nation-states. Any countertrend, such as that found across the peace campaigns, is a significant variation or departure from the general trend.

The main reason for the trend toward local organizing was the great increase across the campaigns in grassroots mobilization. Although not identical with local work, grassroots activism tends to operate through local organizations.

Professional-Grassroots

The peace campaigns mobilized both grassroots participation and professional expertise. They developed these two components to different degrees and in different proportions, just as they did with national and local work. The EPC was mainly a nationally run campaign, run primarily by professionals. The NWFC had a smaller national operation than the EPC, but a much larger grassroots component of 45,000 to 72,000 volunteers. As long as the NWFC remained a locally based campaign, it was also mainly a grassroots mobilization. When it got swept up in national politics, its professional component grew in size and relative influence within the campaign. SANE had the smallest national office of the three and the smallest professional component. SANE's grassroots base of 4,000 to 7,000 volunteers was like its local chapter structure: larger and more independent than those of the EPC, but smaller than those of the NWFC. SANE was more balanced between professional and grassroots elements than were the other two campaign organizations, just as it was more balanced between national and local efforts.

These parallels reinforce the idea that there are affinities between national-level movement organizations and professionalism and between local work and grassroots mobilization. They are not identical.

There are grassroots groups that are nationally focused, and there are local professional groups. CNVA was a purely grassroots group, but it was not a truly local one. There are other social movement groups organized this way, and there are nationally run organizations with some paid staff but a grassroots emphasis. The NWFC started this way and changed over time.

Local professionalism emerged in the antinuclear campaigns. Some SANE chapters and many local and state NWFC organizations hired paid staff, many of whom worked full-time year-round. For SANE and the NWFC, local professionalism developed when large chapters sought to formalize and regularize their activities. Usually, it appears, they hired people who had been volunteers within the chapters. Some local staff developed strong management, organizing, political, and media skills, some did not. Some chapters developed effective fund-raising operations; others did not and had to lay off some or all staff members. The extent, causes, and significance of local professionalism in other organizations and other movements merit further study.

The campaigns varied not just in the size and relative proportion of professionalism and grassroots activism but also in the specific forms in which these broad categories were expressed. The EPC had a large staff and budget, the key aspects of professionalism. There are, however, three important qualifications to the use of this term. First, it was a sponsored professionalism, with the top staff on loan from the peace groups and most of the money coming from these groups' longtime major funders. This qualification applies to the EPC as an organization. It is still significant that the peace movement organizations sponsoring the EPC had substantial professional resources in the 1930s. Second, this was not the sort of "market" professionalism that McCarthy and Zald (1973, 1977) and others discuss, in which different movements compete for staff, funding, and attention. Although some peace staffers moved among peace, labor, and religious groups, they all had long-term ties and strong commitments to the peace movement, as did the key funders. Third, it was a temporary, emergency professionalism. The peace groups made it clear they would not give up their staff and funders for very long. Many staff members who were working for subsistence wages probably would not have continued to do so had the campaign endured.

The EPC mobilized volunteer activism at the local level, but this grassroots component does not correspond to common imagery. There were few large groups of people working together, whether in chapters or outside formal structures. Rather, the EPC engaged a few people in many cities to help run the nationally planned program. Most of these people were leaders of peace or other community groups.

Neither SANE nor the NWFC had access to the professional resources that the EPC had depended upon, but both developed some professionalism. The wealthy Quakers who had funded the peace groups in the 1930s were gone, and their family fortunes had dispersed. The peace groups were smaller at the national level, and so there were fewer experienced professionals in the movement. As SANE and the NWFC were more independent of the peace groups, they were not able to borrow their top staff.

SANE raised small sums and hired a few staff members. Like those of the EPC, most of these men and women came from the ranks of the peace movement. They had less experience running national-level professional operations and more experience as local volunteers or staff. Despite this local background, their initial plans were to run a mostly professional, national-level operation; thus their orientation was not that different from that of the EPC staff. SANE developed an unanticipated grassroots component that differed from that of the EPC because SANE chapters were groups of people acting together and exercising substantial autonomy in setting strategies and tactics. Along with the direct action tactics of CNVA, this gave the test ban campaign a grassroots dimension more vigorous and more closely resembling the usual image than that of the EPC.

Although the professional component of the NWFC grew to a size between the EPC's and SANE's, it began with a different orientation. The NWFC began with a grassroots strategy and hired Randall Kehler as national coordinator to implement this strategy. Other staff hired were expected to share this view and most did, although for various reasons the NWFC later invested heavily in a more professional strategy. Nevertheless, it had and tried to maintain a professionalism that emphasized grassroots organizing more than professional-style lobbying and publicity work. Reflecting this strategy and the grassroots ethos of the campaign, except for Kehler, NWFC staff members did not dominate policymaking. This contrasts strongly with the virtual monopoly on policy making exercised by the EPC staff and the significant role played by several SANE staff members. Furthermore, Kehler's own style helped minimize his role; he was more of a mediator and facilitator than an oligarchical leader.[3]

In trying to keep its staff oriented to grassroots mobilization, the NWFC ran into problems because of the nature of its funding. As the campaign grew, the national office became dependent on major funders who were not integral parts of the peace movement. Instead, foundation support followed market behavior, shifting away from the NWFC as the issue cooled.

The grassroots component of the NWFC was notable not only for its size — there were between 45,000 and 72,000 NWFC activists, about ten times as many as mobilized by SANE — but also for its self-conscious appropriation of the language and ethos of a grassroots movement. The term "grassroots" was constantly used at NWFC policy-making meetings and conferences, in the campaign's literature, and in speeches by leaders. This was not true for SANE or the EPC.

The distinctions identified here, with those discussed earlier, such as Oliver's typology of resources, do not mean that professionalism and grassroots activism are empty terms; they mean that professionalism and grassroots activism are complex forms. There are important variations within each, and these variations have important consequences for the course and outcomes of movements, as the campaign histories showed. Furthermore, the lines between professionalism and grassroots activism sometimes blur. The staff working in the EPC for subsistence were not purely volunteers, but they were not career professionals. Many staff of the NWFC and some of SANE's came from a grassroots background and remained committed to grassroots organizing.

Size, relative proportion and influence, and types of professionalism and grassroots activism all varied. Many of the same factors that made the EPC a nationally centered campaign and the NWFC a locally based one also contributed to the professionalism of the EPC, the grassroots nature of the NWFC, and the in-between status of SANE. The initial state of the movement organization and the campaign strategy was especially important. Their effects were amplified by the affinities between national and professional work and local and grassroots mobilization.

Beyond this, both SANE and the NWFC experienced the rise of grassroots activism, unanticipated in the first case and planned in the second. The EPC did not. Several factors may account for the different grassroots responses to the campaigns. First, the EPC started during the peak of a cycle of general mobilization, marked especially by labor organizing and by mobilization of the unemployed. SANE and the NWFC started at times of general quiescence. Networks and individuals that might have been available to the EPC were already engaged in existing movements. The antinuclear campaigns had the advantage of working a fairly empty field. Their demands mobilized people and networks that, in retrospect, were ready to protest but had not been reached by existing movements and demands. This scenario contrasts with the claim that, compared to "early risers," movements starting at the peak of a cycle have an advantage because they can capitalize on generalized turbulence, newly energized activists, and the widespread perception that elites are weak and movements can succeed (McAdam 1982, Tarrow, 1989). Under some conditions, late risers may have an advantage in attracting volunteers. The antinuclear campaigns, however, gained some of their grassroots strength from the absence of other mobilizations. The early riser hypotheses may be more consistently true when one looks at movement outcome rather than grassroots mobilization. Grassroots mobilization affects a movement's outcome, but so does the political environment. Had they emerged at times of generalized protest, the antinuclear campaigns probably would have made greater political gains than they did during the lulls in the protest cycle.

Second, the networks available to the campaigns differed. For both the EPC and the NWFC, religious congregations at national and local levels provided many key activists. During the test ban campaign, the religious establishment was more conservative, as was the labor movement that had cooperated with some EPC programs.

Third, all three campaigns tried to present popular messages, but the EPC's call for neutrality was more overtly political than the deliberately neutral messages of the antinuclear campaigns. SANE and the NWFC therefore had more chance to mobilize people from the political center or apolitical people; they also had more opportunity to serve as vehicles for dissent. The popular response to the apolitical appeals, however, may not have translated into enduring activism or the development of deeper analyses and critiques of society.

Finally, the freeze campaign drew on the legacy of the movements of the 1960s and 1970s, including the antiwar movement. Despite the widespread reaction against these movements, protest had become more legitimate. The first wave of the freeze campaign involved many veterans of the previous movements. The test ban campaign did not have these advantages, and began when the cold war still dominated U.S. politics.

These factors combined with the state of the movement organizations and the different strategies of the campaigns help explain the different levels and types of grassroots activism. This activism interacted differently with professionalism in each campaign. In all three, there was some facilitation. Staff members encouraged volunteer activism, indirectly and directly, and provided levels of assistance that ranged from minimal during the EPC to great during the NWFC. Conversely, the campaign's grassroots activists lent the staff credibility and a potential strategic resource.

There were also tensions. The top-down structure and strategy of the EPC may have inhibited grassroots activism. The campaign deliberately avoided encouraging the formation of local chapters. With SANE, the tensions mostly overlapped with those between its national office and local chapters, involving mainly issues of governance. With the NWFC, there were overt conflicts over governance and campaign strategy and structure. For many reasons, including the tensions within the founding coalition, the NWFC did not develop effective decision-making structures. The power of local activists and the grassroots ethos of the NWFC may have inhibited tendencies toward oligarchy. They also kept formalization and centralization below the point necessary for effective decision making. Lack of structure often meant organizational drift, not democracy. National conferences frequently debated small points, not clear choices concerning major issues. In a more complex process, the professional elements of the NWFC contributed to strategic decisions, such as the focus on congressional resolutions, that retarded the campaign's development of a large and effective grassroots base. There were also less-visible tensions, including basic choices between hiring professionally oriented staff such as lobbyists and hiring grassroots organizers.

One key question that would require more research to resolve is what relations developed in local chapters between staff and volunteers. My impression is that, in some NWFC chapters, staff helped to recruit and train volunteers, keeping grassroots participation high in activities and sometimes governance. In other chapters, paid work replaced decreasing volunteer efforts. Some staff may have hastened the decline of volunteer activism by taking over decision making, developing projects based on paid activism, and failing to cultivate volunteers.

Just as the different amounts, proportions, and types of professionalism and grassroots activism shaped the campaigns, so did the relationships of reinforcement and conflict. None of the campaigns managed to develop both a large and effective professional component and a large and vigorous grassroots base, partly because of the tensions between the two. On the other hand, each campaign incorporated some good professional work with significant levels of volunteer activism, partly because of the way these elements reinforced each other.

These cases provide the basis for some speculation about the conditions under which facilitation rather than conflict occurs. As new resources may ease the tensions within a coalition, so they may strengthen professionalism or grassroots activism or both without damaging either. Occurring with the early growth of the NWFC was the rise of grassroots activism along with a strengthened professional component funded by outside money. Although this professionalism later led indirectly to a neglect of grassroots organizing, this neglect is not a necessary consequence. The outcome depends on what is done with the new funds. What is done may depend on what strings, if any, come attached to the funds. Some outside funding represents an effort to domesticate a movement, and developing professionalism may play a part in that process.[4] On the other hand, organizations may have some latitude in whether to use new money to hire lobbyists or organizers, for example.

In principle, the presence of paid organizers represents another condition under which professionalism reinforces grassroots activism, but the role of professional organizers in social movements remains underexplored. Of the three campaigns, only the NWFC had fulltime organizers, and only two were in the field. This provides little basis for generalization, although I know of grassroots-based local and state freeze groups that were helped by the work of the NWFC's field staff. An organization that chooses to may use some of its professional resources effectively to strengthen its grassroots base, although there are limits to the ability to create grassroots activism and there are potential tensions between staff and volunteers, as between the structures needed to support each.

Under some circumstances, then, professionalism may sustain grassroots activism. Staggenborg (1986, 1988) believes that professionals help organizations survive by formalizing them, making them more efficient. Some local freeze groups that did hire staff took advantage of the consequent stability to maintain some level of grassroots activism. Staggenborg also argues that professionalism facilitates the formation of coalitions. This was true for the peace campaigns, which were initiated by staff members from peace groups. These clearly energized the movement and led to the rise of grassroots activism in varying amounts. Staff also contributed to tensions within coalitions because of their concerns in maintaining the relative strength of their home organizations.

A last set of issues involves trends over time. Since McCarthy and Zald claimed, in 1973, that social movements had been professionalizing, scholars have debated the level and significance of movement professionalism. Many of the movements of the 1960s were substantially grassroots in origin; but there is also evidence that, since the early 1970s, professionalism has become more significant within many movements and movement organizations (Marwell and Oliver 1992).

The peace campaigns show a tendency that is the opposite of that suggested by McCarthy and Zald. Both in the number of volunteer activists and in their relative influence within the campaign, the trend across the campaigns was toward a greater grassroots role. The significance of professional-style activism and the influence of paid staff decreased. This finding does not disprove the McCarthy and Zald thesis. Possibly, there has been a larger trend toward professionalism and, at the same time, a countertrend toward more grassroots involvement within the peace movement, for reasons that may be unique or at least unusual.

First, the peace campaigns reflected the composition of the sponsoring movement in many ways, including the size and type of professional and grassroots activism. The peace groups of the 1930s were unusual in that they had access to significant amounts of major donor money, with Quakers funding the pacifist groups and the CEIP funding the internationalists. It is unlikely that other social movement groups of the time had this kind of support. Perhaps general trends in the availability of resources, leaders, and activists that have increased professionalism over time have not been as important for the peace movement as the specific circumstances that facilitated professionalism in the 1930s. Moreover, the larger trend toward professionalism may partly account for the differences between SANE and the NWFC, which had a larger professional component and took greater advantage of new technologies, including direct mail and canvassing.

Second, the countertrend may be an artifact of the timing of the peace campaigns relative to general cycles of mobilization. The grassroots component of the EPC was relatively small and less autonomous because the campaign emerged during the peak of a general mobilization cycle. The later peace campaigns began during quieter times. Other movements, timed differently in relation to general cycles, might not show a trend toward greater grassroots participation.

Finally, there was a trend toward professionalism at the local level. Many local NWFC chapters hired paid staff. None of the EPC chapters and few of the SANE chapters did. This trend is missed by studies that focus only on national-level organizations.

The peace campaigns, then, to some degree and in some ways went against what have been called major trends toward professionalism and toward an emphasis on national-level activity. These findings do not disprove the claims about the existence or significance of the more general trends. One case or a few cases cannot do this. Rather, these findings show first, that it is important to recognize the complexity and diversity of the social movement scene and the complexity of apparently simple concepts such as professionalism. Sweeping claims about professionalism and national social movements may point to important trends, but they tend to overgeneralize and oversimplify. Second, further empirical research is needed before there can be much confidence in claims about general trends, even allowing for exceptions and for variations in form. For the peace movement alone, it would be necessary to look at the trends I have found to see whether and to what degree they apply to specific movement organizations, and to the movement during times other than campaigns. Beyond the peace movement, solid information is needed about many different movements and movement organizations, not just to identify trends but also to analyze their causes and significance.

Third, whatever larger trends may exist, a movement may mobilize substantial grassroots activism through the use of appropriate structures, strategies, and tactics, under favorable conditions. This activism may help create the conditions for future waves of grassroots mobilization in that movement or other movements.

Organizational Tensions — Conclusion

Large social movement organizations face problems of managing the tensions between local activism and national work, and between grassroots mobilization and professionalism. The peace campaigns faced the additional task of maintaining a coalition while developing one or more campaign organizations. In each case, although the initial coalition gave the campaign a strong start, tensions within the coalition and between the coalition and the new organization(s) eventually weakened the campaign both directly and indirectly: directly, by reducing the unity and focus of the movement; indirectly, by contributing to the development of structures unable to manage the other two sets of tensions for long. This task, inherently difficult, was complicated by the short-term orientation imposed on the campaigns by the coalition members.

The EPC was explicitly limited to two years to ease the tensions within the founding coalition. The struggle for neutrality and international economic cooperation would be continued beyond the end of the campaign through other structures. The antinuclear campaigns, however, were designed as open-ended efforts to achieve particular goals. They had no explicit timetable; their leaders thought in terms of a few years. They spoke, as had the EPC leaders, of creating a movement and not an organization. Although they saw the need to create formal structures to manage the campaigns, they did not focus their attention on developing structures capable of sustaining activism for more than a few years, structures that could better handle organizational tensions.

In part, this lack of attention to organization may have been the result of miscalculation: overoptimism concerning political prospects and an understandable failure to anticipate the magnitude of the grassroots response to the campaigns. It also reflected both the reluctance of the coalition members to create an organizational rival, and, during the freeze campaign, the fact that organizational rivalries prevented the emergence of strong leadership. Structures that worked well at the start of campaigns collapsed or did not work well after their first two or three years, partly because of the weaknesses inscribed at the outset by their origins in coalitions.

Campaign organizations face peculiar problems because of the advantages and disadvantages of coalition sponsorship, but all SMOs grapple with how to build structures that can sustain activism. Scholars have examined only small parts of this problem, mainly focusing on whether and how SMOs can avoid the Weber-Michels scenario of oligarchization and bureaucratization. These cases show the importance of other dynamic issues, especially the problems of managing national-local and professional-grassroots tensions, and, for campaigns, the additional issues raised by coalitions. Understanding these specific tensions and studying some of the ways in which they interact and play out help in assessing the larger question of how to mobilize intense activism over the short run and also build to sustain mobilization over the longer term. This question, central to the campaigns, is also a key to the relationship between the campaigns and the peace movement.

Beyond the ability of the campaigns to achieve their manifest goals, or at least to create structures that would have maximized their chances to do so, is the question of their role, if any, in helping the peace movement achieve its long-term goals. Social movement campaigns have ways to pursue immediate campaign goals that may help in building toward larger movement goals. There are also potential conflicts between the two. The campaign vs. movement issue has both an organizational, movement-building component and a strategic component of education and political reform.

The campaigns centered on one or two key goals or political reforms were seen as inherently important. Campaign leaders also hoped that achieving the overt goals would contribute toward more comprehensive changes, both by generating political momentum and by establishing structural reforms that would increase public participation in the policy-making process. One key structural reform would be strengthening the role of Congress relative to that of the executive. Some claim that the freeze campaign made progress in this direction, although the permanence of any changes is an open question.

The danger in emphasizing short-term goals, however, is that either failure or success may, under some circumstances, decrease political momentum. Failure may frustrate activists and change public and elite perceptions of the campaign's strength, as happened with the freeze. Winning purely symbolic or severely limited victories, such as the nonbinding congressional freeze resolution and the partial test ban treaty, also may be demobilizing. Even substantial reforms may prove counterproductive in the long run, if they coopt leaders and incorporate oppositional movements into institutionalized politics. Concerns in this direction were raised about the relationship between the freeze movement and the Democratic party.

Campaigns and movements create social change not just through their immediate impact on policy and the policy-making process but also through a slower process of the education of activists, the public, and elites. Here also short-term changes may facilitate long-term change, but there also may be tensions between the two. The peace campaigns presented their goals in terms that were simple and easily communicated, using language that was moral, practical, or technical, but not heavily political, to make their appeals as broad and immediate as possible. They succeeded in raising the salience of their issues and in mobilizing significant public support, although for the antinuclear campaigns especially this support proved to be shallow. Leaders had hoped that the campaigns also would promote the underlying philosophies and values of the peace movement (although they differed among themselves over what these might be). They hoped that some activists and members of the public would undergo a learning and politicizing process that would start with the simple overt goals and themes of the campaigns and end with a more profound analysis and a belief in internationalism, nuclear disarmament, pacifism, and so forth. Some did develop this way, but for some members of the public the campaigns had little long-term effect; for others, they may have backfired, translating fear into support for isolationism and unilateral military strength.

There is no evidence that the campaigns affected the thinking of significant segments of the elite. We also do not know whether the campaigns had much influence on deeper cultural currents, something Gusfield (1981) suggests social movement scholars should look at more often. The most important educational effect of the campaigns may have been upon some activists. They may have helped to translate short-term activism into sustained commitment — although no systematic research has shown the extent or depth of this effect. We must consider not just individuals' changes in attitudes and commitment, but also their development of knowledge, skills, experience, and personal networks. Many of these changes may not show up until another wave of mobilization occurs within the peace movement or other movements, when people who have not stayed a part of the organized movement again become active.

Beyond individuals, the organized peace movement was both strengthened and weakened by the campaigns. The existing peace groups were overshadowed by the campaigns, and during the EPC they lost resources. During all the campaigns, however, many peace organizations gained members, at least for a while. During the antinuclear campaigns, especially the freeze, they raised more money. A variety of new organizations was created, ranging from direct-action groups to educational and lobbying groups of professionals, such as PSR. The net impact of all this on the peace movement is again something that would require systematic research to puzzle out. Many, however, agree that the peace movement has lacked a continuing mass-membership group. SANE/FREEZE, created by a merger of the umbrella organizations that survived the antinuclear campaigns, aspires to be such an organization. How large and how effective it will be remains to be seen.

Although there may not be inherent tensions between the short-term and long-term aspects of movement building comparable to those involved in pursuing political reforms and education, the impact of the peace campaigns on the peace movement is unclear. From one perspective these campaigns were repeated exercises in frustration for the peace movement, merely vehicles to continue the movement's cyclical history. Some would even argue that they proved to be traps for a movement that should have been slowly building a base for fundamental alternatives to the current system but keeps getting drawn into apparent opportunities that dilute its message and burn out and demoralize its supporters. From another perspective, the campaigns that fell short of their goals did take advantage of political opportunities to raise key issues, provide a hearing for alternatives, and slowly build an opposition movement.

The peace campaigns faced organizational and strategic tensions involving both the campaigns themselves and their relationships with the long-term development of the peace movement and the achievement of its various goals. They also operated within constraints determined by larger political and social structures and by the inherent difficulties in mobilizing activism. Facing these tensions and constraints, leaders and activists made decisions about strategy and structure that strongly influenced the course and impact of the campaigns. The political and social contexts of the campaigns differed greatly, but the tensions and choices confronting them were similar. Leaders and activists could have looked to the movement's past, especially to previous campaigns, to inform their choices; but it appears they did not, at least not in any systematic way or to any great extent.[5] This is odd, especially for the NWFC, which was dealing with the same issues as the test ban campaign. It developed in many similar ways. All the campaigns were started by the same peace groups, which might be expected to perform one key function of a movement halfway house — to reflect upon and pass along the history of the movement.

This ahistorical activism has its reasons. The sponsoring groups were the same, but the key individuals were not. The campaigns were separated by a change of generations in the leadership of most peace groups, although there was some continuity. Movement organizations usually look ahead, not behind. After the decline of the campaigns, leaders and activists tried to salvage what they could and cope with the next set of organizational and strategic problems. Individuals thought and even wrote about what had been and what might have been; the movement organizations did not do so in a way that would ensure passing on these thoughts.[6] New activists prefer to make their own history and are often suspicious of more experienced activists.

What if anything would have been different had activists developed more of a sense of history is hard to say. Organizational and strategic tensions are inherent in campaigns, and there are no ways simply to resolve them. By recognizing the nature of these tensions, anticipating the kinds of decisions to be made, and understanding the consequences of decisions made by earlier campaigns, activists in the future may be able to match the successes of past efforts as they avoid some of the problems that affected the Emergency Peace Campaign, the test ban campaign, and the Nuclear Weapons Freeze Campaign.

Notes
Bibliography
Index

Notes

Preface

1. A note on terminology. In two cases the campaign and its leading organization bore the same name. I will use "Emergency Peace Campaign" or "EPC" to mean both organization and campaign because little activism took place beyond the bounds of the organization. I will use "Nuclear Weapons Freeze Campaign" or "NWFC" to refer to the central organization, and "nuclear freeze campaign" or "freeze campaign" to mean the entire campaign, which did extend beyond the organization. I will call the policy promoted by the campaign as the "freeze proposal" or "freeze idea." Occasionally, I will simply use "freeze" to mean the campaign or the idea, if the context makes clear which is meant. The test ban campaign presents no similar problem, as its key organization was SANE.

2. In 1982 and 1983 I was an activist with the Students for Nuclear Disarmament at the University of Wisconsin-Madison. I served on the board of directors of the Wisconsin Nuclear Weapons Freeze Campaign from 1983 until spring 1989, with one term as vice-president. I spent two summers as a paid, part-time door-to-door canvasser for the Wisconsin Freeze, a job I took more as an activist hoping to earn money than as a scholar seeking new insights, although insights were a side benefit. I participated in national conferences of the NWFC from 1983 through its merger with SANE in 1987 and served on the national board of SANE/FREEZE from Jan. 1988 through spring 1989.

1. Modern American Peace Campaigns

1. In formal terms, this study is a heuristic, comparative case study (George 1979). Such studies are inductive in-depth analyses of a few cases of a class of events with the goal of generating both specific explanations and broader insights that may be generalizable. The specific explanations involve the identification of causal patterns and the conditions under which they occur, the first step in the construction of what George (1979) refers to as "rich, differentiated theory," or typological theory. This is theory cast in the form of contingent generalizations rather than universal laws or tendencies, typically the goal of positivist, deductive research. Because comparative case studies emphasize the importance of context, practitioners of this method tend to deny the possibility of the development of universal laws. See also Mouzelis

(1967), Ragin (1987), Sayer (1984), Skocpol and Somers (1980), and Walton (1973) for good discussions of the comparative case study method.

2. Aminzade (1992) discusses several ways in which historical sociology deals with time.

2. The American Peace Movement

1. DeBenedetti (1988) says estimates of the number of "citizen peace activists" range from one-half of one percent to two percent of the American population. This seems reasonable, although he does not define the term activists, and the number of people mobilized by the movement has varied tremendously with the cycles of the movement. The core of the movement has probably consisted of fewer than one-half of 1 percent, if measured by membership in peace groups throughout the modern era. None of the peace campaigns mobilized more than two percent, nor did the protests against the Vietnam war, which ultimately included "several million," according to DeBenedetti and Chatfield (1990, 389).

2. Morris (1984) shows the key role played by organizations such as the AFSC and the WRL in the rise of the civil rights movement.

3. This threefold categorization of peace traditions is adapted from DeBenedetti (1984), who lists conscientious objection as a fourth tradition. This is so closely identified with pacifism, as he notes, that I do not discuss it as a separate strand.

4. Young (1987) identifies ten distinct traditions in the western peace movement, including the three I stress here.

5. Terminology is inconsistent in peace movement literature, even in the definition and use of basic terms such as pacifism and internationalism. For example, Young's (1987) taxonomy of peace traditions refers only to liberal internationalism and does not treat conservative internationalism as a separate tradition. My usage here, as in Chatfield and Kleidman (1992), follows Chatfield (1971) in explicitly distinguishing liberal and conservative internationalism.

6. DeBenedetti (1980, 73) claims the Anti-Imperialist League still holds the record as the largest American antiwar organization in ratio of members to total population.

7. DeBenedetti (1980) stresses the reform element in Progressivism and how this fed into the left orientation of the post–World War I peace movement. Patterson (1973) emphasizes how elitism limited the ability of the prewar movement, including its progressive wing, to find a mass base.

8. This discussion follows Chatfield's (1971, 1973, 1978) division of the modern peace movement into pacifist and internationalist wings. DeBenedetti (1980) adds liberal reformers as a third group. For analytic purposes the dichotomy seems most useful: the less-cohesive groups of liberal reformers offered no distinct analysis or proposals, and most of their work fits under the umbrella of one of the two major wings. In the history of the interwar period, however, the third group is mentioned specifically.

9. DeBenedetti (1980, 99–100) places John Dewey and Charles Beard in this group of liberal internationalists.

10. Wittner (1984, 103) cites a 1943 poll showing that although 55 percent of Americans attributed to the United States the key role in turning the tide of war, only 3 percent of the British saw things this way, and most gave the Soviet Union the credit.

11. Of major combatant nations, the United States suffered the fewest casualties as a percentage of 1935 population: 0.8 percent. Percentages for other nations include: Great Britain 1.3, France 1.8, Japan 7.7, USSR 8.3, Germany 14.3. Data cited by Wittner (1984, 109) from P.M.S. Blackett, 1949, *Fear, War, and the Bomb: Military and Political Consequences of Atomic Energy*, New York: McGraw Hill.

12. Cantril (1951, 21–22), cited by Wittner (1984, 132). Similar ambivalent attitudes provided opportunities and problems for later arms control and disarmament movements.

13. Poll cited by Wittner (1984, 142), who also notes that world government was supported by nineteen U.S. senators and fifty to one hundred representatives.

14. On the dual impact of fear, see Boyer (1985), and Sandman and Valenti (1986).

15. A good account of these negotiations and American postwar nuclear policy is found in Herken (1982).

16. LaFeber (1980) and Sanders (1983) provide radical critiques of containment militarism and the role of the United States in the origins of the cold war. Sanders details the evolution from containment to containment militarism.

17. From 1939 to 1945 military expenditures went from less than $1 billion annually to more than $81 billion. Military personnel expanded from less than one-third of a million to more than 12 million. Although postwar demobilization brought these figures down, they never returned to prewar levels. Military personnel have remained above 2 million since the Korean War. Military spending also remained relatively high—between $180 and $220 billion (in 1986 dollars) from 1954 to 1980, and higher under the Reagan administration (Meyer 1988, 1990A). Including part of the budgets for the Department of Energy and NASA, for example, as well as part of the interest on the federal deficit, brings military spending to more than $400 billion annually in the 1980s—more than ten percent of the gross national product, and more than half the federal budget, excluding trust funds such as Social Security (Joseph 1981).

18. Seymour Melman (1965, 1974), among others, has been making this critique since the 1960s. Only in the late 1980s has it received a significant audience among policy makers, many of whom were reached by Harvard professor Paul Kennedy's 1987 book, *The Rise and Fall of the Great Powers: Economic Change and Military Conflict from 1500 to 2000*.

19. Estimates of the magnitude of antiwar protest vary because of differing definitions of protest and because of the decentralized and informal character of the movement. DeBenedetti and Chatfield (1990) note that few organizations kept membership statistics, and estimate that combined membership in peace and antiwar groups increased from 40,000–80,000 in 1962 to 300,000–400,000 in 1972, largely owing to the proliferation of new organizations. They also note, however, that this does not capture most of the activism, which was local and episodic. Including this kind of activism, they estimate that "several million" were involved in antiwar activity. DeBenedetti's earlier book (1980) puts the number at 4 million, working through more than 560 organizations. Joseph (1981) estimates that by 1968 2–3 million Americans had taken part in some action: attending an antiwar demonstration, signing an ad, writing a letter to Congress, etc.

20. Boyer's analysis of the decline of the test ban campaign (Boyer, 1984) emphasizes the discontinuities between that effort, led largely by liberals, and the antiwar movement shaped by the New Left, which was incubated by the test ban campaign.

He also claims that Wittner (1984) and DeBenedetti (1980) stress continuities between the movements. I consider both continuities and differences important. Although the dominant tone of the test ban campaign was liberal, radical activists were a part of the campaign and the antiwar movement. The growth of the New Left did lend the antiwar movement a more radical tone, but as Wittner and DeBenedetti and Katz (1986) discuss, the majority of antiwar protest was carried out by more traditional liberals.

21. In June 1969, for example, SANE did adopt a position calling for unilateral withdrawal.

22. The impact of the antiwar movement on policy is discussed in Joseph (1981), Niedergang (1986), DeBenedetti (1980), and Wittner (1984). Schuman (1972) analyzes the relations between protest and public opinion.

23. The contras in Nicaragua, for example. The Vietnam syndrome continued to shape the conduct of the Persian Gulf War, with the administration visibly concerned to keep the conflict short and the casualties low.

24. Meyer (1988, 1990A) discusses the strategic advantages of local peace organizing in this era.

25. Meyer (1988, 239), quoting Terry Provance of the AFSC. Meyer also notes that Carter's B-1 decision was tempered by his decision to proceed with developing another bomber, which became the Stealth plane, and to deploy nuclear cruise missiles on the B-52 fleet.

26. In the fall of 1988, three major nuclear weapons plants, including Rocky Flats, were closed by the federal government after incidents and reports indicated that these plants had exposed workers and residents of nearby communities to levels of radioactivity exceeding established guidelines. It was disclosed that the plants had a thirty-year history of accidental releases, and the Department of Energy estimated clean-up of the plants would take more than fifty years and cost at least $110 billion (*Nuclear Times,* Jan./Feb. 1989, 5).

27. Meyer 1988, 295. The NWFTF, actually established after MFS, was affiliated with this larger coalition until after the UN demonstration, according to Solo (1988).

28. An obvious comparison is with the nuclear freeze campaign, which did have a simple, galvanizing issue and demand, but it also benefited from a political environment in which nuclear issues were again high on the public agenda.

29. Ferguson and Rogers (1986A) challenge the thesis that public opinion did become more conservative, citing continued support for social spending and other elements of the New Deal legacy. They do concede, however, that elite opinion and major party politics moved to the right.

30. The balance of power is documented numerous places, including Sanders (1983), Aldridge (1983), Bottome (1986), and a number of volumes of the *Defense Monitor,* issued by the Washington-based Center for Defense Information.

31. The term "doldrums" is borrowed from Rupp and Taylor's (1987) analysis of the women's movement.

32. Meyer (1988) emphasizes this aspect of the nuclear freeze campaign.

3. Social Movements, Campaigns, and Organizations

1. Good overviews of the main traditions in the social movement literature: Jenkins (1983), Marx and Wood (1975), McAdam, McCarthy, and Zald (1988), Morris and Herring (1988), and Zurcher and Snow (1981).

2. The term "stormy sixties" is taken from Jenkins (1987).

3. Both resource mobilization and political process refer to a set of perspectives rather than one theory, and there is no clear division between them. Perrow (1979B) divided resource mobilization theories into two broad groups. RMI is an economistic strand emphasizing the role of movement "entrepreneurs" and external resources such as contributions from sympathizers and relying on utilitarian models of behavior. For this view, see McCarthy and Zald (1973, 1975, 1977). RMII theorists, more rooted in political sociology, look to shifting political opportunities to help explain movement cycles, and tend to emphasize the role of indigenous organization and the informal networks and formal organizational infrastructure of aggrieved groups; e.g., Oberschall (1973) and Tilly (1978). The term "political process," introduced by McAdam (1982), in many respects represents an extension of RMII.

Collective behavior theory also responded to the new perspectives, and drew increasingly on theorists such as Turner and Killian (1987) who, as Morris (1984) and Oberschall (1973) point out, worked within this framework without assuming movement irrationality, and recognized the social change potential of movements.

4. Staggenborg (1988) defines a formal movement organization as one with established procedures or structures for the performance of tasks, bureaucratic procedures for decision making, a developed division of labor, explicit criteria for membership, and rules governing subunits such as chapters.

5. Other important critiques claim that these views slight or neglect individual motives for participation as well as the importance of culture and the construction of meaning (e.g., Gusfield 1981, Klandermans 1984, Snow et al. 1986).

6. Marwell and Oliver (1984) critique several alternative candidates for unit of analysis. Besides organizations, scholars have looked at individuals, interest groups, and collective events. I study the peace campaigns because of their importance in the history of the peace movement rather than for methodological reasons, but I agree that campaigns offer a useful unit of analysis that can help build theories of movements.

Campaigns vary in planning and coordination, size, scope, duration, and ambition. The peace campaigns had considerable centralization and coordination; ongoing peace groups and the new campaign organizations were both important. My analysis slights the roles of activists, allies, opponents, and others outside these groups. In looking at the one or two umbrella organizations in each campaign, I de-emphasize the actions of other formal movement organizations. This narrowing of perspective is necessary to come to an understanding of what these central organizations did and why, but further research on other organizations and nonorganizational phenomena will add to an understanding of the peace campaigns.

7. McAdam, McCarthy, and Zald (1988) adopt the term "institutional school" from Perrow (1979A) and make the point that it coexisted with but did not challenge the dominance of the collective behavior school. The institutional school of social movement analysis is related to the institutional school of political science mentioned earlier.

8. Some union positions are notable exceptions to the low compensation rule, of course. Wilson (1973, 215-34) observes that paid staff in labor unions may be more liberal or radical than the rank and file in their interest in a range of social issues but less militant in pursuit of bread-and-butter goals.

9. It appears that the most common use of Piven and Cloward's book is to argue against the antiorganization claim.

10. This is true for grassroots movements. McCarthy and Zald (1973) argue

that formal SMOs can launch a movement even in the absence of grassroots participation.

11. Strategic tensions include issues of goals, strategies, and tactics. The key temporal issue for campaigns—an important one for movements in general—is the tension between emphasizing short-term goals and emphasizing long-term goals. There are also issues of reformist goals vs. transformative goals; narrow, single-issue goals vs. broad, multiple-issue goals; and institutional vs. noninstitutional strategies and tactics. Some of these issues are discussed by Gamson (1990), who uses Ash's (1972) typology of strategic options (which forumlates these issues somewhat differently) in his analysis of the impact of strategy on movement outcome.

12. Wilson (1973, 277) argues that Olson's (1965) logic of collective action may apply more to coalitions as organizations of organizations than to organizations of individuals. Organizations are more likely to act in purely instrumental fashion than are individuals. Therefore, they are more likely to require a specific, material benefit to join a larger organization, i.e., a coalition.

13. Staggenborg (1986) discusses some of these conflicts in connection with the rise of a new umbrella organization to manage the coalition. This development may exacerbate conflicts, but they are likely to arise in any event.

14. The economistic terminology of McCarthy and Zald (1977) has become standard in the literature. Organizations working on similar issues constitute an industry; all SMOs together constitute the social movement sector.

15. Also in contrast to Morris's image of halfway houses, what the movement organizations did not provide to the NWFC was an institutional memory of the test ban campaign and its lessons.

16. Some peace efforts have tried to work underneath or around the nation-state through "citizen diplomacy," the establishment of direct contacts between citizens and organizations in different nations. Alger and Mendlovitz (1983) discuss local vs. global orientations of contemporary peace and other activists, and Young (1987) analyzes trends toward localism in the western peace movement.

17. There is a difference between grassroots and local organizing. Local organizing may focus on local elites. Organizing popular participation almost always does mean working at the local level. Some small action-oriented groups, however, are not rooted in geographic communities. These are "grassroots" in that they mobilize volunteer activism; they are not grassroots in community "rootedness."

18. Cited by Agnew (1987). I have seen a similar statement attributed to Richard J. Daley, former mayor of Chicago.

19. "Incorporation" refers to the process of taming a movement or organization by granting limited concessions; "cooptation" involves individuals including movement leaders.

20. Wilson (1973) discusses types of incentives for movement participation.

21. At the extreme, this can become something of a "franchise" operation; McCarthy and Wolfson (1988) claim it is becoming more common.

22. This and other information about Common Cause comes from McFarland (1984).

23. McFarland estimates the core membership of local and state committees at about four thousand; another seven thousand "activists" are frequent letter-writers.

24. The primary sources for the description of the NAACP are Wilson (1973) and Rudwick and Meier (1972).

25. McAdam (1982) says it led to a neglect of grassroots organizing by these groups.

26. Morris (1984) quotes, among others, Ella Baker, who thought that the predominance of a few charismatic leaders was an organizational weakness, inhibiting the development of other potential leaders, national and local.

27. This was a key work in the development of RMI.

28. Historically, "grassroots" actually has a variety of meanings, according to Alger and Mendlovitz (1983). One older meaning involves "Main Street U.S.A." — small towns, and their backbone institutions and professionals. Grassroots politics, in this sense, is electoral politics channeled through the major parties. A second established meaning adds to rural populism a leftist, even Socialist strand. Grassroots politics here means a drive for equity and participation; it means challenging large institutions through cells, cadres, and protest politics. Grassroots politics also has a newer sense of empowering the urban poor and minorities through less ideological, Alinsky-style organizing.

29. In common imagery, activists are those who are consistently agitating for change. I accept Oliver's broader definition of activists as those people, paid or unpaid, who occasionally take action other than contributing money.

30. McCarthy and Zald (1973) speculated that the rise of movement professionalism might soon be accompanied not only by the expansion of movement careers but also by rationalization and routinization in training and the establishment of professional organizations. I am not aware of any subsequent research on this important topic.

31. Cycles in social movements have become a major focus of attention, in part because of the work of Tarrow (1983A, 1983B, 1989). In claiming that SMOs act to ensure their survival, I am stating, first, that activists — paid and unpaid — often make organizational survival a high-priority goal; and therefore to the extent that these activists control organizations, the organizations do act this way. Second, organizations that fail to find stable resource supplies tend to fail. Wilson (1973, 262) asserts more explicitly that SMOs, like other organizations, seek to maintain themselves. Without explanation this claim tends to reify organizations, endowing them with a consciousness and purpose.

32. McCarthy and Zald (1973) mention that movement entrepreneurs may try to develop at least a paper base of members for their otherwise professional organizations, so that their claims to speak for a constituency appear more legitimate. Paper members are also an important source of funds for many groups.

33. Staggenborg (1988) found that some professional activists in the pro-choice movement recruited and trained substantial numbers of volunteers. I have not found in the social movement literature much discussion of the crucial issue of volunteer training. Volunteer activists who learn movement skills — organizational and political — are an invaluable resource for movements and movement organizations, and the proliferation of skills has implications beyond particular movements and movement cycles.

34. According to Fainstein and Fainstein (1974), paid organizing outside the labor movement is relatively new. It has its origins in two traditions. First, paid organizers played a significant role in the labor movement; then union organizing principles were extended to community organizing, notably by Saul Alinsky. Second, the "nonpolitical" social-work community organizing curriculum and practice was extended in a radical direction by social workers connected with the early poverty programs. Together, these two traditions provided a basis for a broader use of organizers and organizing in the 1960s and beyond. Unfortunately, the empirical and analytical literature on paid organizers and professional activists in general is

rather thin, Not enough is known about who they are, what they do, what kinds of careers and career networks they have developed, etc.

35. Organizational stability earlier seemed to lead to professionalism; here it appears as a consequence of professionalism. Stability can be both consequence and cause: if as an outcome it contributes to the survival of an organization, then through competition and selection it also becomes a cause; and if activists see professionalism as likely to increase organizational stability, they may act deliberately to increase organizational professionalism.

36. Funding is cyclical both for the social movement industry as a whole and for particular movements, as the issue attention cycle moves on. Small-donor giving resembles a competitive market, and individual organizations are no more secure than most small businesses. Large institutions are not reliable sources of ongoing support for most SMOs: many foundations look on grants to SMOs as seed money. Reliance on external sponsors makes organizations dependent upon elites.

37. They actually consider how PSMOs can survive the withdrawal of elite support—which translates into a loss of funds. My discussion deals with loss of outside support for other reasons.

38. This analysis centers on perspective—whether paid staff tend to have deeper and broader views than the typical volunteer. A related issue is motivation. Some resource mobilization theories imply and some collective action theories state that paid staff should be less driven by ideological and purposive factors than volunteers because they receive material benefits. There is, however, no reason to think that material motives exlude others. Oliver (1983) found that paid activists in neighborhood organizations were no less ideologically committed than were volunteers.

39. Taylor (1989) explores how the women's movement survived the "doldrums" from 1945 to 1960. Without discussing the role of paid staff, she does argue that organizational centralization—I suspect it is related to professionalism—contributed to survival of the movement.

40. The nuclear freeze group to which I belonged was required by the federal government to sign a pledge not to sponsor illegal activity in order to receive a tax exemption.

4. The Emergency Peace Campaign

1. The description of the 1920s as a decade of working to build peace and the 1930s as a decade of working to avoid war is taken from Chatfield (1971).

2. Union membership, still only 9.5 percent of the labor force in 1935, was rapidly escalating, as was strike activity, which doubled from 1935 to 1937 in worker-hours lost (Massad 1980).

3. According to Allen (1934), the May 1933 Continental Congress for Economic Restructuring drew four thousand labor delegates representing "hundreds of thousands" of trade unionists, and adopted a strong resolution for unqualified war resistance.

4. Tarrow (1983B, 42) hypothesizes that a social movement is more likely to succeed during the peaks of protest cycles because the political system is more permeable and elites are more malleable.

5. Most internationalists eventually supported American entry into World War I, creating a split in the peace movement similar to what would occur in the late 1930s over World War II.

6. Minutes of Buck Hills Falls conference, Dec. 4–6, 1935, EPC papers, box 1.

7. Williams (1962) discusses national chauvinism; Curti (1959) noted a rise in nationalist feelings.

8. See Domhoff (1983) for a discussion of these policy-formulating bodies, and Shoup and Minter (1977) for a critical history of CFR.

9. The aftermath of Vietnam and Watergate led to greater congressional oversight and participation in foreign policy making, although the executive branch has remained dominant; see discussion in chap. 6, below.

10. Kuusisto (1950, 25–27) provides these figures; the 15,000 cited for WILPF is the average membership in the years 1935–1937.

11. The NCPW was not strictly a pacifist group, but its leaders were pacifists and it supported the pacifist position throughout the 1930s and into the war.

12. The endowment was established in 1910 with an initial gift by Andrew Carnegie of $10 million. High (1938) estimated that for 1938 the endowment would provide $800,000 to the peace movement, or almost 40 percent of its total funding. This would represent the majority of the funding to the internationalists.

13. In his report to the 1938 annual meeting of the NCPW, Frederick Libby reported that from 1920 to the end of 1938 the organization had spent almost $2 million, or an average of $117,000 per year, and that in no year had small contributions exceeded 15 percent of these funds (NCPW papers, box 20).

14. On the World Court see Divine (1962, 83), Chatfield (1971, 102–6), and DeBenedetti (1980).

15. Chatfield's chap. 10, "The Emergency Peace Campaign," is the key source for my narrative of the planning and history of the EPC.

16. Minutes of Buck Hills Falls conference, Dec. 4–6, 1935, EPC papers, box 1.

17. Minutes of buck Hills Falls conference, Dec. 4–6, 1935, EPC papers, box 1.

18. Minutes of November 1935 planning conference, EPC papers, box 1.

19. This position stemmed not from any sympathy with fascism, which the peace groups led in condemning, but from a longstanding analysis of the international scene. Chatfield (1971), Wittner (1984), and other historians show that pacifists were among the first to recognize and formulate strategies to oppose the rise of fascism, and to try to rescue its victims.

20. The pacifist view, although held by a minority, does go counter to the analysis in accounts such as Divine's (1962), which identify neutralism with isolationism. Ferguson (1989), Kolko (1984), and Williams (1962) emphasize economic protectionism rather than isolationism as an important trend in elite thinking. Flynn (1964) notes that ethnic ties to Germany and Ireland led some segments of the public to support neutrality.

21. The $800,000 figure is from High (1938). Ferguson (1989) included the national mass media among capital-intensive businesses sympathetic to internationalism for economic reasons.

22. James Mullin (former assistant to the director of the EPC) interview.

23. Minutes of June 19, 1936 council meeting, EPC papers, box 2.

24. *New York Times,* June 26, 1936, 13, cited in Divine (1962, 163).

25. "Preliminary Report on 1936 Fall Meetings," EPC papers, box 2. Chatfield (1971, 275 n.51) interprets the increase in the number of meetings in spite of limited national assistance as representing an increase in local initiative, although the report makes no such conclusion.

26. "Activities of the Emergency Peace Campaign Adopted by the Council October 13, 1936," EPC papers, box 2.

27. Most local committees differed little from contacts, as they mostly consisted of one or two activists.

28. The account of the 1937 neutrality legislation is taken from Divine (1962).

29. Memo from Fred Atkins Moore to speakers at the outset of the No-Foreign-War-Crusade, EPC papers, box 2.

30. Having read a number of reports from public meetings (in the EPC collection), I have concluded that the meetings failed to generate much income, a conclusion supported by EPC financial reports.

31. Minutes of Nov. 13, 1936 council meeting, EPC papers, box 2.

32. Minutes of Oct. 13, 1936 council meeting, EPC papers, box 2.

33. Minutes of Feb. 2, 1937 council meeting, EPC papers, box 2.

34. "Recommendations by Dorothy Detzer, Chairman of Legislative Work," n.d., but appended to minutes of EPC Council, June 19, 1936, EPC papers, box 2.

35. Minutes of the council meeting, Oct. 13, 1936, EPC papers, box 2.

36. During World War II, 6,000 men were jailed for resistance to the draft or nonregistration, 12,000 joined the military as noncombatants, and 12,000 did alternative service in the Civilian Public Service camps. This total of 30,000, including members of the historic peace churches, represents a modest increase over the World War I total of 25,000, of whom 4,000 were jailed, and 21,000 served in noncombatant situations (there was no CPS program during WWI). Statistics from Wittner (1984) and Chatfield (1971).

37. According to Young (1987), new traditions and philosophies tend to arise within the peace movement during wartime.

38. The pacifists probably made this disproportionate contribution to control the EPC. James Mullin believes, however (personal communication), that they acted not on a Machiavellian calculus but from a sense of urgency and a belief that if they did not sponsor the campaign nobody would.

39. W. O. Mendenhall, in minutes of the Executive Committee of the EPC, Jan. 15, 1936, EPC papers, box 2.

40. Minutes of the meeting of the council, Feb. 2, 1937, EPC papers, box 2.

41. The EPC had by its own estimate about 1,200 local committees and 600 local contacts. Earlier, I used a round figure of two thousand—a rounding-up of the total.

42. There was some debate over whether to create the area offices as semiautonomous agencies. The EPC leadership decided to keep the area offices under the strict control of the national office. Minutes of the EPC Executive Committee, Jan. 15, 1936 and Feb. 6, 1936, EPC papers, box 2.

43. Minutes of the EPC council, June 1, 1937, EPC papers, box 2. The goal for 1937 was to have 2,000 local committees (minutes of the EPC council, Feb. 2, 1937, EPC papers, box 2). The 1,200 local committees formed fell short of this number, though they were supplemented by 600 "contacts" in other cities and towns.

44. Bulletins to area directors, EPC papers, box 158.

45. "The National Peace Conference and the Local Peace Councils," Feb. 1, 1937, EPC papers, box 2. Although this is a question of only one or two people in each community, for the most part, it is important. The answer would indicate how far the EPC was able to extend peace activism, even if only for a short while, beyond the established set of local activists. It will require additional research to try to establish this.

46. During the December 1935 EPC planning meeting, Sayre stated that one goal of the EPC should be to leave local groups stronger. The lack of debate and opposition to this statement was probably owing to the vague way in which it was stated. (Minutes of Buck Hills Falls conference, 12/4-6/1935, EPC papers, box 1.)

47. Minutes of the EPC council, Feb. 2, 1937, EPC papers, box 2.

48. Minutes of the EPC council, Feb. 2, 1937, EPC papers, box 2.

49. The EPC leadership agreed to urge local groups to affiliate with the NPC; it is not clear how many did so once the EPC folded.

50. In 1983 dollars—a baseline for comparing the campaigns—the EPC had a two-year budget of more than $4 million.

51. Total budget from a press release dated Dec. 31, 1937, issued at the end of the campaign, EPC papers, box 2. The two-thirds figure is based on an internal EPC document, "Is a Coalition of Peace Agencies Possible and Desirable?," which reported that as of March 10, 1937, the EPC received $282,250 in thirty-six large gifts ranging from $1,000 to $50,000, and $140,000 in 20,000 smaller contributions. The source of the figures on initial funds is a letter from Kirby Page to local contacts, EPC papers, box 3.

52. I discuss this point in more detail in an article on the EPC (Kleidman 1986).

5. The Atomic Test Ban Campaign

1. Wittner (1984) is the primary source for this section. DeBenedetti (1980) is also very informative.

2. Wittner (1984, chap. 4) adds that expectations before the war were also lower than before World War I, the "war to end all wars," so people were less likely to be disillusioned with the outcome.

3. Senator Arthur Vandenberg is quoted in LaFeber (1980, 54). Some critics of the cold war argue that with the war over, many economic and political leaders feared a return to prewar economic conditions, and favored a continuation of "military Keynesianism" as a way of staving off recession. Others emphasize the role of the military in promoting economic penetration of Europe and the Third World.

4. The use of fear to mobilize activism is seen as a double-edged sword by Sandman and Valenti (1986) and by Wittner (1984).

5. A good account of these negotiations and American postwar nuclear policy is in Herken (1982).

6. Underground tests, requiring more complicated technology than atmospheric tests, were not conducted until 1957; most tests were conducted above ground until the 1963 treaty.

7. The NSC report has never been declassified, but Divine (1978) presents strong evidence that it did favor a test ban.

8. Homer Jack, letter to the author, Nov. 18, 1991.

9. Key secondary sources for the history of SANE are M. Katz (1973, 1986), and for CNVA, N. Katz (1973). Other important secondary sources for the movement and the test ban negotiations include DeBenedetti (1980), Wittner (1984), and Divine (1978).

10. I have seen no indications that the founders of the test ban campaign consciously drew any lessons from the EPC in their planning. Nor, for that matter, did the planning of the nuclear freeze campaign seem to involve any reflections on either the EPC or the test ban campaign.

11. Memo from Lawrence Scott to interested parties, May 13, 1957, SANE papers, ser. B, box 4.

12. The information about Quaker money was provided by Stephen Cary (interview), a Quaker activist and educator, who added that family fortunes tended to erode because children of wealthy Quakers often went into service occupations rather than business. The two Chase sisters, key sponsors of the EPC, by the 1950s had died and left their money to a Quaker meeting in Philadelphia; the trustees of the estate were not as interested in giving large sums to activists.

13. Minutes of the organizing committee, Oct. 8, 1957, SANE papers, ser. B, box 5.

14. Sanford Gottlieb was not present at the meeting where Gilmore proposed the coupons but was confident that this is what had happened.

15. Minutes of provisional committee, June 21, 1957, SANE papers, ser. A, box 4.

16. Some — it is not clear how many — were former Communist party members, disillusioned with the party and looking for an issue around which to organize. Their presence, concentrated in the New York region, became a key issue in 1960 when SANE was torn apart by red-baiting.

17. Figures and quotations are from an internal SANE report dated Jan. 1958, cited by M. Katz (1973, 81–85).

18. Flynn (1964) reports that Gottlieb in 1963 estimated that 80 percent of SANE's members were white collar or professional, and only 5 percent fell into the lowest third in national family income.

19. Morris (1984) details important links between groups such as FOR (which he characterizes as "movement halfway houses"), pacifist-oriented civil rights organizations such as CORE, and leading civil rights figures, including King. The FOR and other peace organizations introduced King and other civil rights leaders to the philosophy and techniques of nonviolence — which the civil rights leaders then transformed into a disciplined, effective mass strategy.

20. One delegate alleged that three people set national policy. Report of Pawling working conference, SANE papers, ser. B, box 13.

21. *SANE-U.S.A.* (1958); report of Pawling working conference, SANE papers, ser. B, box 13.

22. SANE's budget for the fiscal year July 1, 1958, through June 30, 1959, was just over $50,000. Most of this came from mail and individual solicitations and other small gifts, with only $2,100 coming from local committee contributions. SANE budget document, SANE papers, ser. A, box 9.

23. *New York Times,* Feb. 2, 1959, cited by Divine (1978, 250).

24. SANE had few major sponsors, but Lenore Marshall, who had helped SANE get started, loaned the organization $5,000 during this period.

25. Information on these meetings is from the minutes of the second annual national conference, Oct. 25–26, 1959, SANE papers, ser. A, box 9.

26. More precisely, it marked the end of this stage of the quest for a comprehensive test ban. The idea was revived in the late 1970s, and President Carter apparently negotiated a comprehensive ban but did not submit it to the Senate, where it would have been defeated after the Soviet invasion of Afghanistan. Revived during the nuclear freeze campaign, it is currently a negotiating item between the superpowers.

27. Gottlieb, a labor organizer, had responded to SANE's first ad, joining and later chairing the Washington, D.C., chapter and becoming a member of the na-

tional board of directors. As the NWFC did years later, SANE eventually consolidated its offices in Washington.

28. Lear said some members of expelled chapters continued to work with SANE as individuals (M. Katz 1986, 55–56).

29. Donald Keys had resigned as executive director to become program director when Homer Jack was hired as the new executive director. Sanford Gottlieb remained as political director, and Ed Meyerding was hired as development director. Leaders saw this staff increase as giving SANE the ability to manage a much larger program than it could the previous fall, when only the position of executive director existed. "Summary, Third National Conference of the National Committee for a Sane Nuclear Policy, October 14–16, Chicago," SANE papers, ser. A, box 9.

30. Records of discussions from "National Committee for a SANE Nuclear Policy, Minutes of Special Board Meeting—June 16-17, 1961—New Canaan, Connecticut," SANE Papers, ser. A, box 4.

31. The 26,000 included chapter members and others subscribing to the national newsletter, *SANE-U.S.A.*

32. Disagreements over the necessary number and scope of inspections of seismic events proved to be a key factor in excluding underground testing from the 1963 test ban treaty. Glenn T. Seaborg, chair of the AEC under Kennedy, later acknowledged that American proposals would have opened huge areas of Soviet territory to onsite inspection, something he believed the suspicious Soviet regime could not have accepted. He further argued that such inspections were not required to achieve a technically sound comprehensive test ban treaty, but without them pressure from the Right on the U.S. Senate would have killed the ban (Seaborg 1981).

33. "Proceedings, Fourth National Conference of the National Committee for a SANE Nuclear Policy, October 12–15, 1961 New York City," SANE papers, ser. A, box 9.

34. Minutes of Oct. 23 and 30 board meeting, SANE papers, ser. A, box 4.

35. The impression that some of WSP's leaders were disillusioned SANE members is shared by Sanford Gottlieb (interview) and Donald Keys (1965), who adds that although the WSP leadership consisted of longtime activists, most members were new to the movement.

36. Minutes of national board meeting, Nov. 26, 1962, SANE papers, ser. A, box 4.

37. Minutes of national board meeting, Nov. 20, 1961, SANE Papers, ser. A, box 4.

38. This was Spock's first significant participation with SANE; he served as national cochair from 1964 through 1967.

39. "Staff Conclusions about National Student SANE," Jan. 10, 1962, SANE Papers, ser. A, box 19.

40. This issue surfaced again in disputes within SANE and other liberal organizations over cooperation with more radical groups in protests against the Vietnam War and led to the departure of Dr. Spock and the more radical members of SANE in 1967. As Donald Keys (1965, 297) saw it, the generation represented by the student leaders came of political age in the era of McCarthy, and saw issues of exclusionism primarily in civil-liberties terms. Also, they did not have to contend with a large and manipulative Communist party, as had activists of the 1930s, and hence had a more benign view of Communists and the far Left.

41. In fact, this is what happened in 1963.

42. Cousins (1972) offers a fascinating if not very critical insider's view of these contacts.

43. Seaborg (1981, 174) claims the air strike was planned for the next day, Oct. 29; LaFeber (1980, 228) claims it was planned for Oct. 30.

44. Flynn (1964) counted two peace candidates reelected to the House, joined by three from California running as Democrats, vs. nine major-party peace candidates defeated in the general election.

45. "National Committee for a SANE Nuclear Policy Joint Staff Report (Covering Period of Oct. 15, 1961, to Oct. 1, 1962)," SANE papers, ser. E, box 2. Paarlberg (1973) claims that the salience of the nuclear issue peaked between 1961 and 1963.

46. This observation about local problems was actually made in Donald Keys's March field trip report.

47. "National Committee for a SANE Nuclear Policy, Minutes for the National Board Meeting, Nov. 26, 1962," SANE papers, ser. A, box 4. The proposed budget of SANE, which had fewer than a dozen staff members, was $200,000. The SCLC, headed by Martin Luther King, Jr., had a 1963 budget of more than $1 million, and almost one hundred full-time staff members (Morris 1984). Although SANE was the only major test ban campaign organization of national scope, the SCLC was but one of four leading civil rights groups; and at this stage, it was focusing its efforts almost exclusively on the South (although it was also raising funds in the North).

48. See Bottome (1986) for a discussion of these issues. The debates around SDI ("Star Wars") and other aspects of Reagan administration policies in the 1980s followed similar logic.

49. I.F. Stone (1970) argues that Khrushchev was hoping for a major reduction in hostilities with the West, as tensions between China and the Soviet Union were escalating. The United States, however, sided with Adenauer and other German conservatives in rejecting plans for a neutralized Germany and other measures reducing the role of the military in the European cold war. These two powers instead hoped that an escalation of the arms race and other pressures would force the Soviet Union to accept a Germany reunified on Western terms.

50. "Final Report, Joint Campaign for Three Letters," SANE papers, ser. E, box 2.

51. Minutes of Sept. 16, 1963, national board meeting, SANE papers, ser. A, box 4.

52. Homer Jack, "Next Steps in the American Peace Movement," Oct. 1, 1963, SANE papers, ser. A, box 5.

53. M. Katz (1973, 206) quotes Gottlieb as contending that one UWF board member in particular proved to be the stumbling block.

54. For example, Kriesberg (1985, 12) cites surveys showing that in 1962, after the moratorium had broken down and the Soviets had resumed testing, the public seemed prepared to support Kennedy whether or not he decided to begin atmospheric testing.

55. According to Fine (1982), at the outset of the campaign, WILPF and FOR were primarily national organizations with "feeble" local efforts, the WRL was limited to the new York City metropolitan area, for the most part, and the AFSC had a strong constituency in a number of locations, but was unable to develop a core group of leaders and activists. Flynn (1964) estimated that by June 1963, of all the peace groups, only the AFSC could come close to matching the 20,000–30,000 members he estimated SANE had at that time. None had the national funding or staff that gave the

1930s peace groups a strong presence. Sanford Gottlieb (interview) had similar opinions about the weakness of the established movement, noting that of the two major groupings present at the start of the campaign, the pacifists were out of the mainstream, and the world federalists' concern for world order was too structured and mechanistic to interest many. Both were, in his view, narrow and doctrinaire.

56. SANE started with funds of a few thousand dollars; the EPC began with $100,000 (more than $200,000 in 1960 dollars) pacificists had raised.

57. The income of $216,526 was for SANE's 1962-63 fiscal year ("Joint Staff Report Covering Period of Oct. 1, 1962 to Nov. 1, 1963," SANE papers, ser. E, box 2).

58. I use 1984 dollars as a standard for all three campaigns. Direct comparisons between a six-year campaign like SANE's and the two years of the EPC are tricky, but there is no question that the size and scope of the EPC's national-level operation were much greater than SANE's. Note also that the EPC took place during the Depression, and the test ban campaign arose during a period of relative affluence and economic growth. On the other hand, SANE's more extensive and vigorous local chapters did raise and spend some money, but probably not a great deal because only two had paid staff.

59. *SANE-U.S.A.,* May 20, 1958; report of Pawling working conference, SANE papers, ser. B, box 13.

60. New York: "A Meeting of Local Group Leaders, New York—Metropolitan Area Committees for a SANE Nuclear Policy, January 12, 1958," SANE papers, ser. B, box 4. Chicago: Memo from Carol Urner, Oct. 31, 1957, SANE papers, ser. B, box 4.

61. The figures come from a variety of SANE documents, some of which claimed that chapters were being added after 1959. The natural inference, assuming the net figures are roughly correct, is that chapters folded at about the same rate as new chapters were formed.

62. Sanford Gottlieb (interview) and *SANE-U.S.A.,* May 20, 1958; report of Pawling working conference, SANE papers, ser. B, box 13.

63. This conclusion, based on field reports, staff reports, and the interviews I conducted, reflects the perspective of national staff members of SANE both during and after the campaign.

64. "Summary, Third National Conference of the National Committee for a SANE Nuclear Policy, October 14–16, Chicago," SANE papers, ser. A, box 9.

65. Probably just two local chapters had hired paid staff, New York and Chicago.

66. Both Sanford Gottlieb and Homer Jack (interviews) saw nothing unusual in the problems SANE encountered in this regard. Jack remarked on the general problem of "policing" local chapters.

67. The figures come from a number of documents in the Swarthmore collections. An undertermined number of EPC staff were serving at subsistence wages as part of the emergency mobilization against war, and some top staff were paid by their home organizations. Nevertheless, the contrast between the two budgets—the EPC's was almost three times SANE's—indicates that the difference in staff size reflects a real difference in the professional components of the campaigns.

68. The activist figures are estimates, based on the assumption that each of SANE's 175 chapters had a core group of five to ten volunteers and another fifteen to twenty occasional activists, numbers typical of SMOs at their peak.

6. The Nuclear Weapons Freeze Campaign

1. The major secondary sources for this chapter include Leavitt (1983A, 1983B), Meyer (1988, 1990A), Solo (1988), and Waller (1987). The NWFC documents, however, unlike the material from the EPC or the test ban campaign, are not archived in the Swarthmore College Peace Collection. While researching this chapter, I visited the National Clearinghouse of the Freeze Campaign twice and recieved complete access to documents on file. These are cited by title. These documents were later donated to the Western Historical Manuscript Collection at the University of Missouri–St. Louis.

As a participant in the freeze campaign, I have my own experiences to draw upon. I was an active board member of the Wisconsin NWFC from 1983 through 1989, took part in national conferences from 1983 through the 1987 merger with SANE, and served as the Wisconsin member of the national board of SANE/FREEZE from Jan. 1988 through the spring of 1989. For two summers I canvassed door-to-door for the Wisconsin NWFC.

I conducted informal interviews with NWFC leaders and activists to supplement these sources, and have reviewed partial transcripts of interviews of fifty-five key leaders kindly provided to me by Bruce Ferguson. These interviews were the basis of his "Lessons of the Nuclear Freeze Movement" (1987), cited in this chapter. Ken Mack also provided me with transcripts and tapes of interviews he conducted with key leaders, including Randall Kehler and Betsy Taylor, material he used in his undergraduate thesis (Mack 1987).

2. The term "freeze" has three meanings. I will use "Nuclear Weapons Freeze Campaign" or "NWFC" to refer to the central organization, "nuclear freeze campaign" or "freeze campaign" to mean the larger mobilization that involved activists outside as well as inside the NWFC, and "freeze proposal" or "freeze idea" for the policy promoted by the campaign. Occasionally, I will simply use "freeze" to mean the campaign or the idea, if the context makes clear which is meant.

3. Smith (1991) argues that the end of American economic hegemony and the decline of Soviet power changed superpower relations, and that the peace movement in the United States has failed to appreciate both its own lack of success and the likelihood of continued American militarism and interventionism.

4. Ronald Reagan resurrected the B-1 in 1980, with deployment of almost one hundred B-1s at a cost of almost $40 billion a few years later. For a detailed history of the B-1, see Kotz (1988). Both Kotz and Hedrick Smith (1988) view the B-1 as a persistent and ultimately successful exercise in power by the military-industrial complex. In Mar. 1989, the Air Force's fleet of ninety-seven B-1s, costing more than $300 million each, was grounded for the third time by the latest malfunction. One estimate for the cost of fixing the fleet was $11 billion, according to the *Los Angeles Times*, Mar. 19, 1989.

5. Meyer (1988, 239), quoting Terry Provance of the AFSC. Meyer notes that Carter's B-1 action was tempered by his decision to proceed with developing another bomber, which became the high-technology Stealth radar-evading plane, and to deploy nuclear cruise missiles on the B-52 fleet.

6. The main source for membership and other figures (most of them, from 1982 and 1983, reflect growth owing to the freeze campaign) is Leavitt (1983B).

7. Caldicott's riveting speeches, which featured graphic descriptions of the consequences of atomic blasts, were criticized by some activists for appealing too strongly

to fear, and for making unsubstantiated, dire predictions of the near-certainty of nuclear war should measures like the freeze not be enacted. See, for example, Sandman and Valenti (1986).

8. A comprehensive account of the move to conservative voting patterns would require considering many other factors, including Democratic party politics and the rise of the evangelical Right. Ferguson and Rogers (1986A) also argue that while voting and policy moved to the right, most Americans continue to support New Deal-style economic policies that many would consider liberal.

9. As many in the peace movement have argued, and as more recent and more popular interventions have shown, the main concern of the American public and elites has been American lives. Much less regard has been shown for the lives of those living in the Third World.

10. Critics referred to deterrence as MAD, mutual assured destruction. They believed that the threat of a Soviet first strike had been greatly inflated by groups like the CPD, which overestimated the number and size of Soviet missiles. They also believed that the United States would not be as vulnerable as the Soviets to a first strike because a much higher percentage of its nuclear missiles were on submarines, which could not be destroyed by Soviet missiles.

11. Critics argued that war fighting had been United States policy for many years, but public pronouncements had generally been based on simple deterrence (against a nuclear strike only). The release of PD59 alarmed peace leaders and moderates in the arms control groups.

12. This was a trend greatly escalated under Reagan. Real military spending increased another 50 percent from 1980 to 1985.

13. The first-strike element: the Pershings could reach key Soviet facilities in a few minutes; the cruise missiles were supposed to fly low enough to avoid early-warning radar. The announcement of planned NATO deployment of 572 of these missiles in Holland, Italy, Belgium, Great Britain, and West Germany was supposedly designed to pressure the Soviets into withdrawing their new missiles. The Soviet position was that their new SS-20s and SS-22s were a counter to British and French missiles, a position NATO did not accept.

14. In addition to Solo's (1988) views on this matter, Ferguson's (1987) survey of fifty-five leaders found many who believed the freeze campaign suffered from a lack of both leadership and clear, efficient decision-making structures.

15. According to a "Report On Fund-Raising for the Nuclear Weapon [sic] Freeze" dated Feb. 1, 1981 (NWFC papers), contributions to that point, other than the Kay grant, totalled $2,425, plus another $375 pledged. Apparently Kay had stipulated some matching plan: the document states "Submitted to Mr. Alan Kay in fulfillment of fund-raising arrangement for release of his total gift."

16. Cockburn and Ridgeway (1983), who are mostly sympathetic to this critical view, also looked for signs that freeze activists were on a "learning curve," having joined the movement because of the immediacy of the issue then becoming more politicized. Senturia (interview) says that part of the "broad front door" strategy of the freeze was to encourage this process, that many freeze activists did move on to other issues and movements, including Central American "solidarity" work, opposing United States military intervention and supporting indigenous democratic forces.

17. Leavitt (1983A, 28) notes that in the spring of 1981, the clearinghouse could not raise the funds to hire a lawyer to do the campaign's tax work. Campaign documents indicate that fund raising from the March conference through mid-December 1981

totaled only $38,000. Of this, $6,000 was from a grant from the CLW, a leading liberal arms-control lobbying group, and one of the few to give the campaign strong early support. Another $20,000 came from two individual grants of $10,000 each. The first year of the freeze campaign, therefore, was funded for under $50,000 at the national level, in contrast with the EPC's first-year budget of more than $2 million (in 1984 dollars), which included $700,000 raised before the EPC officially began.

18. Kehler, 1981, "Local Organizing: What's Next?" *Freeze Newsletter* 1, no. 3 (Oct.): 4–5.

19. Leavitt (1983B, 5) claims most of the local groups were started by people with little previous social movement experience. This is probably true — so many local groups emerged — it also seems that many people with organizing and other relevant backgrounds helped in this process, certainly more than was the case in the previous two campaigns. Price (1988), who surveyed a North Carolina local NWFC group in 1985, and the national board of SANE/FREEZE in 1987, found that in both groups most members were of the 1960s generation. This group constituted more than 70 percent of the national board, which was composed mainly of people who had been local activists (then state-level activists, in some cases as paid staff) during the start of the freeze campaign.

This is only weak evidence for the claim that veterans of the 1960s movements provided the majority of this early second group of volunteers. My own observations in Wisconsin and at national conferences of the Freeze Campaign (starting, in both cases, in 1983) persuade me that this generation was important both in numbers and in shaping the political culture of the NWFC. Others I have spoken with agree, as do some of Ferguson's (1987) informants. Solo (1988) does not discuss the background of these activists, but the antileadership attitudes she (and others) observed in the campaign can be attributed in part to values of participation prominent in movements of the 1960s New Left. Additional support comes from McAdams's (1988, 203) follow-up study of volunteers from the Mississippi Summer Project of 1964. He found that 61 percent of his sample claimed to be involved in antinuclear activity to some degree (12 percent said they were "very" involved, 18 percent "moderately," and 31 percent "somewhat").

20. Leavitt (1983B, 5) describes the major peace groups.

21. The 20,000 figure, from the "Freeze Progress Line" in the NWFC March 1983 Request for Funding, is reported as the figure for Jan. 1982. Given the looseness of the NWFC network, this is obviously a guess; it may be a high estimate.

22. Gitlin (1987) shows how many New Left activists reacted against what they saw as obsessive anticommunism among the non-Communist Old Left by adopting open structures in organizations such as SDS. The same values influenced some of the early freeze activists.

23. "Nuclear Weapons Freeze Campaign Fundraising Plan, May–December 1982," NWFC papers. The $350,000–$375,000 is my best estimate of total fund-raising plans, based on several partial figures in the document.

24. Total and subtotals are from "Nuclear Weapons Freeze Campaign Request for Funding," Mar. 1983, Summary of Income and Expenditures 1982.

25. Molander did not actually support a freeze, which he saw as a simple, technical-fix approach to a complex problem. He thought the campaign offered a chance to education some of the public about these complexities (Meyer 1990, 128).

26. The rhetoric did not change overnight. Reagan made his famous "evil empire" speech in Mar. 1983.

27. The tactical use of arms control talks was hardly new. Solo (1988, 86) cites activist Sidney Lens who reported that Paul Nitze, a top administration negotiator, had in 1950 suggested that the United States offer implausible deals to the Soviets and use their refusals to justify greater buildups. In the unlikely event that these proposals were accepted, he said, the United States should be prepared to withdraw them.

28. Also by Nov. 1982, the freeze campaign listed endorsements from 11 state legislatures (one or both houses), 321 city councils, and 446 New England town meetings.

29. Waller (1987, 178–179) notes some confusion in the language of the measure passed at the conference. In calling for the United States to enact a freeze, some sections said Congress should make this contingent on similar Soviet restraint; others said Congress should call upon the Soviets to match the American initiative. To Waller, the latter language was political dynamite that could have been used to brand the freeze as favoring unilateral steps. It was, he says, generally ignored by the media.

30. Solo (1988, 119–23) stresses the influence of Waller, Markey's aide, and Jan Kalicki, Kennedy's chief foreign policy advisor, both of whom had been working with Freeze leaders, and of Christopher Paine of the Federation of American Scientists (FAS), a liaison with Senator Kennedy. Waller's own account (Waller 1987) credits himself and Kalicki with some influence in lobbying the conference, and on the merits of the debate takes the "political realist" view criticized by Solo.

31. Solo (1988, 115) reports that as chair of the strategy committee, she drafted a proposal urging a broader focus. Kehler and other national staff members chose to present a more narrowly drawn proposal to the conference.

32. "Decisions Made by the Third National Conference of the Nuclear Weapons Freeze Campaign," NWFC papers.

33. "Nuclear Weapons Freeze Campaign Request for Funding 1984, Summary of Income and Expenditure Dec. 1, 1982 to Nov. 30, 1983."

34. "Nuclear Weapons Freeze Campaign Request for Funding, March 1983," "Nuclear Weapons Freeze Campaign Request for Funding, 1984."

35. "Memo to Executive Committee from Barbara Roche, October 31, 1984," including "Chronology of Outreach and Field Programs," NWFC papers.

36. Two of the four were regionally based organizers who traveled to locals. Two liaisons based in St. Louis did their work by mail and telephone.

37. SDI opponents argued that the program could never prevent a successful first strike by the Soviets, but it might persuade American planners that the United States could strike first and use SDI to intercept the few Soviet missiles that would survive this strike. They saw SDI, therefore, as part of a nuclear war-fighting strategy, not as an alternative to it. The Soviets have opposed SDI, claiming that it is a destabilizing system and that testing it would violate the treaty.

38. Elizabeth Drew's fascinating account of the congressional votes revealed that Les Aspin, then Democratic chair of the House Armed Services Committee, had worked with the administration to orchestrate the timing of the freeze and the MX votes (Drew 1983). Aspin, who claimed to accept the bargaining chip theory, knew that many representatives would vote yes on both to stay in the political middle.

39. During 1983, the campaign added two new offices to the St. Louis clearinghouse and the Washington lobbying office. Kehler moved back to western Massachusetts for personal reasons. Rather than lose his skills in fund-raising and in mediating between different groups in the NWFC, the national leadership set up a separate office for him. The fourth office opened in Denver in May as a base of operations for the new minority outreach coordinator.

40. The conference also voted to encourage any groups and individuals, including NWFC staff members, who wished to do direct action to do so independently of the campaign.

41. Election laws permit some overlap in membership between the two boards. Like many groups the NWFC took advantage of this to provision to try to keep the SMO and the PAC in harmony.

42. Senturia (interview) sees the problems as stemming less from competition and more from a lack of communication between the NWFC and Freeze Voter, a Washington-based organization trying to capitalize on the strength of the freeze movement, the volunteers outside Washington.

43. "Decisions Made By the Fourth National Conference of the Nuclear Weapons Freeze Campaign," Dec. 2–4, 1983, NWFC papers.

44. Analysts, including Ferguson and Rogers (1986A), argue that the perceived recovery was the major reason for Reagan's reelection.

45. The Soviets even hinted that there could be no agreements as long as Reagan was president (Talbott 1985, 352).

46. These discussions would lead to a Jan. 1985 agreement to resume arms control talks.

47. Nationally, Freeze Voter raised almost $1.5 million, and state-level Freeze PACs added almost $2.25 million, giving freeze groups more than half the total of $5.4 million raised by peace and arms control PACs in 1984 (Taylor 1985B). Taylor also noted great variation in the quality of the volunteers recruited and in the ability of recruiting organizations to deploy them skillfully.

48. According to Hertsgaard, the national mass media imposed a "virtual blackout" on the campaign after the 1983 House resolution. He cites statistics showing that in 1982 the three major networks included on their evening news programs ninety-five freeze-related stories. This declines to sixty-one in 1983, thirty-nine of them during the peak of the House debates from March to May, and almost none thereafter. One reason he cites for the media's general reluctance to cover grassroots movements is that such reporting requires a large commitment of time and money. He claims that the exception that proves the rule was the extensive coverage given the civil rights movement.

49. The number of volunteer activists is hard to determine because the NWFC had no national membership program.

50. Comparable increases during 1984, 1985, and 1986 at state and local levels were noted in two related areas: the number of formal offices went from forty to fifty to fifty-seven; the number of paid staff members changed from 66.5 to 115 to 108. These figures are from a series of "Status of State Level Freeze Organization" reports, NWFC papers.

Some of this growth occurred when several state and local organizations developed paid canvasses. Wisconsin, for example shows an increase in staff from three in 1984 to sixteen in 1985. This represented the addition of a paid door-to-door canvassing operation, and counts canvassers as paid staff. Some scholars and activists see canvasses as fund-raising operations; others see them also as educational and organizing tools. Not all canvasses generate more funds than they absorb in salaries and overhead. From the first perspective, therefore, canvass staff should be counted in a different category from other staff. Adding a canvass may not expand the impact of the organization. Unfortunately, NWFC statistics do not count canvass staff separately.

51. In "A Special Message to Local Groups from the Freeze Executive Committee" included with the July/Aug. 1986 local organizers mailing, the committee reported, "Foundation supporters (providing over 80% of our budget) had hoped grassroots Freeze supporters would provide a larger share of the budget and that at some point they could begin to provide less. This spring [1986], foundation support dropped dramatically and grassroots support, while growing steadily, could not fill the gap."

52. Chavez did note that the UFW took help from sympathizers in handouts of food and small contributions. This account of his speech is from notes I took at the conference.

53. Solo (1988, 159–60) makes similar observations about the national conference debating minor points rather than focusing on key issues, a problem I observed at the conferences I attended between 1983 and 1986.

54. The structure task force's report also called for the removal of decision-making power from the national conference, and the reconstitution of the national committee as a board of directors-type organization with final authority. After heated debate, this part of the report was rejected. Solo (1988), a member of the task force, does not separate the conference's rejection of this part of the report from its acceptance of the rest.

55. Forsberg, who distanced herself from the NWFC, had served as president of the board of Freeze Voter.

56. The only category showing a significant increase was direct mail, which went from $45,000 in 1983 to $199,000 in 1987.

57. SANE's total revenue for 1987 was slightly more than $4 million, with receipts broken down as follows (in rounded-off numbers): membership dues, $1.9 million; contributions (phone, mail, and other solicitations), $1.1 million; grants $580,000, plus other miscellaneous income. The "grants" category lists $546,000 in contributions to SANE's tax-exempt education fund. I have not looked into how much of this came from foundations, which tend to give to education funds rather than to the parent organization (this was also the case with the Freeze; figures I reported combined these two).

58. Seymour Melman (1965, 1974), a board member of SANE, had been a pioneer in developing ideas about "economic conversion" to a peace economy.

59. Don Shaffer, SANE treasurer, replied to Judis in a letter to In These Times, (Aug. 5–8, 1987). A reply from Judis restated his criticisms.

60. I observed this clash while serving as a national board member of SANE/ FREEZE in 1988. It seemed to me that SANE had been influenced by the Old Left, and the NWFC by the New Left.

61. A former field director for the NWFC described this process to me as illustrating the differences in perspective between national and local activists. The former had failed to adequately consult the latter, who rebelled.

62. An internal or membership PAC could be run by the organization's staff and board. A large membership would minimize the limitations of an internal PAC, especially the inability to solicit funds from nonmembers.

63. The 1988 national congress elevated economic conversion to the organization's top goal. The 1991 national congress set a goal of a 50 percent cut in military spending over the next five years.

64. Even though SALT I had a built-in expiration date and SALT II was never ratified by the Senate, both sides had abided by their limits.

65. According to Waller (1987, 302) "some of this congressional activity would

have occurred without the movement. . . . But there is no doubt that more congressional activity occurred because of the freeze."

66. Senturia (interview) believes that this may be the NWFC's most important legacy.

67. Solo (1988) emphasizes this lack of planning.

68. Solo (1988, 88) asserts that even as early as 1982, the established peace groups lost funding as the NWFC grew, but she does not document this claim. Many groups did gain new activists during the rise of the freeze campaign.

69. Kehler (1984). *Nuclear Times,* a journal begun in 1982 accompanying the upsurge of the freeze movement, suspended publication in 1989 for financial reasons and resumed in the spring of 1990. Reflecting changes in the movement, it shifted focus beyond nuclear disarmament to issues of "global security," including international political and economic relations, the environment, and human rights. *Nuclear Times,* however, ceased publication in 1992.

70. Because of the absence of formal affiliation in the early stages of the NWFC, there are not good figures available for the number of local chapters. The NWFC counted more than 1,300 in Oct. 1984, and recorded an increase to more than 1,800 in mid-1986. This increase, after the peak of the public campaign, may represent an increase in those groups formally or informally affiliating with state organizations, rather than a continuing growth in the formation of local chapters.

71. Nuclear Weapons Freeze Campaign Requests for Funding 1983–1987, summary of income and expenditure, NWFC papers.

72. One plan, for example, called for charging each state a fixed dollar amount per member. Leaders of the Wisconsin Freeze, which had recruited more than 10,000 members in a paid door-to-door canvas, and leaders of similarly structured groups objected that this plan would penalize them and reward states that had not established a formal membership program.

73. State and local NWFC groups employed both full-time and part-time staff. Together they worked the equivalent of sixty-six full-time employees. "Status of State Level Freeze Organizations, October, 1984," NWFC papers.

74. Solo (1988) strongly criticizes the leadership and strategy process of the NWFC. Others have similar criticisms, although they may analyze the causes and evaluate particular groups, people, and incidents differently.

75. Several leaders interviewed by Ferguson (1987) identified this as a problem, as did Solo (1988). On the basis of my observations as a participant in the NWFC, I agree with this critique.

76. Senturia (interview) maintains that a key lesson of the freeze is that once you tell a locally based movement that had emphasized local, short-term goals that success depends on Washington, you lose control of the movement.

77. Foundation grants for research and education on "international security and the prevention of nuclear war" increased from $16.5 million in 1982 to $52 million in 1984. More than 70 percent came from five major "multi-nationally oriented" foundations: MacArthur, Carnegie, Ford, Rockefeller, and W. Alton Jones (Ferguson and Rogers 1986B). Although most of this money supported research, an important part directly or indirectly funded activism, through activist groups' tax-exempt arms, such as the NWFC Education Fund.

78. Ferguson and Rogers (1986A, 1986B) and Wright, Rodriguez and Waitzkin (1985) reduce the NWFC to an instrument of these elites.

79. From the national staff list included in the "Nuclear Weapons Freeze Campaign Request for Funding, 1984," NWFC papers.

80. Similarly, Jenkins and Eckert (1986) conclude that in the 1960s, elite support of the civil rights movement followed the rise of indigenous activism and influenced the course of the movement by encouraging moderate professional activism rather than radical grassroots groups.

81. Solo (1988) makes the strongest critique on these lines.

7. The Organizational Dynamics of Modern American Peace Campaigns

1. All budget figures are in 1984 dollars for ready comparisons.

2. NWFC employees were almost all full time. The statistics for state and local employees are in full-time-equivalents — the figure may represent more than sixty-six individuals.

3. Solo (1988) and other observers agree on Kehler's style, although they disagree on how well this worked in giving the campaign leadership and direction.

4. Jenkins and Eckert (1986) claim that this process occurred in the civil rights movement.

5. None of the minutes of the major planning sessions of the campaigns that I have looked at reflect any consideration of previous campaigns.

6. Frank Blechman, a field organizer for the NWFC (interview), emphasized this as one reason for the NWFC's lack of historical reflection.

Bibliography

Manuscript Collections

Swarthmore College Peace Collection, Swarthmore Pa.:
    Emergency Peace Campaign (EPC)
    Committee for Nonviolent Action (CNVA)
    National Council for Prevention of War (NCPW)
    SANE, A Citizens' Organization for a Sane World [Formerly The Committee for a Sane Nuclear Policy] (SANE)
Western Historical Manuscript Collection, University of Missouri–St. Louis:
    Nuclear Weapons Freeze Campaign (NWFC)

Interviews

Frank Blechman, telephone, Mar. 12, 1991
Stephen Cary, telephone, Jan. 30, 1990
Sanford Gottlieb, telephone, Nov. 24, 1986
Homer Jack, telephone, Nov. 28, 1986; Dec. 19, 1987
James Mullin, Iowa City, IA, May 5, 1989
Ben Senturia, telephone, June 20 and July 2, 1991

Books and Articles

Adams, Gordon. 1982. *The Politics of Defense Contracting: The Iron Triangle.* New Brunswick, N.J.: Transaction.
Agnew, John A. 1987. *Place and Politics.* Boston: Allen & Unwin.
Aldridge, Robert C. 1983. *First Strike!* Boston: South End.
Alford, Robert R. 1985. *Powers of Theory.* Cambridge: Cambridge Univ. Press.
Alger, Chadwick F., and Saul Mendlovitz. 1983. "Grass Roots Activism in the United States: Global Implications." *Alternatives* 9:619–46.
Allen, Devere. 1934. "The Peace Movement Moves Left." *Annals of the American Academy of Political and Social Science* 175:150–55.

Americans Talk Security Project. 1988. *Americans Talk Security.* Winchester, Mass.: ATS Project.

Aminzade, Ronald. 1992. "Historical Sociology and Time." *Sociological Methods and Research* 20, no. 4:456–80.

Ash, Roberta. 1972. *Social Movements in America.* Chicago: Markham.

Ayvazian, Andrea, and Michael Klare. 1986. "Decision Time for the American Peace Movement." *Fellowship,* Sept.:12–14.

———. 1990. "The Civilization Crisis: Activists Voice Their Hopes for a New Era." *Nuclear Times* 8, no. 1:11–17, 52–53.

Barkan, Steven E., William H. Whitaker, and Steven F. Cohn. 1988. "Problems of Mobilization in National Membership Organizations: The Local Chapter as a Possible Solution." Paper presented at Workshop on Frontiers in Social Movement Theory, Ann Arbor, Mich.

Benford, Robert D. 1988. "The Nuclear Disarmament Movement." In *The Nuclear Cage,* edited by Lester R. Kurtz, 237–65. Englewood Cliffs, N. J.: Prentice Hall.

Berry, Jeffrey M. 1977. *Lobbying for the People.* Princeton: Princeton Univ. Press.

———. 1978. "On the Origins of Public Interest Groups: A Test of Two Theories." *Polity* 10, no. 3:379–97.

Bottome, Edgar G. 1986. *The Balance of Terror.* Boston: Beacon.

Bowers, Robert Edwin. 1947. "The American Peace Movement, 1933–1941." Ph.D. diss., Univ. of Wisconsin–Madison.

Boyer, Paul. 1984. "From Activism to Apathy: The American People and Nuclear Weapons, 1963–1980." *Journal of American History* 70, no. 4:821–44.

———. 1985. *By the Bomb's Early Light.* New York: Pantheon.

———. 1987. Review of *Ban the Bomb,* 1986, by Milton S. Katz. *American Historical Review,* June:774–75.

———. 1989. "Arms Race as Sitcom Plot." *Bulletin of the Atomic Scientists,* June:6–8.

Boyte, Harry C. 1980. *The Backyard Revolution: Understanding the New Citizen Movement.* Philadelphia: Temple Univ. Press.

———. 1982. "The Formation of the New Peace Movement." *Social Policy,* Summer:4–8.

Bürklin, Wilhelm P. 1987. "Why Study Political Cycles?" *European Journal of Political Research* 15:131–43.

Caldicott, Helen. 1980. *Nuclear Madness.* New York: Bantam.

Campbell, W. Joseph. 1987. "Anti-Nuclear Movement Pauses to Reflect and Regroup." *The Philadelphia Inquirer* (reprinted from the *Hartford Courant*) Aug. 30:15A.

Cantril, Hadley, ed. 1951. *Public Opinion: 1935–1946.* Princeton: Princeton Univ. Press.

Carden, Maren Lockwood. 1978. "The Proliferation of a Social Movement: Ideology and Individual Incentives in the Contemporary Feminist Movement." *Research in Social Movements, Conflict and Change* 1:179–96.

Carlin, David R., Jr. 1982. "Civil Disobedience, Self-Righteousness, and the Antinuclear Movement." *America,* Sept. 25:152–54.

Chatfield, Charles. 1965. *Pacifism and American Life: 1914–1941.* Ph.D. diss., Vanderbilt Univ.

———. 1971. *For Peace and Justice. Pacifism in America, 1914–1941.* Knoxville: Univ. of Tennessee Press.

———. 1973. "Alternative Antiwar Strategies of the Thirties." In *Peace Movements in America,* edited by Charles Chatfield, 68–80. New York: Schocken.

———. 1978. "More Than Dovish: Movements and Ideals of Peace in the United States." In *American Thinking About Peace and War,* edited by Ken Booth and Moorhead Wright, 111–34. Hassocks, England: Harvester.

———, with the assistance of Robert Kleidman. 1992. *The American Peace Movement: Ideals and Activism.* New York: Twayne.

Clotfelter, James. 1986. "Disarmament Movements in the United States." *Journal of Peace Research* 23, no. 2:97–101.

Cockburn, Alexander, and James Ridgeway. 1983. "The Freeze Movement Versus Reagan." *New Left Review,* no. 137:5–21.

Colwell, Mary Anna C. 1986. "Peace Movements and Public Policy." Paper presented at First Annual Conference on Applied Social Psychology, Univ. of California, Santa Cruz.

———. 1989. *Organizational and Management Characteristics of Peace Groups.* San Francisco: Univ. of San Francisco Institute for Nonprofit Organization Management, Working Paper No. 8.

Cooney, Robert, and Helen Michalowski. 1977. *The Power of the People: Active Nonviolence in the United States.* Culver City, Calif.: Peace Press.

Corn, David. 1982. "A Directory of Antinuclear Groups." *Nation,* May 1: 525–26.

Cortright, David. 1991. "Assessing Peace Movement Effectiveness in the 1980s." *Peace & Change* 16, no. 1:46–63.

Cousins, Norman. 1972. *The Improbable Triumvirate: Pope John, John F. Kennedy, Nikita Khrushchev.* New York: Norton.

Curti, Merle. 1959. *Peace or War.* Boston: Canner.

DeBenedetti, Charles. 1980. *The Peace Reform in American History.* Bloomington: Indiana Univ. Press.

———. 1984. "Peace History, in the American Manner." *History Teacher* 18, no. 1:75–110.

———. 1986. Review of *Ban the Bomb,* by Milton S. Katz. *Library Journal,* July:91.

———. 1988. "American Peace Activism, 1945–1985." In *Peace Movements and Political Cultures,* edited by Charles Chatfield and Peter van den Dungen, 222–29. Knoxville: Univ. of Tennessee Press.

———, and Charles Chatfield. 1990. *An American Ordeal: The Antiwar Movement of the Vietnam Era.* Syracuse: Syracuse Univ. Press.

Deming, Barbara. 1960. "The Peacemakers." *Nation,* Dec. 17:471–75.

Detzer, Dorothy. 1948. *Appointment on the Hill.* New York: Henry Holt.

Divine, Robert A. 1962. *The Illusion of Neutrality.* Chicago: Univ. of Chicago Press.

————. 1978. *Blowing on the Wind: The Nuclear Test Ban Debate 1954–1960.* New York: Oxford Univ. Press.

————. 1987. Review of *Ban the Bomb,* by Milton S. Katz. *ISIS,* Mar.:94–95.

Domhoff, G. 1983. *Who Rules America Now?* New York: Simon & Schuster.

Downs, Anthony. 1972. "Up and Down with Ecology—the 'Issue-Attention-Cycle'." *Public Interest* 28:38–50.

Drew, Elizabeth. 1983. "A Political Journal." *New Yorker,* June 20:39–75.

Evans, Peter B., Dietrich Rueschemeyer, and Theda Skocpol, eds. 1985. *Bringing the State Back In.* Cambridge: Cambridge Univ. Press.

Fainstein, Norman I., and Susan S. Fainstein. 1974. *Urban Political Movements.* Englewood Cliffs, N. J.: Prentice-Hall.

Ferguson, Bruce. 1987. "Lessons of the Nuclear Freeze Movement." Unpublished paper prepared for the Institute for Defense and Disarmament Studies, Brookline, Mass.

————. 1988. "Different Agendas, Styles Shape SANE/Freeze." *Nuclear Times,* Apr.: 26–30.

Ferguson, Thomas. 1989. "Industrial Conflict and the Coming of the New Deal: The Triumph of Multinational Liberalism in America." In *The Rise and Fall of the New Deal Order, 1930–1980,* edited by Steve Fraser and Gary Gaerstle, 3–31. Princeton: Princeton Univ. Press.

————, and Joel Rogers. 1986A. *Right Turn.* New York: Hill and Wang.

————. 1986B. "Big Business Backs the Freeze." *Nation,* July 19/26:43–47.

Fine, Steven. 1982. "Peace Coalition Politics: The Liberal Experiment, 1954–1965." Unpublished History Honors Thesis, Oberlin College.

Fireman, Bruce, and William A. Fireman. 1979. "Utilitarian Logic in the Resource Mobilization Perspective." In *The Dynamics of Social Movements: Resource Mobilization, Social Control, and Tactics,* edited by Mayer Zald and John D. McCarthy, 8–44. Cambridge, Mass.: Winthrop.

Flynn, James R. 1964. "The U.S. Peace Movement: Its Electoral Prospects." *Political Science (New Zealand)* 16, no. 1:61–80.

Freeman, Jo. 1983. "A Model for Analyzing the Strategic Options of Social Movement Organizations." In *Social Movements of the Sixties and Seventies,* edited by Jo Freeman, 193–210. New York: Longman.

Gamson, William A. 1987. "Reframing the Debate." *Nuclear Times,* July/Aug.: 27–30.

————. 1988. "Political Discourse and Collective Action." *International Social Movement Research* 1:219–44.

————. 1990. *The Strategy of Social Protest.* Rev. ed. Homewood, Ill.: Dorsey.

George, Alexander L. 1979. "Case Studies and Theory Development: The Method of Structured, Focused Comparison." In *Diplomacy: New Approaches in History, Theory, and Policy,* edited by Paul Gordon Lauren, 43–68. London: Free Press.

Gerlach, Luther P., and Virginia H. Hine. 1970. *People, Power, Change: Movements of Social Transformation.* Indianapolis: Bobbs-Merrill.

Gitlin, Todd. 1980. *The Whole World Is Watching: Mass Media in the Making and Unmaking of the New Left.* Berkeley: Univ. of California Press.

Ground Zero. 1982. *Nuclear War: What's in It for You?* New York: Pocket Books.

Gusfield, Joseph R. 1981. "Social Movements and Social Change: Perspectives of Linearity and Fluidity." *Research in Social Movements, Conflicts and Change* 4:317–39.

Healey, Richard. 1988. "Melted Freeze." *Nuclear Times,* Nov./Dec.:23.

Heberle, Rudolf. 1951. *Social Movements: An Introduction to Political Sociology.* New York: Appleton-Century-Crofts.

Herbers, John. 1983. "Grass-Roots Groups Go National." *New York Times Magazine,* Sept. 4.

Herken, Gregg. 1982. *The Winning Weapon.* New York: Vintage.

Hertsgaard, Mark. 1985. "What Became of the Freeze?" *Mother Jones,* June: 44–47.

High, Stanley. 1938. "Peace, Inc." *Saturday Evening Post* 210.

Holborn, Frederick, and Mark Niedergang. 1985. "Citizen Movements and Congressional Action on Arms Control: The Test Ban and The Freeze." Unpublished paper, Johns Hopkins Univ., School of Advanced International Studies.

Holloway, Vernon Howard. 1949. *American Pacifism Between Two Wars: 1919–1941.* Ph.D. diss., Yale Univ.

Howlett, Charles F. 1985. *The American Peace Movement: History and Historiography.* Washington, D.C.: American Historical Association.

Jack, Homer. 1961. "New Frontier." *SANE-U.S.A.* 4, no. 2 (Feb.): 2.

———. 1963. "Where Do We Go from Here." *War/Peace Report,* Sept.

———. 1987. "The Nuclear FREEZE is a SANE Proposal." *Christian Century,* Dec. 16:1133–35.

Jenkins, J. Craig. 1977. "Radical Transformation of Organizational Goals." *Administrative Science Quarterly* 22:568–86.

———. 1983. "Resource Mobilization Theory and the Study of Social Movements." *Annual Review of Sociology* 9:527–53.

———. 1985. *The Politics of Insurgency.* New York: Columbia Univ. Press.

———. 1986. "Stirring the Masses: Indigenous Roots of the Civil Rights Movement." *Contemporary Sociology* 15:354–57.

———. 1987. "Interpreting The Stormy 1960s: Three Theories in Search of a Political Age." *Research in Political Sociology* 3:269–303.

———, and Craig M. Eckert. 1986. "Channeling Black Insurgency: Elite Patronage and Professional Social Movement Organizations in the Development of the Black Movement." *American Sociological Review* 51: 812–29.

Joseph, Paul. 1981. *Cracks in the Empire.* Boston: South End.

Judis, John. 1987. "The Freeze Movement Closes Ranks." *In These Times* June 24–July 7:3.

Katz, Milton S. 1973. *Peace, Politics, and Protest: SANE and the American Peace Movement, 1957–1972.* Ph.D. diss., Saint Louis Univ.

———. 1986. *Ban the Bomb: A History of SANE, The Committee for a SANE Nuclear Policy, 1957–1985.* Westport, Conn.: Greenwood.

———. 1989. "Reply [to Thiede 1989]." *Peace and Change* 14, no. 1:140–46.

Katz, Neil H. 1973. "Radical Pacifism and the Contemporary American Peace Movement: The Committee for Nonviolent Action, 1957–1967." Ph.D. diss., Univ. of Maryland.

Kehler, Randall. 1984. "The Freeze: Three Years After." *Fellowship,* July/ Aug.:8,9,35.

———. 1984. "We Need A Common Voice." *Nuclear Times,* June:9–10.

Kennedy, Paul M. 1987. *The Rise and Fall of the Great Powers: Economic Change and Military Conflict from 1500 to 2000.* New York: Random House.

Keys, Donald F. 1964. "Detente Brings New Challenges to SANE." *Sane World,* Apr. 15:4.

———. 1965. "The American Peace Movement." In *The Nature of Human Conflict,* edited Elton B. McNeil, 295–306. Englewood Cliffs, N. J.: Prentice-Hall.

Klandermans, Bert. 1984. "Mobilization and Participation: Social-Psychological Expansions of Resource Mobilization Theory." *American Sociological Review* 49:583–600.

———. 1989. "Introduction: Social Movement Organizations and the Study of Social Movements." *International Social Movement Research* 2:1–17.

———, and Sidney Tarrow. 1988. "Mobilization into Social Movements: Synthesizing European and American Approaches." *International Social Movement Research* 1:1–38.

Kleidman, Robert. 1986. "Opposing 'The Good War': Mobilization and Professionalization in the Emergency Peace Campaign." *Research in Social Movements, Conflicts and Change* 9:177–200.

———. 1990. "Organization and Mobilization in Modern American Peace Campaigns." Ph.D. diss., Univ. of Wisconsin–Madison.

Kolko, Gabriel. 1984. *Main Currents in American History.* New York: Pantheon.

Kriesberg, Louis. 1985. "Peace Movements and Government Peace Efforts." Paper prepared for the Conference: Social Movements as a Factor of Change in the Contemporary World, Uniwersytet Jagiellonski, Krakow, Poland.

Kuusisto, Allan A. 1950. *The Influence of the National Council for Prevention of War on United States Foreign Policy 1935–1939.* Ph.D. diss., Harvard Univ.

LaFeber, Walter. 1980. *America, Russia, and the Cold War.* New York: John Wiley.

Leavitt, Robert. 1983A. "The Genesis of a Mass Movement," from "Freezing the Arms Race." Unpublished Kennedy School of Government Case Study, Harvard Univ.

———. 1983B. "A Structural Guide to National Organizations Active in the Freeze Campaign and the Anti-Nuclear Movement," from "Freezing the Arms Race." Unpublished Kennedy School of Government Case Study, Harvard Univ.

LeBon, Gustave. 1960. *The Crowd.* New York: Viking.

Libby, Frederick J. 1969. *To End War.* Nyack, N.Y.: Fellowship.

Lipset, Seymour Martin, Martin Trow, and James Coleman. 1956. *Union Democracy.* New York: Free Press.

Lofland, John, Mary Anna Colwell, and Victoria Johnson. 1990. "Change-Theories and Movement Structure." In *Peace Action in the Eighties: Social Science Perspectives,* edited by John Lofland and Sam Marullo, 87–105. New Brunswick: Rutgers Univ. Press.

McAdam, Doug. 1982. *Political Process and the Development of Black Insurgency, 1930–1970.* Chicago: Univ. of Chicago Press.

McCarthy, John D. 1988. *Freedom Summer: The Idealists Revisited.* New York: Oxford Univ. Press.

———, John McCarthy, and Mayer Zald. 1988. "Social Movements." In *Handbook of Sociology,* edited by Neil J. Smelser, 695–737. Newbury Park: Sage.

———. 1987. "Pro-Life and Pro-Choice Mobilization: Infrastructure Deficits and New Technologies." In *Social Movements in an Organizational Society,* edited by Mayer N. Zald and John D. McCarthy, 49–66. New Brunswick, N.J.: Transaction.

———, and Mark Wolfson. 1988. "Exploring Sources of Rapid Social Movement Growth: The Role of Organizational Form, Consensus Support, and Elements of the American State." Paper presented at Workshop on Frontiers in Social Movement Theory, Ann Arbor, Mich.

———, and Mayer Zald. 1973. *The Trend of Social Movements in America: Professionalization and Resource Mobilization.* Morristown, N.J.: General Learning.

———, and Mayer Zald. 1975. "Organizational Intellectuals and the Criticism of Society." *Social Service Review* 49:344–62.

———, and Mayer Zald. 1977. "Resource Mobilization and Social Movements: A Partial Theory." *American Journal of Sociology* 82:1212–41.

Mack, Kenneth E. 1987. "An Analysis of the Nuclear Weapons Freeze Campaign." Unpublished paper, School of Social Science, Hampshire College.

McFarland, Andrew. 1984. *Common Cause.* Chatham N.J.: Chatham House.

Mansbridge, Jane J. 1986. *Why We Lost the ERA.* Chicago: Univ. of Chicago Press.

March, James G., and Johan P. Olsen. 1984. "The New Institutionalism: Organizational Factors in Political Life." *American Political Science Review* 78:734–49.

Marullo, Sam. 1988. "Leadership and Membership in the Nuclear Freeze Movement: A Specification of Resource Mobilization Theory." *Sociological Quarterly* 29, no. 3:407–27.

———. 1992. "Political, Institutional and Bureaucratic Fuel for the Arms Race." *Sociological Forum* 7, no. 1:29–54.

————. Forthcoming. *Mobilizing for Peace: The Nuclear Weapons Freeze Campaign and the Peace Movement of the 1980s.*

Marwell, Gerald, and Pamela Oliver. 1984. "Collective Action Theory and Social Movements Research." *Research in Social Movements, Conflicts and Change* 7:1–27.

Marx, Gary T., and James L. Wood. 1975. "Strands of Theory and Research in Collective Behavior." *Annual Review of Sociology* 1:363–428.

Masland, John W. 1940. "The 'Peace' Groups Join Battle." *Public Opinion Quarterly,* Winter:664–73.

Massad, Timothy G. 1980. "Disruption, Organization, and Reform: A Critique of *Poor People's Movements.*" *Dissent,* Winter:81–90.

Melman, Seymour. 1965. *Our Depleted Society.* New York: Holt, Rinehart and Winston.

————. 1974. *The Permanent War Economy: American Capitalism in Decline.* New York: Simon and Schuster.

Meyer, David S. 1988. "The Nuclear Freeze Movement in the United States, 1979–1984: Political Opportunity and the Structure of Social Mobilization." Ph.D. diss., Boston Univ.

————. 1990A. *A Winter of Discontent: The Nuclear Freeze and American Politics.* New York: Praeger.

————. 1990B. "How We Helped End the Cold War." *Nuclear Times* 8, no. 4:9–14.

————, and Robert Kleidman. 1991. "The Nuclear Freeze Movement in the United States." *International Social Movement Research* 3:231–62.

Michels, Robert. 1962. *Political Parties.* New York: Collier.

Molander, Earl A. 1987. "An Equilibrium Theory to Explain Development of the Anti-Nuclear War Movement of the 1980s — I." Paper presented at annual meeting of the American Sociological Association, Chicago, Ill.

————, John Parachini, and Theo Brown. 1988. "Network-Building and Maintenance in the Anti-Nuclear War Movement." Paper presented at annual meeting of the American Sociological Association, Atlanta, Ga.

Molander, Roger C., and Earl A. Molander. 1987. "An Equilibrium Theory to Explain Development of the Anti-Nuclear War Movement of the 1980s — II." Paper presented at annual meeting of the American Sociological Association, Chicago, Ill.

Morris, Aldon D. 1984. *The Origins of the Civil Rights Movement.* New York: Free Press.

————, and Cedrick Herring. 1988. "Theory and Research in Social Movements: A Critical Review." *Annual Review of Political Science* 2:137–98.

Mouzelis, Nicos P. 1967. *Organization and Bureaucracy: An Analysis of Modern Theories.* Chicago: Aldine.

Moynihan, Daniel P. 1969. *Maximum Feasible Misunderstanding: Community Action in the War on Poverty.* New York: Free Press.

Muste, A. J. 1960. "The Crisis in SANE." *Liberation* Pt. 1, July-Aug.:10–13; pt. 2, Nov.:5–8.

Nelkin, Dorothy, and Michael Pollack. 1981. *The Atom Besieged.* Cambridge: MIT Press.

Niedergang, Mark. 1986. "The Origins, Impact, and Legacy of the Anti-Vietnam War Movement in America." Unpublished U.S. Foreign Policy Thesis, Johns Hopkins Univ., School of Advanced International Studies.

Nielsen, Waldemar A. 1972. *The Big Foundations.* New York: Columbia Univ. Press.

Oberschall, Anthony. 1973. *Social Conflict and Social Movements.* Englewood Cliffs, N.J.: Prentice-Hall.

Oliver, Pamela. 1983. "The Mobilization of Paid and Volunteer Activists in the Neighborhood Movement." *Research in Social Movements, Conflicts and Change* 6:133–70.

———. 1988. "Pam Oliver's Reflections on the CBSM [Collective Behavior and Social Movements] Section [of the American Sociological Association]." *Critical Mass Bulletin* 13, no. 2:1–3.

———. 1989. "Bringing the Crowd Back In: The Nonorganizational Elements of Social Movements." *Research in Social Movements, Conflicts and Change* 11:1–30.

———, and Mark Furman. 1990. "Contradictions Between National and Local Organizational Strength: The Case of the John Birch Society." *International Social Movement Research* 2:155–78.

———, and Gerald Marwell. 1992. "Mobilizing Technologies for Collective Action." In *Frontiers of Social Movement Theory,* edited by Aldon D. Morris and Carol McClurg Mueller, 251–72. New Haven: Yale Univ. Press.

Olson, Mancur, Jr. 1965. *The Logic of Collective Action.* Cambridge, Mass.: Harvard Univ. Press.

Paarlberg, Rob. 1973. "Forgetting About the Unthinkable." *Foreign Policy* 10 (Spring):132–40.

Paine, Christopher E. 1985. "Lobbying for Arms Control." *Bulletin of the Atomic Scientists,* Aug.:125–30.

Peck, Keenan. 1985. "First Strike, You're Out: An Interview with Daniel Ellsberg." *The Progressive,* July:30–35.

Perrow, Charles. 1979A. *Complex Organizations: A Critical Essay.* Glenview, Ill.: Scott, Foresman.

———. 1979B. "The Sixties Observed." In *The Dynamics of Social Movements,* edited by Mayer N. Zald and John D. McCarthy, 192–211. Cambridge, Mass.: Winthrop.

Piven, Frances Fox, and Richard A. Cloward. 1979. *Poor People's Movements.* New York: Vintage.

Price, H. Edward, Jr. 1988. "Historical Generations in the Mobilization of the Nuclear Weapons Freeze Campaign." Paper delivered at Workshop on Frontiers in Social Movement Theory, University of Michigan, Ann Arbor, Mich.

Ragin, Charles C. 1987. *The Comparative Method: Moving Beyond Qualitative and Quantitative Strategies.* Berkeley: Univ. of California Press.

Ratcliff, Richard. 1985. "Community Organizing and Political Change." Paper presented at annual meeting of the American Sociological Association, Washington, D.C.

Rizzo, Renata. 1983. "Professional Approach to Peace." *Nuclear Times,* Aug./Sept.:10-13.

Rosi, Eugene J. 1965. "Mass and Attentive Opinion on Nuclear Weapons Tests and Fallout, 1954-1963." *Public Opinion Quarterly* 29:280-97.

Rudwick, Elliott, and August Meier. 1972. "Organizational Structure and Goal Succession: A Comparative Analysis of the NAACP and CORE, 1964-1968." *Social Science Quarterly* 51:9-24.

Rupp, Leila J., and Verta Taylor. 1987. *Survival in the Doldrums: The American Women's Rights Movement, 1945 to the Present.* New York: Oxford Univ. Press.

Salisbury, Robert H. 1969. "An Exchange Theory of Interest Groups." *Midwest Journal of Political Science* 13:1-32.

Salomon, Kim. 1986. "The Peace Movement—An Anti-Establishment Movement." *Journal of Peace Research* 23, no. 2:115-27.

Sanders, Jerry W. 1983. *Peddlers of Crisis.* Boston: South End.

Sandman, Peter M., and JoAnn M. Valenti. 1986. "Scared Stiff—Or Scared Into Action?" *Bulletin of the Atomic Scientists* Jan.:12-16.

SANE-U.S.A. 1958. "Nationwide Organizing Conference for a Sane Nuclear Policy," 1, no. 1(May 20):1-2.

Sasson, Theodore. 1987. *A Mile Wide and an Inch Deep: The Rise and Decline of the Freeze Movement.* Unpublished Honor's Thesis, Sociology Department, Brandeis Univ.

Sayer, Andrew. 1984. *Method in Social Science: A Realist Approach.* London: Hutchison.

Schuman, Howard. 1972. "Two Sources of Anti-War Sentiment." *American Journal of Sociology* 78, no. 3:513-36.

Seaborg, Glenn T. 1981. *Kennedy, Khrushchev, and the Test Ban.* Berkeley: Univ. of California Press.

Shoup, Laurence H., and William Minter. 1977. *Imperial Brain Trust.* New York: Monthly Review.

Skocpol, Theda, and Margaret Somers. 1980. "The Uses of Comparative History in Macrosocial Inquiry." *Comparative Study of Society and History* 22, no. 2:174-97.

Smith, Allen. 1991. "No More 'No More Vietnams.'" *Capital Area Peace Studies Chronicle* 2, no. 5:2-3.

Snow, David A., Burke Rochford, Jr., Steven K. Worden, and Robert D. Benford. 1986. "Frame Alignment Processes, Micromobilization, and Movement Participation." *American Sociological Review* 51:464-81.

Solo, Pam. 1988. *From Protest to Policy.* Cambridge, Mass.: Ballinger.

———. 1989. "The Reagan Era: The Freeze Campaign and Political Power." *Annual Review of Peace Activism,* 1-9.

Staggenborg, Suzanne, 1986. "Coalition Work in the Pro-Choice Movement." *Social Forces* 33, no. 5:374–90.

――――. 1988. "The Consequences of Professionalization and Formalization in the Pro-Choice Movement." *American Sociological Review* 53(Aug.):585–606.

Stone, I. F. 1970. "The Test-Ban Comedy." *New York Review of Books* 14.

Talbott, Strobe. 1985. *Deadly Gambits.* New York: Vintage.

Tarrow, Sidney. 1983A. *Struggling to Reform: Social Movements and Policy Change During Cycles of Protest.* Western Societies Program Occasional Paper no. 15. Ithaca, N.Y.: Center for International Studies, Cornell Univ.

――――. 1983B. "Resource Mobilization and Cycles of Protest: Theoretical Reflections and Comparative Illustrations." Paper presented at annual meeting of the American Sociological Association, Detroit, Mich.

――――. 1988. "National Politics and Collective Action: Recent Theory and Research in Western Europe and the United States." *Annual Review of Sociology* 14:421–40.

――――. 1989. *Struggle, Politics, and Reform: Collective Action, Social Movements, and Cycles of Protest.* Western Societies Program Occasional Paper no. 21. Ithaca, N.Y.: Center for International Studies, Cornell Univ.

Taylor, Betsy. 1985A. "Learning Electoral Lessons." *Nuclear Times,* Sept./Oct.:16–19.

――――. 1985B. "'If We Can't Change the Politicians' Minds . . . Let's Change The Politicians!'" An Analysis of Six Peace PACs and Their Political Impact in 1984." Unpublished paper, Harvard Univ., John F. Kennedy School of Government.

Taylor, Verta. 1989. "Social Movement Continuity: The Women's Movement in Abeyance." *American Sociological Review* 54(Oct.):761–75.

Terkel, Studs. 1985. *The Good War: An Oral History of World War II.* New York: Ballantine.

Thiede, Barbara. 1989. Review of *Ban the Bomb,* by Milton S. Katz. *Peace and Change* 14, no. 1:135–40.

Tilly, Charles. 1978. *From Mobilization to Revolution.* Reading, Mass.: Addison-Wesley.

――――. 1984. "Social Movements and National Politics." In *Statemaking and Social Movements,* edited by Charles Bright and Susan Harding, 297–317. Ann Arbor: University of Mich. Press.

Tilly, Chris. 1990. "The Politics of the New Inequality." *Socialist Review* 90, no. 1:103–20.

Turner, Ralph, and Louis Killian. 1987. *Collective Behavior.* 3d ed. Englewood Cliffs, N.J.: Prentice-Hall.

Tygart, C. E. 1987. "Participants in the Nuclear Weapons Freeze Movement." *Social Science Journal* 24:393–402.

Waller, Douglas C. 1987. *Congress and the Nuclear Freeze.* Amherst: Univ. of Massachusetts Press.

Walton, John. 1973. "Standardized Case Comparison: Observations on

Method in Comparative Sociology." In *Comparative Social Research: Methodological Problems and Strategies,* edited by Michael Armer and Allen Grimshaw, 173-91. New York: John Wiley.

Wechsler, James. 1938. "War In the Peace Movement." *Nation.* Pt. 1,: Mar. 19:323-54; pt. 2, Mar. 26:352-54.

Wehr, Paul. 1986. "Nuclear Pacifism as Collective Action." *Journal of Peace Research* 23, no.2:103-13.

Wilensky, Harold L. 1956. *Intellectuals in Labor Unions.* Glencoe, Ill.: Free Press.

Williams, William Appleman. 1962. *The Tragedy of American Diplomacy.* New York: Dell.

Wilson, James Q. 1973. *Political Organizations.* New York: Basic.

Wittner, Lawrence S. 1984. *Rebels Against War.* Philadelphia: Temple Univ. Press.

Women's Action for Nuclear Disarmament (WAND). 1986. *Turnabout: The Emerging New Realism in the Nuclear Age.* Arlington, Mass.: WAND Education Fund.

Wright, Talmadge, Felix Rodriguez, and Howard Waitzkin. 1985. "Corporate Interests, Philanthropies, and the Peace Movement." *Monthly Review* 36, no.9:19-31.

Young, Nigel. 1984. "Why Peace Movements Fail." *Social Alternatives* 4, no. 1:9-16.

———. 1987. "Peace Movements in History." In *Towards a Just World Peace,* edited by Saul H. Mendlovitz and R. B. J. Walker, 137-69. London: Butterworths.

Zald, Mayer N. 1987. "The Future of Social Movements." In *Social Movements in an Organizational Society,* edited by Mayer N. Zald and John D. McCarthy, 319-36. New Brunswick, N.J.: Transaction.

———, and Roberta Ash. 1966. "Social Movement Organizations: Growth, Decay, and Change." *Social Forces* 44:327-41.

———, and John D. McCarthy. 1980. "Social Movement Industries: Competition and Cooperation Among Movement Organizations." *Research in Social Movements, Conflicts and Change* 3:1-20.

Zurcher, Louis A., and David A. Snow. 1981. "Collective Behavior: Social Movements." In *Social Psychology,* edited by M. Rosenberg, 447-482. New York: Basic.

Index

ORGANIZING FOR PEACE

was composed in 11 on 13 Baskerville on Digital Compugraphic equipment
by Metricomp;
printed by sheet-fed offset on 50-pound, acid-free Glatfelter Natural
and Smyth-sewn over binder's boards in Holliston Roxite B,
with dust jackets printed in 2 colors
by Edwards Brothers, Incorporated;
designed by Victoria M. Lane;
and published by
SYRACUSE UNIVERSITY PRESS
SYRACUSE, NEW YORK 13244-5160

Syracuse Studies on Peace and Conflict Resolution
Harriet Hyman Alonso, Charles Chatfield, and Louis Kriesberg, *Series Editors*

A series devoted to readable books on the history of peace movements, the lives of peace advocates, and the search for ways to mitigate conflict, both domestic and international. At a time when profound and exciting political and social developments are happening around the world, this series seeks to stimulate a wider awareness and appreciation of the search for peaceful resolution to strife in all its forms and to promote linkages among theorists, practitioners, social scientists, and humanists engaged in this work throughout the world.

Other titles in the series include:

An American Ordeal: The Antiwar Movement of the Vietnam Era. Charles DeBenedetti; Charles Chatfield, assisting author

Building a Global Civic Culture: Education for an Interdependent World. Elise Boulding

The Eagle and the Dove: The American Peace Movement and United States Foreign Policy, 1900–1922. John Whiteclay Chambers II

From Warfare to Party Politics: The Critical Transition to Civilian Control. Ralph M. Goldman

Give Peace a Chance: Exploring the Vietnam Antiwar Movement. Melvin Small and William D. Hoover, eds.

Intractable Conflicts and Their Transformation. Louis Kriesberg, Terrell A. Northrup, and Stuart J. Thorson, eds.

Israeli Pacifist: The Life of Joseph Abileah. Anthony Bing

Mark Twain's Weapons of Satire: Anti-Imperialist Writings on the Philippine-American War. Mark Twain; Jim Zwick, ed.

One Woman's Passion for Peace and Freedom: The Life of Mildred Scott Olmsted. Margaret Hope Bacon

Peace as a Women's Issue: A History of the U.S. Movement for World Peace and Women's Rights. Harriet Hyman Alonso

The Road to Greenham Common: Feminism and Anti-Militarism in Britain since 1820. Jill Liddington

Timing the De-escalation of International Conflicts. Louis Kriesberg and Stuart J. Thorson, eds.

Virginia Woolf and War: Fiction, Reality, and Myth. Mark Hussey, ed.

The Women and the Warriors: The U.S. Section of the WILPF, 1915–1946. Carrie Foster